Béla Bartók-

The American Years

(FORMERLY TITLED: THE NAKED FACE OF GENIUS)

by

Agatha Fassett

Dover Publications, Inc.

New York

To Ditta

Illustrations will be found following
page 180

A catalogue of Bartók's works appears
on pages 363-367

Published in Canada by General Publishing Company, Ltd.,
30 Lesmill Road, Don Mills, Toronto, Ontario.
Published in the United Kingdom by Constable and Company,
Ltd., 10 Orange Street, London WC 2.

This Dover edition, first published in 1970, is an unabridged
republication of the work originally published by the Houghton
Mifflin Company in 1958 with the title *The Naked Face of
Genius: Béla Bartók's American Years*. The present edition is
published by special arrangement with the Houghton Mifflin
Company. One new photograph has been added to this edition.

International Standard Book Number: 0-486-22530-5
Library of Congress Catalog Card Number: 77-127848

Manufactured in the United States of America
Dover Publications, Inc.
180 Varick Street
New York, N. Y. 10014

1

Deep in the hall closet of my Vermont house hangs an old knobby cane with a broadly curved handle, and above it a shapeless white cotton sun hat with a transparent green shield in its floppy brim. Untouched for many years, they have so completely blended with their surroundings and with each other that they seem to have rooted themselves there in the semidarkness, and taken possession. At first they were left alone in the hope that their owner would come back for them, but when I knew he never would, there was no tearing them from that life of their own in the dim and sheltered enclosure.

I do not know where that crabbed staff came from; perhaps a farmer carved it when he was laid up with a broken leg, or with an attack of rheumatism in his old bones. The hat was bought by Ditta Bartók and myself for twenty-nine cents in a five-and-ten-cent store in Montpelier. When she brought it home, Bartók tried it on unwillingly, complaining about its stiffness, and pointed out that its shape did not correspond to the shape of his head. Nevertheless, he put it on and took it off over and over again. Then he carefully folded strips of measured newspaper and placed them experimentally inside the leather band until he found a satisfactory adjustment. After that he went to work on the brim. Though he bent it this way and that with patient determination, he could not give its limpness the exact angle he desired. But he wore the hat, although not entirely pleased with it, that same day when he took his afternoon walk, and from then on he never left the house without it.

The cane, on the other hand, delighted him from the moment I handed it to him. Leaning on it with his full weight, he was visibly pleased with the strong support it gave him, and he adopted it instantly for his own.

And so the hat, the stick and Bartók became inseparable and were often seen that summer by the inhabitants of our Vermont hillside. To this very day when they stop me as I pass by to talk about one thing or another, they seldom let me go without mentioning once more the man who used to walk around here wearing such a queer white hat and carrying that old walking stick. Wasn't it a strange thing, they are apt to say, how he would stare at an ordinary leaf on an ordinary tree just as if he'd never seen anything like it before, and the way he'd stand still for the longest time listening to the call of some bird or the sound of a woodpecker hammering noisily on the trunk of a dead tree. And the way he'd hold a pine cone to his ear as if it were a fancy seashell — what on earth could he have heard in it? And they ask me if I know why he should have wanted to pull the pine cone apart and stare at each bit of it, as if he were going to discover some new wonder in every piece.

There are other things, too, they remember, like his poking into cow dung, digging deep into it with that stick of his. What did he expect to find there anyway?

Wouldn't it be nice to see him again standing over there as if he had grown right out of the ground? Too bad he is gone — well, we all have to go sooner or later —

"Yes, he died," I answer, as I walk away, amazed and moved

that they too remember those things: the ordinary leaf on an ordinary tree, the pine cones, the cow dung.

"There is life in this dried-up mound of dung," Bartók would say. "There is life feeding on this dead heap." And he would crumble it apart with his cane. "You see," he would say, scrutinizing it intently, "how the worms and bugs are working busily helping themselves to whatever they need, making little tunnels and passages, and then soil enters, bringing with it stray seeds. Soon pale shoots of grass will appear, and life will complete its cycle, teeming within this lump of death. Once in a mound like this I found a tiny shoot of an apple tree growing, springing up with so much confidence — a long time ago, in Hungary. It could be bearing fruit by now, but more likely its life was crushed out almost as soon as it started, for Nature takes life as abundantly as she gives it."

Nature takes life as abundantly as she gives it! These words, so lightly spoken, planted themselves in my mind as they kept on growing into the characteristic life-and-death theme of Bartók's own that I finally learned to recognize in his most fragmentary remarks throughout the five years I knew him.

And out of these roots comes my own story, the only one I can tell, the story of five years of Bartók's life. For these last five years, as they slowly unfolded before me, attained in an unrelenting cycle the roundness of a lifetime, as massive and preordained as a Greek tragedy. And his wife Ditta, linked in the same chain of circumstances, inevitably shared in her own way the anguish of Bartók's destiny.

Bartók remained permanently lonely here, since he was not the kind to transplant well, and every step was made harder — for although he did not know it, soon after he arrived here the seed of his fatal illness, leukemia, was within him, and wherever he went he was followed by the doom of his tightly numbered years.

Perhaps for this reason his final five years here grew into shapeless length, with the most trivial things taking on great importance, completely out of proportion if measured by the ordinary flow of time. There was, besides, the monumental weight of Bartók's past, insistently trailing along with him, adding its full weight to the present, that enlarged out of bounds the smallest motions of the fatally disappearing days.

The words of Bartók were to remain with me, together with the many shades of his moods, tied to the places where they were spoken, preserved in their own characteristic rhythm that was as dominant and unfailing in Bartók's speech as in his music. And this accumulating storehouse of words, as it gathered impact and meaning, slowly led me to think of Bartók as the mysterious and resonant instrument itself, constructed with secret and tremulous accuracy to sound the music that grew out of him.

He was fifty-nine years old when he came here in 1940 as a voluntary exile, before the Nazi invasion reached Hungary. There was still, and there always remained, a strange newness about him as if he had just emerged from the unknown. The cloud of mystery which engulfed him from the very beginning was not lifted by the years, but remained settled in heavy layers around him, preserving the source of excitement that never seemed to give out, and burst forth with fresh energy whenever a new opus came to life. The controversy over his work never quite died away, but was carried on by adversaries and followers alike with a conviction both violent and unbending.

Yet it had all begun so smoothly and without a jolt at the beginning of the century.

"It seems to me that I always played the piano, and always seriously," Bartók said one winter evening in New York, "that

I always dug up fragments of music I considered my own; and it was never anything else but an intensely consuming occupation. So it was, perhaps, the most natural event of my life when I first appeared before the public as pianist and composer when I was nine years old.

"What I remember most distinctly from that occasion is the awareness I had of being confined within certain uncomfortable boundaries, and how I tried to console myself with the thought that this was just a temporary condition, an obstacle caused by my limited knowledge, and that it only rested within myself to break through these boundaries into a greater freedom. And the desire to do so filled me with an impatience so unbearable that it was almost physical pain.

"Nothing could speak more eloquently of my innocence at this time than the belief that I could make my boundaries disappear. For only much later comes the discovery that one remains confined, to a lesser or greater degree, forever, and the wings of one's conception are always clipped."

Bartók was born in Nagyszentmiklós in 1881. He began his own musical education as soon as he was able to hold his hands on the keyboard, but his first lessons were given him by his mother. As his relationship to music grew deeper it filled every need of his childhood, spent in complete isolation, for during the first six years or so of his life he suffered from a skin disease that made him reluctant to be seen by anyone else but his mother.

His father died when Bartók was only seven years old, and it was left entirely in the care of his mother to forward his musical training. He took in the vast complications of music with such swift penetration that it became increasingly difficult to keep pace with him. His mother therefore found it necessary to move, together with Bartók and his only sister, from one provincial town to another in search of a place that offered opportunities for more extensive learning. And after long years of continuous moving, finally in 1894 they settled in the city of Pozsony, where they found the cultural atmosphere they were looking for.

Separating himself from his mother for the first time, Bartók went in 1899 to Budapest to continue his studies at the Royal Hungarian Musical Academy, and when he graduated in 1902 he was already accepted as an outstanding pianist. In 1907 he was appointed professor of piano at this same academy, and he remained there for three decades.

It was in 1904 that his *Kossuth* Symphony was performed with instant success in Budapest and in Manchester, England, too. By that time Bartók was known as a young promising composer and, above all, as an outstanding pianist both inside and outside Hungary. In 1905, as Bartók himself loved to quote, he was hailed with the appearance of his piano pieces *Abrand* and *Scherzo* as "the future master of the most charming salon music." And it was at just about this time that Bartók's successful romantic period came to an end.

In the spring of 1906 Ferenc Vecsey, a young violinist who was a world-famous prodigy at the time, went to Spain on a concert tour, and Bartók traveled with him as his accompanist. After the tour was over, before returning to Hungary, Bartók could not resist taking this opportunity to wander for a while on his own. Fascinated by Portugal, which he called "half-Africa," it was a quite natural next step to cross over from Gibraltar to Africa itself.

"Reaching this distant-sounding place, a country with such a strange and strong flavor, I could not stop wandering tirelessly each day from morning until night," Bartók told the story almost forty years later, with the same fresh excitement as if it had happened only a short time ago. "And at the close of one long day, thirsty and tired, I went into a dark and dingy inn and, happy to lean back and rest, I almost fell asleep in that musty, heavy-smelling atmosphere. But all at once, I found myself fully awake, startled and whipped into wild attention, as there came to my ears the singing of a group of old men I could barely see through the smoky mist at the other end of the room. Listening to their songs, and their unknown Arab words, I was overcome by something of such significance for me that I knew instantly this would have to be followed up and investigated to the utmost, even if it should take my entire lifetime.

"And it was right there and then, sitting impatiently on the rickety bench, I felt myself swept into a cause that filled me with a more consuming excitement than I had ever known. And with immediate clarity I could see a mapful of lines tying together widely scattered and up till now unconnected native songs and transforming them into a semblance of order.

"And this was, incidentally," Bartók added, "the very moment when 'the future master of the most charming salon music' was sent on his way, and without any blessing, to be sure, as he was made to realize not too long after."

Bartók went to Africa again in 1913 to spend the summer among the nomads of Biskra, whose language he knew well by then, for he had been planning for a long time to go there to collect their songs. Through the years he had worked out a concrete science of collecting and of classification, and assimilated and abstracted into his own music the spirit of the folk songs. By now he had measured fully the importance of those songs that lay hidden underground in every country, "the most precious possession and purest ore of all."

At the beginning he only had the vision of what the ancient Hungarian folk songs might have been from the scattered melodies he heard here and there, sung mostly by servant girls of the faraway provinces. And the surprising discovery fol-

lowed that these perfect little songs he was becoming acquainted with bore no resemblance to anything he had heard
before. They were a world apart from the so-called Hungarian
songs and from the shapeless art songs, from all those loqua-
cious tunes distorted even further by the equally ornate presentations of gypsy bands.

"What could point out more clearly," Bartók once said,
"how unrelated to Hungarian folk songs these forms of expression really are than watching the joy and sorrow reflected
on the faces of those reserved peasant singers who overcome
their shyness and identify themselves completely with the
pure emotions of the songs that are their own.

"How unfortunate it is that, instead of the authentic Hungarian folk songs, the rootless and synthetic imitations of
them, presented in the unwholesome style of the gypsy bands,
became accepted inside and outside our country as the very
spirit of Hungarian music."

Although he began to write down folk melodies as early as
1904, in the summer of 1906 he gave himself up completely
with all his inspired force to collecting this hidden material,
not only forging his way closer to the songs, but finding with
amazement that they were deeply related to what he himself
had already imagined before he realized that the concise
strength and majestic simplicity of the songs so strangely co-
incided with his own dreams.

His entire being was shaken by the wild joy of finding the
ancient villages together with the ancient songs and a whole
slow-moving life still close to its original form, underneath
the shadow of snow-covered mountains and far within overgrown forests and in the endless fields on the fringes of
unbroken estates. While he wandered among the small whitewashed mud houses with their clean-swept earthen floors, Bartók, who had spent most of his twenty-five years in cities, felt

as if he had discovered the scene where he was most at home, and could not drink in enough of this world he was beginning to adopt as his own.

He grew used to the deep calm, and in the falling darkness, the sound of the almost forgotten instrument of the shepherds, the *tilinko*, in the strong quiet evening, made even more quiet by the vibrant and unceasing drone of the miniature orchestra of insects and the heavy sleep of the friendly animals, the "good cows and self-sacrificing horses."

Just about the same time there was another important composer who independently conceived a plan to seek out the folk songs of Hungary, Kodály Zoltán. And it was most natural for these two young men to form a friendship that lasted for a lifetime, constantly strengthened and renewed by their intensive determination to follow these songs to their sources.

From the beginning each had his own conception of where the end of the source lay, for Kodály never felt the necessity to seek farther than the borderlines of Hungary. No sooner did Bartók begin, however, than the idea was taking shape in him that it is possible to evaluate fully the folk song material of one country only if the folk songs of those countries that lie beyond are known equally well. His great desire to investigate the folk songs throughout all of Eastern Europe was from the first the only logical conclusion for him.

Even while this idea was developing into a definite plan, Bartók did not miss any opportunity to emphasize the importance of making up for the long-lost years when the simple and genuine folk expression was completely forgotten, nor did he fail to point out the necessity of exerting a tireless effort to follow the network of songs all the way to its roots in order to realize the full impact of this irreplaceable material. Only then could the great need be fulfilled to refresh and purify the prevailing superficial style with the elements of unpretentious peasant songs, marked by the rigorous absence of all that was unnecessary.

"But it would have been a task beyond the strength of a Hercules," Bartók reflected once during his last five years in America, when his thoughts so often returned to one phase or another of his past, "to change the dusty taste of an indifferent public, settled comfortably for so long into the sentimental sound of gypsy music as in the fumes of heavy wine, to open wide the windows and doors and let in the fresh breeze from the fields, and allow the sober clarifying sunlight to seep into every stagnant corner. To disturb a whole society drugged with monotony and static self-satisfaction could not be accomplished without arousing angry, bitter and lasting fights."

But there were even more serious considerations that Bartók did not stop to take into account, the ill will and jealousies and mutual hatred of those nations crowded so close together that they virtually infringed upon each other's territory. And all this while Bartók remained oblivious to the danger of daring to dream about friendship among these nations at this especially crucial time, when even the idea of artistic or scientific cooperation was all wrong, an unforgivable sin.

The events during those foreboding war years worked even more strongly against his dreams. Neither did he realize, when as early as 1907 his own compositions began to ring out with a new, original strength, that the outburst of anger which came from the public, the eagerness to hurt him with almost personal venom, had reasons predetermined by his own far-reaching aim rather than by the mere dislike of the idiom of his music.

Perhaps he did not hear because he had no time to take in the full implications of the steadily mounting antagonism, for there was no end to what he wanted to do as he became increasingly alive to the tremendous upheaval taking place within himself, opening the channels into his own resources. Already materializing in his consciousness was the vision of what his own voice had to say. By 1908 his music was beginning to sound in its full originality.

And bound only by a belief in this new path Bartók was clearing, a small army was gathering behind him, inside and outside Hungary, convinced by now that he was bringing into being a new expression, unmistakably suggesting the outline of its immense proportions.

During the sad and hopeless years of a losing war, in a country completely walled in around him, with no road left open to the outside world, he was weaving a dream of bringing about an interchange among well-educated collectors covering all parts of the world whereby one could become acquainted with the folk song heritage of every country. Meanwhile for him all hope of any further collecting was shattered for a long time to come, if not really ended for ever.

And in this darkened and closed world, amidst worry and fear and isolation, his own work grew boundlessly and broke through the closed walls and emerged and spread like a flood. And this flood, sweeping beyond the borders of Hungary, flowed back again with even greater force, and for this new idiom to be accepted even in his own country was for him a silent triumph.

Time passed and ripened his importance.

2

ON A LATE September evening in 1940, I was standing at the door of a New York apartment for a long time, hesitating to ring the bell. Ever since Ernő Balogh had asked me to come and spend an evening there I had thought of nothing else but that approaching visit. For it wasn't an ordinary invitation that he extended to me on the telephone, since he had said at the same time, "Bartók Béla and his wife arrived here just a few days ago, and I am sure you will be glad to hear that they are coming too."

My reaction was much more than gladness. It was a growing excitement, calling to mind a half-forgotten childhood, early enthusiasms, passionate creeds — all connected with the name Bartók Béla. Many years had trickled into the gap separating me now from my very young student days at the Academy of Music in Budapest when Professor Bartók was chosen by many of us as an idol, the symbol of greatness and of all things that were new and electrifying and to be believed in. Although there had been long periods of time when I did not think about it at all, yet I had never lost this belief in him, for I had only to hear his name mentioned and it all came to life again.

I had seen him only once, on a narrow winding street of Buda, in the dull light of a fall afternoon. I was walking home, my music under my arm, with another student, who suddenly stopped and whispered to me excitedly, "Do you know who that is?" She nodded toward a man approaching us as he descended the hill, a figure thin and straight, so obviously unaware of his surroundings that one could not hope for a glance from him. "It's Bartók Béla!"

By the time I had realized what she was saying he had almost passed us, but for one intense second I had seen the beautiful precision of his features and the compressed brilliance of his eyes, preserving his aloofness like a sheet of glass.

I turned to watch as he descended the sloping curve of Tudor Street, struck by the way he moved along the public thoroughfare as if within the walled privacy of his own room.

I was not the only one for whom Bartók was a myth and a cult — the effect of his presence at the Academy had reached all the students, even us, the youngest in the elementary grades. The reverberations of the controversy between his passionate followers and equally passionate opponents were so stormy and loud that no one could help but choose sides and be fired with blind enthusiasm either for or against him.

In this period, although my musical understanding and my knowledge of Bartók's work was limited, I nevertheless took a strong stand among the circle of his followers. I was instinctively drawn to the few small piano pieces I myself played, and on those rare occasions when I listened to a performance of his music, the strange new sounds filled me with joy and I became fired with the conviction that here among us, in our own time, lived one who was destined to become one of the immortal creators of music.

Hypnotized by the strong force of my memory, I completely abandoned myself to the past, and was moving there with such gliding ease that it was a heavy jolt to find myself in the present again, confronted by the reality of the closed door of a New York apartment. My hand on the bell, at the last moment another question came into my mind. Although my early instinctive feeling about Bartók's importance as a composer had proved to be overwhelmingly accurate, what about his personality? Would the impression left by the swift glance that was caught and illuminated two decades ago seem exaggerated to the eye of an adult who had left the scene of the controversies over his work even before growing up, and whose preoccupation was no longer music alone? Would the poetry of those few moments that survived through the years be sustained, or collapse beneath a more lasting scrutiny and under a more sober light?

I rang the bell. There was no relation between my excitement and the friendly greeting of Malvina Balogh as I entered the familiar quiet of her hall. When she led me into the sitting room, I barely acknowledged Ernő Balogh's casual wave of the hand, so immediately was I aware of Bartók standing near the piano. For a moment I felt as though faced by an apparition from the past, visible to me alone. But in that moment, swiftly and without a jolt, the apparition turned into a living figure: *he was exactly as I remembered him,* slighter and paler perhaps, but exactly the same in essential substance.

I was struck again by his complete detachment. He was standing now at ease and part of a friendly group, and still he did not blend with these surroundings any more than he had with the casual passers-by on the street. Although he was talking with animation to a group who gave him complete attention, his interest was not focused on his listeners but concentrated entirely upon the object he held in his hand. I was still standing in the doorway, looking at the scene as if it were on a stage, and I had a momentary impression that Bartók and the object he was discussing were suspended on a different plane from that of the others, isolated and alone.

At first glance I thought he was holding a football, until I heard him say, "But how could this be a coconut? In the first place, all the coconuts I have ever met with before were smaller and rounder in shape than this elongated thing, and were covered with coarse hair instead of smooth cool bark."

A laugh, surprisingly clear, made me glance around. I saw a girl sitting on the edge of the sofa, her hair the color of ripe wheat, braided around her head softly enclosing a fragile heart-shaped face. Her intent blue eyes fixed on Bartók, she was prolonging her laughter as if to encourage the gaiety. As Malvina Balogh introduced her, "Mrs. Bartók," she lifted her eyes to me and took my hand with such friendly warmth that it seemed as though we had met many times before.

But Bartók would not be interrupted by an introduction. Unwilling to abandon his line of thought, he abruptly held out, instead of his hand, the object under dispute for my inspection.

"Would you call this a coconut?" he asked. His voice was low, vibrant, and precisely focused.

Relieved at the unexpected turn this anxiously awaited meeting had taken, I accepted the coconut he was holding so gently and said in a weak voice, "I don't know. It doesn't feel at all like a coconut to me — it's too smooth and too big." As soon as I had said it, I realized that I had only repeated his own words.

"Well," he suggested helpfully, "would you then call it a naked giant of a coconut?"

Overwhelmed by his intensity, I became even more hesitant. "Why, I suppose so."

"But did you ever see anything like it before?" he insisted, indifferent to my confusion. At last he took the coconut back and balanced it on the palm of his hand for all of us to admire.

Looking at it now from a little distance, its shape of a human head stirred in me a memory. "Yes, I have," I said, groping slowly for the words. "Once I saw something like it, almost the very thing, but that one was transformed into a weird-looking Indian head with teeth and eyes and a feather head-dress too." I stopped then, for Bartók's smile had vanished.

"That's one bit of information that might have been left unremembered," he said. His pleasure and gaiety gone, he put the coconut on the piano and turned away. I could not have been more dazed if this fruit had fallen on me with all its weight from its original treetop.

As he had given me no hint of why he had taken offense, I could not imagine any reason why it had occurred. Much later I discovered that this abrupt rejection was not at all unusual, and could happen to anyone at any time conversing with Bartók. However, this was my first conversation and my first fiasco, and I had the feeling that I had committed a sacrilege, if not willingly, at least from unforgivable ignorance or insensitivity, and my discomfort was acute.

Withdrawing to the farthest corner of the room, I sat down on a sofa and found myself next to Ditta Bartók.

"I'm so sorry," I apologized. "I just don't see what was so wrong with what I said."

"It wasn't bad in the least," she laughed to reassure me, "but it couldn't have been worse. For how could you have known that your innocent remark would hurt him in so many tender spots? American Indians, you must understand, have long been a sensitive issue with Béla. His sympathies are always with those who are undeservedly abused. To him that decorated coconut head of yours must have symbolized the terrible humiliations which they suffered. Besides, he hates any distortion of natural things."

She took such pains to make me feel better that I suspected

she herself must have lived through many similar uncomfortable situations, and therefore was able to sympathize thoroughly with me.

"He discovered that coconut in a small store this morning and has carried it around all day long. He was so fascinated by it that he decided to bring it as a present for Malvina Balogh. And do you know," she said, leaning toward me confidentially, whispering into my ear like a child giving away a secret, "Malvina told me that it really is a coconut, in its original husk. But of course we didn't want to spoil Béla's fun by telling him that. He was so interested in that thing he has even forgotten to think about our trunks for a while."

"Your trunks?" I asked. "What about them?"

"Didn't you hear? They are lost. Somewhere along the way they disappeared." Her voice had risen, but with a glance at Bartók she lowered it again. "And what a tragedy it is, for one of them was filled with Béla's manuscripts, the bulk of his unpublished Romanian folk song collection."

"Are you sure?" I said, "that they are really lost? Isn't it too soon to tell?"

"It's not me, it's Béla . . ." she began, but was interrupted by Bartók turning to her from the other side of the room and saying, as if he had heard every word of our conversation, "Please, don't even talk about those trunks any more." The coldness of his voice did not conceal the underlying anguish he was feeling.

"Just because they didn't arrive with you is no indication that they are entirely lost," Ernő Balogh put in.

Balogh, the well-known concert pianist, was a former pupil of Bartók's and there was a long-standing friendship between the two men. I did not know then how unusual it was for Bartók to be as easily outgoing as he appeared throughout that evening. But the warmth of Balogh's personality flowed with such naturalness toward him that it would have been almost impossible for Bartók to put up his customary barriers. Their discussion of the Bartóks' urgent problems was so exclusively between the two of them that the rest of us were not even an audience — we were forgotten except when Ditta interrupted with some question of her own.

Inevitably, along with the other problems, the matter of the trunks came up again and Bartók's attitude was, as before, uncompromisingly hopeless.

"You shouldn't be so ready to welcome calamity," Erno Balogh protested. "Hasn't it occurred to you — the most obvious thing — to try to trace them?"

"Trace them indeed!" Bartók answered. "What a futile effort that would be! If you could see as I have seen the endless piles of baggage of all kinds filling the holds of ships, bulging out of railroad cars, spreading over entire lengths of railroad platforms in senseless confusion from one end of the world to the other, you wouldn't be so optimistic about tracing two trunks out of the millions, either. Remember that we are not the only ones who are trying to rescue from Europe a handful of our own most precious possessions. Only a heap of papers, in my case, but nonetheless the work of a lifetime." When, after a long silence, he spoke again, his voice seemed to be rising from many springs of sadness. "It's not only the collection of songs that is gone; gone too is the entire stretch of time that made it possible, for even if I had another lifetime before me and could start all over again, the results would not be the same. The sources I tapped no longer exist, the people who sang these songs are gone. The places where they were sung have either disappeared entirely or changed beyond recognition."

He got up restlessly, walked around the room and sat down next to Balogh. "After all, Ernő, we must realize that everything that linked us to the past is broken, and we must admit, at least to ourselves, that what brought us here this time was not merely our coming concert tour but actually a mass migration in which we are only an incidental part. It's as though we had been caught in a storm at sea, and to make it complete, our possessions have been scattered. And now here we are, blown to shore with no more than the clothes on our backs."

"Don't you think, Béla," said Ernő, "that in describing your situation here so darkly you are making it seem much worse than it is? Aren't you disregarding the most important thing of all? Clothes on your back or not, you are Bartók Béla! Surely that fact alone carries great weight wherever you go."

"Bartók Béla, Bartók Béla!" he said impatiently. "But to begin with I am not Bartók Béla here, I am only Béla Bartók. To make Béla Bartók mean here what Bartók Béla stands for at home will surely take ten or fifteen years again. You can't blame me that I am unhappy to throw away fifteen years to establish myself in this strange country — every minute of which I urgently need to round out my own work, rather than to scatter myself on sidelines. If, with good luck, I have that many years left!"

Sensing that Ditta was about to protest his last remark, he stopped her with a wave of his hand and went on.

"Here I have a faint chance — I am sure of that. But still the fact that I had no other choice — for if I had stayed at home I could not have worked at all under the menace of Hitler's shadow — is no real cause for rejoicing, it's merely the lesser of two evils."

"All this is sad and true, Béla," Ernő replied. "But now you must make the best of it and not give up even before you have started. Of course your problems are many and very complicated, but if you don't insist upon unraveling all of them at once and instead deal with them one by one, no doubt they can be solved."

Then Ernő Balogh promptly started to enumerate all the difficulties, returning bravely to the misplaced trunks, inquiring about receipts and all the details. Although Bartók did not object this time, he was just as unwilling as before to admit there was any hope of ever seeing his trunks again. And his thoughts had already become involved with another urgent problem.

"I keep on wondering as I walk the noisy streets of New York," he said directly to Balogh, "if there is a quiet corner anywhere in this city where I could feel at home enough to sit down to my work again. In those dark noisy prison cells at the hotel where we are staying, I find it impossible even to think."

"Remember, Béla," said Balogh, "that you don't know this city. You've only been here for brief visits during concert tours and you had no reason then to investigate New York as a possible place to live. With your love for exact figures, I wish I could tell you precisely how many apartments there are in the city and the vicinity, but I assure you there are a great many, and I have no doubt that there is something somewhere that will fill your special needs."

Bartók did not answer, but Ditta did.

"A very special need is a room for Péter — don't forget that."

"Who is Péter?" I asked.

"Why, Péter is our little boy — our son," she said, delighted to talk about him.

"I didn't know you had a child."

"Well, not really a child any more, I'm afraid, though I still think of him as one. He's fifteen years old now."

"Fifteen!" I was astonished. The animation with which Ditta spoke of him made her look scarcely fifteen herself. And then I remembered that Bartók had been married before — this must be the son of that former marriage.

But Ditta quickly made it clear that this was not so. She was indeed talking about her own child, for she said, "Yes, fifteen! Such a big boy, and he looks so like Béla — but he looks a little like me, too."

And when I asked her where he was now and whether he had come over with them, she explained further. "We thought it was wiser to leave him in Hungary until we get settled here. He's at boarding school — one that specializes in English, so that by the time he gets here he will speak the language."

"Don't start looking for him too soon," Bartók warned her.

"But I hope it will be soon, Béla," she answered. "You're always talking about the possibility of the war spreading — "

"I don't claim to be a prophet," Bartók said quickly.

"And a good thing too," Balogh broke in. "You'd stop at predicting nothing short of the end of the world. Don't listen to him, Ditta, or you won't have any hope left, either."

"Hope?" Bartók said. "These are not exactly hope-inducing times."

"True enough," Balogh said, amiably, "but I still insist that it's not the right thing to start your life here in such complete despair."

Bartók, in spite of himself, was not unaffected by this steady stream of reassurance from a friend who understood so well how to approach him, and presently he remarked in a somewhat lighter mood, "I can see that if I listen to you long enough, the only thing that will be left for me to worry about is rationing my wishes. I only hope I don't end up like the poor woodcutter of the fairy tale with a yard-long sausage grown to the tip of my nose."

Many times after this first evening I was to see Ernő Balogh, with sympathy and resourcefulness, ease the tragedy that was pressing ever closer around the Bartóks. His steady warmth and devotion became indispensable as the difficulties, only foreshadowed this evening, deepened into realities, when the war closed in on America and the Bartóks were not able to have access to their funds at home, and Bartók was too sick to work any more. And how much Ditta needed these qualities of Balogh's in those days when she had to stand by in times of sickness when there was urgent need of immediate help, doctors, a good hospital, money.

"Yes, Ditta, I know, I know," Balogh would say. "I understand, but there must be a solution." And Ditta listened, trusting, the lines of care on her face slowly relaxing.

Balogh was one of those who suggested turning to ASCAP (American Society of Composers, Authors and Publishers) when finding a solution could no longer be put off. As it happened, this organization was the one that took care of everything — doctors, hospitals, sanitariums — all the very best, and yes, a funeral too.

But on this fall evening of 1940 these things were still buried in the future.

By the time we sat down to dinner at the Baloghs' cheerful table, there was no trace left of Bartók's gloom. I was surprised at the fresh gaiety of his voice.

"Isn't this," he remarked, digging his fork into a handsome baked orange filled with sweet potato and topped with a perfectly browned marshmallow, "a classic symbol of American abundance! Goodness upon goodness!" he exclaimed. But I noticed that in spite of his enthusiasm, he still tasted it with extreme caution.

"Talking about American abundance," Ditta remarked, "where I find it most overwhelming is in the shop windows, especially since all my clothes are in the lost trunks, and I am badly in need of many things — most of all shoes."

"Shoes!" Bartók picked up the word. "Why women need so many pairs of shoes is a mystery to me." He was not complaining, but seemed to be moved only by pure curiosity. "I don't see why two pairs won't do for anyone — one pair of brown shoes with laces for everyday wear, and one pair of little black pumps for gala occasions." We all laughed, but that merely made him more serious. "Overemphasis on such unimportant things causes so many difficulties in our lives. We are all needlessly weighed down by trifles, and when I say that, I'm not thinking only of personal possessions."

"For that matter, you need shoes too," Ditta said to him, smiling. "Although we have our concert clothes in our small suitcase, all the accessories are in the other lost trunk. You need a black cravat, and black silk socks, and yes, shoes too."

"That's just what I was talking about," Bartók continued. "Why do we performing artists have to button ourselves into frock coats and all the rest of this ridiculous paraphernalia? Could it be that these things are as important to our profession as the long cape is to the magician? Could it be that without all this finery we couldn't conjure up our doves, one after the other, to circle around in the air and blind the audience to our limitations?" He shrugged his shoulders. "Well, perhaps all this is as it should be and it's foolish to imagine it possible for the life around me to be as uncomplicated as I desire it for myself."

He sighed, and I saw once more that loneliness on his face that never quite disappeared, although his mood shifted from gloom to gaiety and back time and time again in the course of that one evening.

When the Bartóks left, I went along with them. Down on the street, while Ditta and I stood making plans for a shopping expedition the next morning, Bartók walked slowly back and

forth studying this particular fragment of New York with concentrated curiosity. Suddenly he turned toward us.

"I smell horses," he announced.

"Horses?" said Ditta. "In the middle of Sixty-sixth Street?"

"Yes, horses," answered Bartók, and turned to examine the
street lined solidly on both sides with shiny cars, then he
started to cross over to the other side.

"Béla is always smelling and hearing things no one else can
smell or hear," Ditta confided. "The strange thing is that no
matter how wrong he seems, he's always right."

We watched him disappear into the doorway of a large
silent building. "He's right this time, too," I said, remembering then that this was the stable of a riding academy.

When we caught up with him, he was standing in the dimly
lit hall where the smell of horses was strong and penetrating.

"What a peaceful, natural smell," he said, inhaling deeply,
"sleeping horses." He leaned against the wall, relaxing, as if he
had reached a point of destination and was there to stay for a
long time. "How powerful a smell it is," he said. "Even the
synthetic breath of the city can't annihilate it. Different as it
seems, combined with gasoline fumes and asphalt, far out
of its natural element, still it remains essentially intact . . ."

Surrounded by the smell he seemed to know so well, he was
slowly becoming content. Realizing now how much it meant
to him, I remembered hearing of his long years of wandering,
collecting folk songs. I tried to imagine how it must have
been, traveling on foot or on carts, at first in the remote villages of old Hungary, and then on into Romania and other
nearby countries, in his desire to trace songs back to their
original sources. For some songs flow as freely as rivers and
just as unmindful of boundaries from one country into the
other.

"Isn't it nice in here!" Ditta said, touching my arm lightly as the three of us stood close together under a single naked light bulb. For a moment I felt I belonged with them.

"It's a smell with many layers," Bartók said, still preoccupied with the same theme, "but it is altogether different here far away from fields and open roads among the city stones of New York, in the United States of America." He smiled as he added, "And Anno Domini Nineteen-forty."

Outside again, he bade a formal goodnight. But as I was walking away, he called after me, "Sleep well — and don't dream about Indian heads."

3

NEITHER HORSES NOR Indian heads — nor any one thing that could be named — but everything together had caught me up in one great web of excitement. I was conscious only of an essence emanating from the Bartóks, an essence that I felt was distilled from stronger and purer ingredients than I had ever encountered before, and which for some reason now occupied my whole being. Their world was a world where the ordinary was no longer ordinary; there was nothing trivial, nothing that was unimportant. It was not what they said, it was a certain quality of their existence. There was something about the earnest searching way Bartók pronounced his words that gave to his speech an unforgettable rhythm, a rhythm that with a sudden twist and turn could transform the tragic into the humorous and just as swiftly reverse them again. He spoke his thoughts without restraint, seeming almost unaware that anyone was there to listen to him. And above all there was a simplicity, shared by Ditta too, a simplicity that hinted of a vulnerability that would be far too easy to trespass upon.

I was therefore both eager and uneasy the next morning as I entered the lobby of the Buckingham Hotel exactly at the hour Ditta and I had agreed to meet. But she was not in the lobby, and did not appear. When I finally called her on the house telephone, she apologized for not being ready, and asked me to come upstairs. She and Bartók were at breakfast in a dark sitting room, where the walls seemed to press close about the large piano.

"Have a cup of coffee," Ditta said, greeting me as an old friend, and poured me a cup from the pot on their breakfast tray. As I sat down and began to sip my coffee, Ditta's lively conversation easily obliterated the hours that had elapsed since our farewell of the evening before; but those same hours seemed to have erased all memory of our previous meeting from Bartók's mind, and he looked at me as though an introduction were in order.

"Tell me all about it," Ditta went on, not at all disturbed by his aloofness. "Where are you taking me? I can see it's not going to be as simple as just going around the corner."

"I'm afraid not," I replied, although for a moment I almost forgot what I originally had in mind. Overcome with a sense of strangeness, and in spite of Ditta's warm welcome, I still felt like an intruder. Neither could I understand the compulsion I was charged with to proceed with extreme caution as far as the spending of money was concerned. And furthermore it seemed impossible to explain what the equivalent would be in Budapest of a New York downtown bargain basement.

Finally, still somewhat uncertain of my ground, I said, "I hope it won't be against your taste to go into those inelegant places I'm thinking of, where at the price of a little discomfort we might be able to save quite a bit of expense."

"I'm prepared for anything!" Ditta answered, laughing, and as I looked up I saw a smile on Bartók's face too. It seemed to me that this speech of mine appealed to him more than anything I had said since we met.

Yet as Ditta and I faced each other across the aisle of a

jolting subway train, I wondered how well prepared she actually was. The midmorning subway was not crowded, and except for the roaring sound not really unpleasant, so that it surprised me to see a look of fear on her face. She sat there huddled into herself, as if trying to shut out the whole experience. And as we climbed the stairs to the street, she clung to my hand so tightly that I realized her fear went deeper than I had thought.

This disturbance disappeared as soon as we found ourselves in the whirl of riotous displays and carried along in the stream of determined shoppers — a scene for me much more bewildering than the subway train. For Ditta, however, to my surprise it seemed to be a relief, and, quickly initiated into the rough procedure, she was amused and gay and altogether in high spirits, enthusiastic about every little purchase she made.

How many pairs of shoes and whatever else we bought I don't remember, but I do remember that, loaded with packages and completely exhausted, we finally went into Childs 14th Street restaurant for tea, and sat down in a quiet corner.

"All I can see is heaps of shoes!" Ditta said, leaning back and closing her eyes. "I don't dare to think what it would have done to Béla to wade through such a chaotic confusion. But I loved every minute of it," she added, opening her eyes as the waitress came to stand at our table. "Let's celebrate and have champagne!"

"Champagne?" the waitress asked, catching the word.

"Yes, two champagne cocktails. And one without ice, please."

"Without ice, it's a quarter extra, miss," the waitress told her.

Ditta turned this information over for a moment, not quite understanding, and then said, "Oh, that's all right." As soon as the girl was gone, she began to laugh. "Did she really say that without ice it costs more? I've never heard of anything so funny. And how strange to mention the price beforehand!"

"I'm afraid I didn't bring you to a very elegant place," I said apologetically.

"But I love this place," Ditta quickly reassured me. "I've loved the whole expedition — except of course the subway. Brrr," she shivered, remembering. But she smiled again immediately as she went on. "This day was really a joy. It made me feel free as a bird. That's the remarkable thing about being here — I seem to enjoy everything. All my fears evaporated just as soon as I landed. And there were so many things I feared — almost everything — expecting it all to be terribly strange. But those very things I dreaded turned out to be easy and natural. I seem to be refreshed and renewed. Everything is stimulating, even to go into our hotel here without being greeted as celebrities. At home we could never just go anywhere, we always put in an appearance, we were always received. And here when we ask for our keys at the desk, the clerk does not even catch our name until we repeat it a few times."

The champagne with ice and the champagne without ice had now arrived. After taking a few sips, Ditta continued. "Actually if it weren't for Béla, I would feel very much at home. But you saw yourself last night the way Béla is affected by the actuality of finding himself here, away from home. And not just for the short period of a concert tour or a lighthearted summer vacation, but here to stay for an amount of time that cannot possibly be foretold — so indefinite, the outcome of it so uncertain, that one cannot even guess how it will end or when."

She stopped, but went on before I found anything to say.

"If it were only up to me, I'd like not to think about it at all — merely accept it like the migrating birds arriving at their winter home." She leaned back against the chair, her eyes closed.

"But won't the fact that you so instinctively feel at home here have some effect on Bartók?" I asked.

She laughed at me good-naturedly as one would at some silly remark of a child, but by the time she answered she was serious once more.

"I'm sure he's glad that I made my own transition so easily, but his feelings cannot be affected by mine. For that matter, I have never known anyone who could change the course of Béla's reactions, even in the smallest matters."

For the first time that day, she looked tired and worried. She began to speak rapidly and confidentially now, and I felt that she was as anxious to straighten out problems in her own mind as to explain them to me.

"Béla seems to have reached a depth of hopelessness — I have never seen him so apprehensive, so thoroughly lost before. It began to show itself on the boat coming over, and turned into real despair when we landed. I thought it was at least partly because those trunks were lost. Now I realize that the root of it all lies far back somewhere. It began a long time ago, when Hitler was coming nearer and nearer to our borders, and Béla realized that the problem would have to be faced sooner or later, and the decision made, a decision even harder to make, for he had no other reason to flee from the Nazis than his own revulsion against their cause. I remember all those discussions he had with Kodály — they both felt the same horror, though they never quite agreed on how it should be met. Neither of them could resign himself to live and work under the Nazis, but Béla was much more prepared to leave Hungary, even though this too was something he could not face. To tear himself from home, where he was so deeply rooted, and survive, seemed impossible to him. And there was his mother, his tremendous attachment to her, and she was in bad health besides."

Here Ditta stopped and hesitated for a moment, but she decided to go on.

"Maybe those things don't seem so terrible as I relate them, but in reality it was a nightmare. And finally the death of his mother was a blow so terrific that even to this day I can only guess the full weight of it. When it actually happened he was stunned, completely calm and quiet for a while, and it was impossible to know what was going on inside him. But it clarified one thing — his decision to leave was made. If his mother had stayed alive I do not think he ever could have left, no matter what happened. But after her death, he was eager to go. Whatever agony he suffered was hidden in the deep silence that descended on him when she died. But I felt, somehow, that he had an unconscious desire to mix the pain of leaving his country with the pain of losing his mother. I sometimes wonder how he survived it all."

She fell silent, and I wanted to say something to comfort her, but what good, in the face of such painful complexities, could my small reassurance do? Still, I sensed that no matter how meaningless my few words of sympathy might be, she would receive them gratefully — as I was to learn later on she always did.

"But now that the break has been made," I said tentatively, "perhaps the worst is over."

"In a way that's true, of course," Ditta quickly agreed. "On the other hand, I'm afraid he's only just beginning to realize what the real consequences of his decision are going to be. Right now it's not a question of adjusting himself to the sacrifice of an easier existence for a harder one, but of being able to exist at all. For Béla, to live is to work, and he seems possessed now by the thought that he will never be able to work here."

"But what makes him feel that way?" I asked.

"Above all, of course, his overwhelming homesickness. And then, so many different needs have to be adjusted before he is able to work. And these needs, though surely modest, are very definite and uncompromising. First of all, for Béla to have peace of mind, it's absolutely necessary to have a steady income, no matter how small, as long as he can depend on it. Only then does he know that his work can always be done in an undisturbed continuity. You know," she laughed, "that at home, with his concert fees, royalties from his music, lecture fees — no matter how these added up — it was always his comparatively small salary from the Academy and the thought of the pension he could look forward to so confidently that gave him the security he needed. Of course," she added, "by the time he would have retired, there should have been plenty for him to live on without that pension, but the idea of that small steady sum somehow meant everything to him. Maybe this sounds exaggerated to you, but that's the way Béla is, and one has to accept it."

"Didn't I hear something about a Parry Collection, and Harvard, and Columbia?" I asked.

"Oh, yes, that's the other thing that makes Béla so discouraged." And she took great pains to explain how it had been arranged the previous spring, when Bartók was in America for a short time and played with Szigeti at the Elizabeth Sprague Coolidge Festival in the Library of Congress, that the Parry Collection of mid-European folk songs, collected, on records only, by a young Englishman and now owned by Harvard, would be loaned to Columbia and Bartók would take it all down on paper from the records.

"And now," she explained further, "the whole project has become doubtful because Columbia can't seem to find a way to assure Béla a small salary. But it's still in progress, and not hopeless at all, though Béla thinks so of course — he's so easily dejected when dealing with matters like this."

"What a perfect solution that would be!" I said.

"But even if that does work out, there are a lot of other things that must be solved. Our most urgent need is for a place to live in — a simple, spacious place, calm and quiet, where Béla can work undisturbed. Is there an apartment like that anywhere in this city, and if there is, I wonder could it be found as easily as shoes?"

She was waiting for my answer, but as it was slow in coming, she went on, "You didn't know, did you, what a complicated shopping tour this would turn out to be, and how far beyond shoes it would go? Are you sorry?" she asked me seriously. "I want you to tell me truly what you think. Is it all too much? An imposition? Do you have the time? Everyone seems to be busy here. You teach piano, don't you?"

"Yes, I do, but not very much, and I have plenty of free time left to do anything I can," I reassured her quickly.

We sat for a long time there in our shadowy corner. There was another round of champagne, and pancakes, and many cups of coffee. The lights went on outside, the sidewalk became less crowded, still we talked on, and no matter how trivial our words were, we seemed to be strengthened by them and linked closer together in a single purpose that perhaps as yet we could not even name.

4

IT WAS ONLY when we started our quest for a furnished apartment that I realized that a "simple and spacious place" was the least simple thing to find. Each apartment we looked at seemed more hopeless than the one before. My ideas, it seemed, of what was suitable were too exalted and at the same time not exalted enough. It was a long time before I found out what qualifications an apartment had to have before the Bartóks would call it a "simple and quiet place."

Finally one day when I happened to be looking by myself, I came upon an apartment on East 57th Street that appeared promising enough to call Ditta about it and arrange a day to look at it together. It was black and rainy as I waited in the lobby of the apartment house for her to come. But to my surprise and dismay, I found myself confronted by Bartók himself, accompanied by his manager, Mr. Schulhoff. Ditta, it seemed, had gone off to Forest Hills to inspect another apartment with someone else. Cold dislike was written all over Bartók's face as we stood waiting in the overdecorated hall for the elevator to come.

"If I have to wait this long for the lift whenever I come home or leave, I'll spend half my life in this terrible place."

At last when the elevator had slowly carried us to the fifth floor and we were greeted by the effusive woman so anxious to sublease her apartment, Bartók would not budge farther than the foyer. Stepping at last on the threshold of the living room, he said, "Very pretty indeed," staring with obvious horror at the crowded decor. With a still more polite "Thank you very much," he turned and hurried off with Mr. Schulhoff close at his heels, leaving me to explain to the disgruntled woman what I myself did not altogether understand. When I finally was able to make my exit and hurry out, Bartók and Schulhoff were still waiting for the elevator.

"Thank you just the same," Bartók said, as we stood for a moment in front of the house. The hard rain had stopped but a sharp whistling wind was blowing through the streets, and it was much colder than before.

Bartók pulled his old flannel scarf around his neck all the way up to his chin, and I only realized after he had already walked away how disappointed he was.

Meanwhile Ditta's day proved more fruitful. "We have an apartment! It's a pleasant little place, furnished with brand-new things — in a new building," she told me with excitement on the telephone that evening. "Béla won't be able to see it before he leaves for the concert, but he's delighted to have a place to return to, and you must come the moment we move in."

As soon as she had moved in, she called again. Her enthusiasm of the first day was gone, and I could sense that she was struggling hard to hide her disappointment. She was talking rapidly and lightly. "The pianos were tuned. They really sound very well . . . I was practicing all afternoon. Béla is coming some time this evening. Everything is unpacked, put away, complete order." There was a pause. "Only one thing."

She hesitated. "There seem to be too many automobiles. I don't understand," she went on. "The entrance to this house is on a quiet little side street, but the windows are facing a boulevard. That's what got me so mixed up, I think. A steady flow of cars, making a steady rumbling. Do you think because it's raining? It seems to me it's the wet pavement that's sending the noise right up here. It couldn't be like that all the time. But still it's a sweet little place. You'll see when you come."

But before I was able to come, there was another call. "Just to tell you that Béla dislikes the place intensely. Rain or shine the cars sound just the same, and without any letup. And there are radios and all kinds of other things. One should spend twenty-four hours on sentry duty before taking a place for Béla. He is wearing his ear plugs all the time, but it's no help." She sounded openly gloomy, and there was no use trying to hide it any more.

It was a cold evening when I finally went out to see them. After changing subways several times, I walked along suburban streets strangely bleak with the undecided snow flurries of early winter. The apartment house seemed new enough, as Ditta had said, so new that it might have sprung up, fully occupied, the night before. Of course, it may have merely been freshly done over, for as I entered the foyer, I was struck by the raw smell of plaster and paint not yet dried into the flimsy walls.

Bartók opened the door and greeted me with his usual formality. I stood hesitantly in one place in the hall, not daring to cross the shiny floor with my wet galoshes, and as I looked around, my eyes wandered to a long chain of painted Mexican gourds hanging from a nail on the wall. "How nice," I said automatically.

Bartók glanced at the gaudy ornament.

"If that's your conception of Mexican folk art, then I am

sure the rest of the place will be exactly to your taste." Turning to Ditta, who appeared at that moment, he went on, "Your friend has just been expressing her admiration for that dangling decoration."

"It makes Béla sick every time he walks through the hall," Ditta remarked.

"Then why don't you take it down?" I asked.

"We don't dare. According to our lease, we're held responsible for every single article in the apartment. That wretched thing looks so fragile we're afraid it might break or chip if we move it, and then we'd have to pay for it as well. But why are you standing here? Come in. Take off your things."

I took them off in a small living room crammed with two pianos, a sofa, and several chairs. Then Ditta led me through another narrow hall to a tiny kitchen that glittered with new equipment. "Why, this is fine," I began, but stopped when I heard Bartók's voice from a farther room.

"Come along and admire the rest of it too. Here is something you shouldn't miss." In the bedroom on a small table near the window were laid out sharply pointed pencils and neat piles of blank paper, indicating that this was also his workroom. He stood in the open window listening. From below came a steady rumble of traffic and the sharp blasts of random horns. "Of course this is delicate compared with the early morning performance. The day begins with trucks, with the roar of rolling trucks that obliterates all other sounds from my memory." He leaned far out as if to intensify his suffering.

"Come, Béla, you'll catch a cold," said Ditta.

"I have my choice, you see," he said, closing the window. "Outside noises or inside noises." And then indeed I became aware of radio sounds on all sides, some soft, some loud, seeping through the walls that might have been made of cheesecloth for all the protection they gave. Overhead, heavy footsteps sounded. Bartók followed them with his eyes as they passed from one end of the room to the other.

"And noise isn't the only thing," he continued with a sweeping gesture. "Every inch of this shiny surface is saturated with smells so viciously synthetic that even in my dreams I can't escape into my natural self any more." He sat down at his desk and stared at the little piles of paper. "During my first long night here, I was thinking that if by some demonic miracle the birds and fishes were forced to exchange their natural elements with one another, they would suffer the same slow torture that I am suffering here."

Ditta, after a moment, turned abruptly and led us back to the living room. "Dinner is ready, I believe," she said. "Why don't we eat now?"

But as she placed a table in front of the sofa and began to set it, she said apologetically, "I have a headache. I am afraid I won't be able to eat with you, but why don't you two begin just the same."

"I'm not hungry," I said quickly. "Let me help, and I'll eat later too."

"Oh no! I wouldn't hear of it," she protested firmly, and disappeared into the kitchen.

"Why don't you sit down?" Bartók said, settling himself on the sofa as I still stood undecided. "Tell me the truth now," and his speech began to show that special humorous rhythm, "is it really lack of appetite, or are you too overcome by the 'great composer' to sit down to a meal with him?" He took my wan smile for a confession and went on with brightness in his eyes. "In that case, you had better forget about it. You'd have to wait a hundred years even to make a guess about any composer's final importance. Bach is too obvious to mention, Mozart and all the others too. Looking backward, it's so easy to pick out the great ones; looking forward is quite another matter." His voice took on a teasing tone and he smiled as he went on. "There's one prophecy I'll risk making, however: very likely in twenty-five years from now you won't find it trying to sit down next to America's current favorite, Sibelius himself — and eat to your heart's content without batting an eyelash."

I laughed and sat down at the far end of the sofa. As Ditta came in with a steaming dish of food, he said, "Sit down with us, even if you don't feel like eating yet." And she promptly did, smiling with relief at the change in his mood, and filled our plates.

"Chicken *paprikash!*" he exclaimed. "How out of place it is in these surroundings. But what kind of food would be appropriate here? Chili con carne to match our Mexican folk art? But that's real food too, and not any better suited to this synthetic atmosphere."

"How about straw?" Ditta suggested with some bitterness. "Plain straw — dry and tasteless."

"Straw? Dry and tasteless?" Bartók looked up. "For me, straw has other associations — the warm, steaming beds of animals sheltered in barns and stables against the cold of winter. Straw alive with fermentation — a smell so active that it actually verges on becoming sound."

We began to eat as he went on developing his theme. "I remember an acacia tree with thick clusters of white flowers giving off a scent of such intensity that I always seemed to feel its vibrations as though they were waves of sound. I knew it well for many years. It stood at the edge of a village where the houses left off and the fields began. I never missed a chance of paying the tree a visit whenever I traveled that way. What a source of delight it was to the birds and insects that hovered around it in a cloud."

Sounds and smells of memory were returning, pushing wide

invisible doors through which he escaped into the past, free at last to wander there among the people, the villages and fields, the stables, and the trees of his native land. There Ditta and I were able to join him in a rarely sustained mood that lasted on well into the evening. Yet even while he enjoyed this illusory journey, present sounds — harsh, actual and malignant — assailed him from all sides, wearing out his fragile nerves with their combined strength, until by the end of the evening he could no longer hold them in abeyance. When he retired to his room, it was as though he had again awakened to complete exhaustion in the same prison cell of inescapable reality.

At about this time the lost trunks suddenly turned up, but Bartók already was so deeply enmeshed in the complexities of his new life that the recovery of the all-important folk song collection gave him no more than a momentary relief — and in addition brought with it a new problem. Because of its tremendous size, storing it in the apartment was out of the question, and yet it had to be kept safe somewhere.

"I don't know why I should have been so concerned about it," he said, at the very moment that concern over its loss was ended. "What use is it over here, anyway? Just another dead load perhaps, like all those other trunks being dragged from one end of the world to the other. What is their purpose except to point to the bitter realization that in order to give joy again they would have to be transported back to the very places they came from — together with their owners, of course."

As winter settled in, bitter weather made the distance from Forest Hills to New York seem even longer. It was more often I who waited in the drafty subway stations to spend an afternoon with Ditta, since her horror of the subway had grown even stronger. We scarcely took time to greet each other those days, we were so eager to resume our conversations where we had left off at our previous meeting. It became a pleasant ritual to sit in the Bartóks' neat kitchen conversing endlessly over our coffee. On one of these occasions, our preoccupation was so deep that we hardly noticed Bartók, evidently attracted by the aroma of fresh coffee, appearing in the doorway. He greeted me with that stiff nod I knew so well by now, and I was startled by the blazing intensity of his eyes in contrast to the icy stillness of his face. Without a word he found himself a cup, filled it, and carried it out of the kitchen. As he disappeared, his fragile figure seemed to leave behind a visible trail of despair.

Ditta and I reacted with a single emotion to this momentary apparition. "It is not any one thing," she said with a sigh, "it is everything together. Nothing seems to be going right for us; the first thing, one would have thought would surely go well, is the concerts. Oh, they are received well enough in a lukewarm fashion, and Béla has his followers of course, an enthusiastic small group, somewhat the same as he had at the beginning of his career. Yes, he mentioned himself that the entire atmosphere reminded him of those early days at home, but without the excitement, without the feverish controversies that were so promising — more negative somehow, and this is the very quality that he finds so depressing."

She looked at me quizzically for some moments.

"I hope you are not one of those who simply dismiss Béla's reactions with the usual remark that he is a born pessimist, for he is not a pessimist at all. I don't really know how to describe it, but it is something quite different. He has a way of understanding the nature of his difficulties, and with that strange accurate awareness of his he can see the present in terms of future development, and never deludes himself into believing that those things which are truly wrong in the pres-

ent can be remedied by an unexpected good turn, suddenly, between one day and another. He expects that things will only
change by very small degrees, and single difficulties solved only
slowly by means of inevitable over-all changes that occur in the
course of time. So the immediate future looks completely
hopeless. Too many things must change to relieve the situation. It's like a long heavy bulk of darkness ahead of him
reaching into our years to come here.

"To make you understand what I mean, I merely have to
mention, for instance, his reaction to the reviews of our various
concerts, and the reviews, too, of performances of his compositions. Whether the criticism is fair or outrightly antagonistic
doesn't seem to make any difference to him. What he is concerned with is the quality of the reviews — or rather the lack
of quality in this case. Favorable reviews mean nothing to him
unless they show insight and understanding. As it is, he is
horrified with what he calls the musically illiterate reviews that
appear in the daily papers. 'Just words,' he says, 'put together
without any sense or knowledge.' The fact that all the reviews
show a consistent misconception of his work makes him feel
that even if his compositions were performed more often they
would not be presented in their true meaning to the public.
For reviewers, he believes, have the temporary power of either
slowing down or speeding up the progress of a composer in his
own time, though in the long run they have no weight at all.
The future is its own judge."

She laughed without mirth. "To sit and wait for the future,
you see, is not exactly an easy existence. And what makes it
worse in our new situation, so far away from home, is that I
have to live with this utter hopelessness — for I have learned
by now that Béla's dark predictions are seldom wrong. His
present dejected mood seems to seep into my own nervous
system, although I am so entirely different from him. My way

has always been to believe that everything that was wrong with today would disappear when a new day came. And when I was unable to believe that, I couldn't fall asleep. I couldn't go on. And I never stopped to take into consideration all the things which had not changed for the better during many thousand and one nights before. I could not help believing that all would turn into happiness tomorrow. That's why I have always gone to sleep smiling. And when the new day arrived again, I never questioned why it didn't bring the things it promised — I merely transferred my hopes to the next tomorrow.

"But getting back to Béla, the single thing he is able to hope for now is the promised work at Columbia, for that depends only upon money being made available. It would be a terrible disappointment to him if Columbia were not able to raise money enough for six months' salary — and I don't know when they will. If ever — as Béla would undoubtedly say!"

She stopped, but it took her only a few seconds to gather her thoughts again. She had to speak, a heavy weight seemed to be lying on her mind waiting to be dissolved into words. My answers were wholly unimportant, a yes or no, and she waited for them occasionally merely out of politeness.

"This long stretched-out uncertainty is irritating and frustrating, but that is a small matter compared with his dread of what is happening in Europe — the dread of what will come next, the next week, the next day, the next minute. His anxiety that America won't enter the war in time is always with him — every moment of delay means the spread of Nazism, and every country that is affected must be liberated ultimately, and perhaps destroyed in the process. And so with Hungary too — Hungary, not merely a country on the map but a part of himself, the entire stretch of it covered by foot, the whole of it known to him by heart as well as you or I would know and remember a street of our own town. Just think of that very acacia tree he never failed to visit multiplied a thousandfold in terms of other places, other things and people, just as dear to him. Every bit of ground he covered was a bit of his work-room, where people sang their songs for him. The place where he slowly, painfully made his way on his single lonely track until at last, without any compromise, always doing what he had to do, he became himself, and found recognition too. And then there are intimate memories of performances of his music from the very beginning, not the flawless outstanding concerts only, but countless other occasions — for instance, when he heard one of his choruses for children sung by the pupils of a public school. It was the first time he had actually heard children sing his music, and the surprise and joy for once sur-passed his own expectation of the intended effect, and brought tears to his eyes."

She paused for a moment, and her own eyes were filled with tears now. "And our home in Buda, Péter playing the piano, learning those first little compositions — it was for him, you know, that Béla began to write the *Mikrokosmos*. Soon we were both teaching it to him. He was no more than six at the time, but so cunning, so clever. I remember one day I came in while he was practicing, and found him sitting at the piano barefoot. His shoes he had carefully placed at opposite ends of the keyboard, with the toes pointing inward. 'A well-directed and perfectly executed symbolic kick!' Béla remarked, when I told him about it afterward.

"If only Péter were here now," she said with a sigh, the spe-cial sigh that always went with Péter's name. Sometimes the sigh came first, sometimes the name, but they were inseparable.

So our conversation, as almost always, ended with Péter, for Péter meant hope, and Ditta's optimism was unfailing; you never had to look for it, it flowed above ground. While Bartók's optimism was much more subterranean, so much harder to discover, nevertheless it was strong and always alive. He was a pessimist only as the small day-by-day obstacles confronted him.

All of his faith was centered upon the organic power of all small increments to grow slowly and in concord toward inevitable fulfillment. And so he never counted on nor hoped for those sudden isolated miracles, those happy strokes of good luck that most of us, in spite of ourselves, expect to happen. He stood firm and calm on the ground that nourished his far-spreading and deep-growing roots.

5

ALTHOUGH BY THE END of the winter I knew through one of my pupils that the large and pleasant apartment her family occupied in Riverdale would soon be available, the thought that it might possibly fill the needs of the Bartóks did not at first occur to me. For one thing, whenever I had mentioned an unfurnished apartment, Bartók had always rejected the idea emphatically.

"Out of the question!" he would insist. "How on earth could we ever furnish an apartment? We couldn't afford anything like that."

And when I tried to explain how cheaply and well I had furnished my big summer house in Vermont by picking up everything in secondhand stores and at auction sales, he would shake his head, refusing to believe me.

"You remember how it is at home," Ditta explained. "All our furniture came down to us from one side of the family or the other. Except for those few things that were carved for him by a shepherd, everything we had was old pieces he had known all his life. Perhaps he never heard of people buying furniture at auction sales. As far as he knows, it would cost a fortune even to buy a bed."

This remark about buying a bed must have stuck in an out-of-the-way corner of my mind, for when I happened to hear that two "almost new" studio couches were to be left behind in the Riverdale apartment, then this apartment that I had hardly noticed before all at once appeared to me in a new light, and I realized this might be that quiet and simple place the Bartóks had so often talked about with longing.

That same evening I went to tell Ditta about my discovery. As we talked, the two studio couches somehow kept on multiplying until they finally suggested the magical phrase "partly furnished."

"You couldn't have brought your news at a better time," Ditta exclaimed. "We had a nightmare of a day. Since Béla is always complaining about the smell here, this afternoon I brought home a bottle of one of those green liquids that are supposed to purify the air, but when I opened it, it made Béla feel terribly faint. We have had to keep all the windows open to get rid of the fumes, and now he's running water full force in the bathtub trying to drown out the traffic noises. I think I'd better turn it off now so we can go in and talk with him."

Bartók, pale and harassed, was sitting up in bed with dozens of little slips of paper spread out over the blanket in meticulous order as though playing an immense solitaire. "Tell Béla all about it," Ditta urged me as we sat down, not giving him a chance even to say hello. "Bring your chair closer!"

"Tell all about what?" he asked.

But in her eagerness she couldn't wait for me to start. "Agota has found a wonderful apartment, and above all it is partly furnished!" She didn't look at me as she added this bit.

"And exactly what makes it so wonderful?" Bartók asked with mild interest as he gathered up his papers.

Having got us over the worst hump, Ditta turned to me to provide the details.

"For one thing," I began, carefully choosing my words, "it's beautifully situated, almost in the country. Yet it's right in New York City and much nearer to the center of things than this place. It's the entire first floor of a two-family house."

"How many rooms?"

"Six or seven — I'm not quite sure."

"You know we can't afford to pay much."

"It's cheaper than this apartment."

"Exactly how much is it per month?"

"Seventy dollars, I think."

"Well, you'd better tell us now what's wrong with it!"

"Nothing at all!"

It was I, now, who did not look at Ditta, but I knew she was smiling.

"Would you please draw me a picture of it?" Bartók asked, and handed me a pencil and a slip of paper, but still trying hard to hide his growing interest.

"I'm afraid I'm not very good at drawing."

"That's all right. I assure you I don't expect a masterpiece, just a floor plan of the rooms."

I made an outline of the rooms, and while he was studying it, amused myself by drawing a picture of the outside of the house, showing roses climbing over its walls and encircling the windows in great profusion. I sketched the two trees in front, and narrow strips of garden on either side. At the back I managed to get in a suggestion of the wild growth of trees that stood on a descending slope.

"What are these?" he asked, pointing to one of my painstaking smudges.

"Roses," I said.

"I like the truth, you know — the truth without trimmings."

"But what if trimmings are part of the truth?"

A smile flitted across his face. "You mean to tell me that the roses are really there, and the trees and the garden too?"

"Yes, at least they will be by spring. And everything is taken care of by the owner, an old Italian who lives in the basement. He loves to putter in the garden all day long."

"Are you sure we can get it?" he asked, unable to restrain his enthusiasm any longer.

"I am quite sure."

"You must remember, Béla," said Ditta cautiously, "that we would have to buy a little furniture. It won't cost much, I promise."

Bartók chose to ignore this remark. "When can we see it?" he demanded.

"The people who are in it now are moving out tomorrow," I said. "We could go out the day after — that's Sunday."

"All right," said Bartók. "Then let it be Sunday."

To avoid the long subway ride from Forest Hills to Riverdale, I telephoned friend after friend until finally I hit upon one who had time to drive us and the gasoline too. That was a rare combination in those days of rationing.

As we approached Riverdale early that Sunday morning, the grayness of the city slowly gave way to the fresh green of trees and bushes already showing their buds. When the car stopped in front of a faded pink stucco house at 3242 Cambridge Avenue, Bartók was the first to get out.

He stood on the sidewalk for a while, just looking at the house. Then he began to walk back and forth, inspecting everything with the utmost care, pausing particularly to examine the little garden in which pansies and bleedingheart were almost ready to come out into the early sunshine. Assuring himself that the climbing roses actually were there, growing on the wall in tightly closed clusters of pink half lost among their new green leaves, he glanced at me with a smile.

Back on the sidewalk again, he looked up and down the whole uneven slope of the street. "See, Ditta," he said, "how completely these tall rows of bushes separate and hide the houses from one another."

Leaving our friend in his car, I went up the steps to the door and opened it, and we walked in.

The hall was dark except for a strip of sunbeams coming from the large square room to the right that was filled with dazzling sunlight. Another room of the same size extended at the side into a narrow sun parlor that looked toward street and garden. At the end of the hall there was a large kitchen with an open porch that ran across the entire back of the house. From it could be seen a patchwork of roofs, treetops, and squares of lawns and strips of gardens. And in the far distance the heavy structure of the elevated drew a long dark line against the horizon.

Bartók studied the view for some time and then went back into the kitchen. He disregarded its worn and uneven floor as his attention was immediately caught by a battered white table standing near the wall. "Is this part of the furniture you were talking about?" he asked, obviously delighted.

"O yes!" I said brightly, happy to find this humble contribution adding its weight to the two bare mattresses and springs, and surprised by Bartók's enthusiasm over the unimposing object.

"Very good," he said. "But are you sure that nobody will take it away?"

"Oh no!" I said, as reassuringly as I could. "Nobody will, I'm positive."

"But why did they leave it here, I wonder? See how steady it is." He leaned against it to test its strength.

"Come on, let's look at the bedrooms," Ditta urged impatiently.

Three bedrooms were at the left of the hall. The front one,

large, cheerful and sunny, contained the two studio couches. Bartók sat down on one, then tried the other. "Why, they are really comfortable! Aren't we lucky!"

Ditta and I exchanged glances of profound relief as we followed him through the complete emptiness of the second bedroom.

At the back of the house, we entered the smallest of the three. One of its windows was almost obscured by overgrown bushes. Bartók opened the other and looked out. "Well!" he said. "You failed to mention the best thing of all — there's a little vegetable garden down there." He pointed to a well-turned patch of brown earth on which the growing things were hardly more than straight green lines.

"How quiet it is in here — how far away from everything. This is just the room for me." When Ditta pointed out how dark and small it was, he only smiled. His mind was made up.

"The middle room we'll save for Péter," he said, "and yours, Ditta, will be that front one we saw first. With all that light and sunshine it should be just right for you."

As Bartók now found everything to his liking, I became more and more disturbed by the cracks that were showing on the ceilings, the paint that was peeling from the walls and woodwork, and by the large patches where mirrors and pictures had hung before. "Some paint and a little plaster will do wonders," I said.

"We have no money for such things," he protested.

"Oh, but you wouldn't have to pay for it — that's the landlord's responsibility."

"Perhaps so, but in the end I'm sure we'd have to pay for it one way or the other. How much did you say the rent was?" he asked, turning to me abruptly.

"I think it's seventy dollars; but I'd better go and ask the owner. He's in the basement, I hope."

"You mean you still don't know the exact amount? I can just see you coming back with the news that it's twice as much as you told me."

Prodded by his eyes, I fled toward the basement, sorry now that I had failed to get a definite figure from the landlord beforehand. I had been so preoccupied with the problem of persuading Bartók to rent an unfurnished apartment that it had never occurred to me he would want to take the place in such a hurry.

The Italian landlord was waiting, only too ready to do business. Old, fat, and polite, with white hair, and dressed in his Sunday best, he told me that the rent was seventy-five dollars. I recognized the routine approach to a bargaining session, and hurried back to warn Bartók, but the landlord was close behind me and already smiling in the door before I could say a word in private.

Bartók greeted him in Italian, and introduced him to Ditta. They all shook hands with great formality, and Bartók continued to talk in Italian and I stood by uncomprehending, fearful lest the transaction be closed entirely to the Bartóks' disadvantage. Finally I broke in and said, "There are no children," knowing from my pupils that the owner regarded all children as born enemies of his gardens, "so I think you ought to let the place go for seventy."

"No, seventy-five," he said, shaking his massive head.

"All right, seventy-five then!" said Bartók at once. "That's fine. Shall we settle everything right now?"

But the old man shook his head again. "Can't take a deposit without my son. I'll have to telephone him."

Bartók looked at me as though I had brought on the delay myself. "I knew something would go wrong," he said.

When the son could not be located by telephone I was greatly relieved, and suggested that I could come back next day to conclude the arrangements. But Bartók wouldn't hear of it, and the landlord told us to return in an hour — which meant that we could not ride back with our patient friend who had to go home to a Sunday dinner with his family. As we walked out to the car, I suggested that we look at other places for rent in the neighborhood, if only to pass the time.

"Why should I look for other places when I have already found the one I want?" Bartók asked impatiently.

And so we sat down to wait on the front steps, Bartók maintaining a complete silence. I could feel the delay fraying our nerves in the Sunday stillness, and was glad when Ditta finally spoke. "Isn't it a lot like Buda?" she asked Bartók.

At first I thought he had not heard as he continued to look off down the street, but after a moment he answered her. "Yes, perhaps." And after another moment, he went on with unexpected intensity, "Of course the trees here are not so old, and the gardens don't have the same depth . . . and . . . somehow the sky doesn't seem so big. Still, I suppose the way I remember Buda now is too blurred and personal to compare with anything real — not because I am separated from it by so great a time or distance but by so small a hope ever to see Buda again."

It was a shock to me that Ditta's chance remark should so easily have broken through the bright surface of this expedition to Riverdale, and I glanced toward her fearfully as she said, "Béla, how can you say such a thing?" But it was a casual protest, and it was apparent that she had rejected his statement of despair as something that must crush her if she allowed it to touch her at all. "It's so lovely here," she added vaguely, quite as though she had really dismissed what he had said.

"Oh, yes, it is fine," Bartók reassured her, "a lot better than I expected."

We sat again without words, and then Bartok turned to me

abruptly. "Shouldn't we see if the landlord has found his son yet?" I saw that he had returned to the importance of the immediate problem, to the impatience with practical details that was the only protection he could raise against an insoluble hopelessness.

I got up to try to find the landlord again, when all at once he appeared himself to tell us that his son had agreed to the seventy-five a month, and we went into the apartment again to close the deal. "But you will paint, of course," I said, quickly.

"Paint, yes," he said, looking around the kitchen door where we were standing, "but no floors."

"Why, just look at these floors!" I cried, but Bartók stopped me with a warning glance before I could protest further, and held out three ten-dollar bills to the old man.

"Paint, yes," said the landlord with finality as he accepted the money, "but no floors."

He scribbled a receipt for the deposit, pulled a ring of keys from his pocket and handed it to Bartók with an expansive flourish. He was all friendly smiles as he shook hands and departed. Bartók, looking deeply relieved, put the keys in his pocket and then led us out of the house into the sunshine.

He walked quickly at first, with long easy strides, but slowed down by the time we reached the end of the street. We stopped there and wandered around for a while among the empty lots overgrown with thick underbrush, the ground spread with long and faded last year's grasses.

"Even a place for picnics!" Bartók pointed toward a group of tall trees. "You are invited to come to the first one with us," he said, turning to me, "though I wonder if you really deserve a picnic after almost losing that house for us. What if he had refused us just because of those floors! What was wrong with them anyway?"

"Oh come along, Béla," said Ditta. "We've got to get back to Forest Hills."

"Must we?" he asked, stopping altogether. "How about going back to our new house and taking a real look at it this time?"

So we turned back, Bartók leading the way. He unlocked the door and we followed him into the hall, where the long rays of sunshine were even brighter than before. It was his discovery — Ditta and I were being shown around for a first look. As we went from one room to another, Bartók stopped suddenly in the sun parlor. "Why didn't you show me this before?" he asked. "It ought to be a good place for the two pianos, Ditta." Of course he must have seen it before, though not taking it in fully in the first moments of confusion.

Then wandering through the kitchen, he noticed, evidently also for the first time, the usual row of cabinets extending across the entire length of one wall. He opened and closed the glass doors appreciatively. "I'll keep my papers here," he said.

"But Béla, this is the kitchen!" Ditta objected. "These closets are meant for dishes and things."

"We have no dishes," he said almost joyfully, "and we don't need many, either. Surely a few cups and half a dozen plates will be enough." His voice had the same light tone as he walked back through the hall. "Come and see how big the bathroom is!" he called, and we found him examining the old-fashioned bathtub standing on its claw feet. He turned on one of the faucets and let the water run over his hands. "Why, it's hot!" he exclaimed in pleasant surprise. "What a waste to keep the water hot in an empty apartment."

Finally he returned to the room he had chosen for himself. Although still sunless, it was filled with soft light tinted green by the bushes outside the window. Going over to the radiator in the corner, he touched its rusty surface. "This will keep me warm when winter comes," and he stood a long while in the empty room.

As we started on the long downhill walk to the 231st Street subway station, Bartók said, "I don't see why we have to wait two weeks. Why can't we move in tomorrow?"

"It will take at least that long to get the apartment painted and furnished, Béla," said Ditta.

"I don't know about the painting, but certainly buying a few tables and chairs shouldn't take so long." I was surprised to see how easily he accepted the fact that the apartment was virtually unfurnished. Apparently the two rickety chairs on the porch, the battered old kitchen table and the two bare couches were almost enough for him.

Walking along the edge of a park separated from the side-walk by a low stone wall, Bartók noticed a parallel path running through the park. "Let's go back and find the entrance," he said. "I'd like to walk on that path." Quickly retracing our steps, we found the entrance and soon were walking among trees and bushes and smooth expanses of well-kept lawn. At the end of the park we were separated only by a highway from a wide business street leading directly to the subway. There was the usual collection of neighborhood stores, but because it was Sunday most of them were closed.

"Here is everything one could possibly think of!" said Bartók, looking at the displays in the windows. "One could spend a whole life here, and be amply provided for without ever having to leave this one street." Stopping in front of a sta-tionery store, he ran his eyes over the various piles of papers, notebooks, pencils and pens. "Now this is luck — a plentiful supply of everything." And then his attention was caught by a towering pyramid of oranges in a fruit market. "Just look at that!" Turning suddenly to Ditta, he asked, "Do we still have that orange squeezer Jóska sent us?"

"Why of course we have it. Szigeti sent it to us when we arrived," she explained to me, "together with a huge basket of oranges."

"Well, with that squeezer," Bartók said, "we have something to start housekeeping with."

Near the subway we passed a little Greek restaurant and the smell that escaped to the street made us realize that we had not yet had lunch. Although the place was dark and narrow, and everything reeked of burned grease, Bartók ate a thick ham sandwich and drank a cup of muddy coffee with enjoyment. Nothing could displease him, it seemed — not even the subway when we finally reached it. The subway, as I had failed to explain to them, was an elevated this far out, the very elevated that we saw in the distance from the back porch of the new apartment. "But it goes underground after only three stations," I added.

"Three stations above ground are better than none," he replied cheerfully.

While we stood waiting on the platform, his eyes traveled back across the long uneven rows of rooftops, half hidden by the arms of trees, as if he were trying to separate the house that was now their own from all the others.

"How far this city stretches in every direction!" he said to Ditta. "And it seems to have a different face at every turn."

As the train clattered along, we made no attempt at conversation, but when it drew into the 116th Street station, Bartók looked at his watch. "Only twenty-two minutes from 231st Street," he said. "How easy it will be to get to Columbia — I won't mind the trip even if I have to make it three times a week."

Ditta smiled at me, for once carried beyond her fear of the subway, and her eyes were bright. "You know," she said, "in our excitement we didn't even tell you that it is almost certain now that Béla's work at Columbia will actually begin soon."

"We'll see what will come of it. We'll see," said Bartók more soberly, as the subway jerked into motion again.

6

LIKE BEACHCOMBERS, Ditta and I searched in the warehouses of the city, through endless heaps of discarded household belongings waiting to be auctioned off — furniture sufficiently worn and faded not to be very desirable or sought after, but still containing some usefulness or even a hint of dormant beauty.

Luck was with us from the beginning. On our very first day, we picked up a dining room set at a warehouse auction on 125th Street — a round walnut table, a china closet of similar finish but lighter tone, five chairs almost but not exactly alike, and a sideboard that had nothing in common with the other pieces but scratches and a complete lack of style.

When I called out our bid of twenty-five dollars, Ditta seized my hand as we braced ourselves for all the competing bids. After we had waited for what seemed to us a very long time and none came, we realized that what meant everything to us at that moment meant nothing to anyone else in that crowded room. When the auctioneer knocked it down to us, Ditta smiled at me in triumph, though I for my part was wondering whether we might not just as easily have had it for ten dollars. "I just can't believe it!" she said, as we pushed our way through jumbled piles of furniture to get to our lot. "Why it cost no more than a pair of shoes!" She could hardly wait to get close to it, leaning forward to touch the top of the table, and to stroke the back of a chair with her fingertips, for once unmindful of dust and dirt. Then she hurried me out of the warehouse, unable to face another such ordeal of suspense that day.

When we came out on 125th Street from the chill of the warehouse, the trolley tracks, darkly marked by the shadow of the elevated, were abstracted into an unexpected vista that seemed to us mysterious and beautiful.

Turning into the nearest cafeteria, we snatched food with the lunch hour crowd and searched for two empty chairs. Ditta balanced her tray of food with an easy skill that made me realize how far she had come since that afternoon at Childs when I had felt that its lack of elegance called for an apology. In a moment we were sitting at a small table opposite two men who were gulping coffee. Ditta was completely oblivious of their presence and talked about our luck without restraint.

"That round dining room table!" she said. "If we could only find a big work table for Béla as easily as that — one that's actually big enough for him to spread out his papers the way he likes to."

Now that we had actually bought so much for so little, to furnish the apartment was no longer a dream that might or might not come true, but a reality. As our plans began to materialize, the apartment took on a more definite shape, and our vision of it seemed to expand even further with each new load delivered to the door. For once fulfillment went far beyond the original conception.

These were happy days, although tiring ones — never had I seen Ditta so completely lighthearted, and she seemed so

much at home in this buoyant mood I could not help feeling
that happiness indeed was her natural, rightful element.

And then one morning, after I had waited a long time for
her at the warehouse where we had planned to meet, she failed
to appear. When at last I telephoned, it was Bartók who
answered me. "But she left hours ago." He sounded apprehensive. "I hope nothing went wrong. Please call me instantly when she arrives. Or call me anyway, in a little while."

I hurried back to the entrance of the warehouse, and all at
once I saw her coming slowly down the street, with no sign of
her usual vigor. Nor did she make any attempt to hasten her
steps, although I ran toward her, eager in my relief. The
clear blue of her eyes was cloudy as if mixed with muddy
green, her cheeks burned with red spots, and her hands were
clammy as they grasped mine. She looked as if she had been
wandering for hours.

"It's rather late," I began, but she didn't hear me.

"I want some coffee, I must sit down somewhere," she said
almost in a whisper.

She didn't speak again as we walked down 135th Street from
Riverside Drive to Broadway and found a cafeteria. It was
almost empty, and she dropped into a chair at the first table.
I hurriedly got the coffee, and then as I sat down I asked her
what was wrong.

"I don't know," she said, looking at me blankly. "What
do you think?" I was lost for an answer. "What will all this
come to?" she went on. "What will become of Béla? This is
all make-believe, it will never come to any good, I am sure
of it. Something will happen to him. You'll see, something
will. I can't even follow through my thoughts to the terrible
end of it all."

I had never seen her like this before, but I sensed that however I might try to reach her, I would not succeed. "What

makes you think something is wrong?" I asked, making the attempt just the same.

"Tell me that what I feel is not true," she answered. "Tell me that there is no terrible end here, that there is a way, that Béla will be all right, that nothing fatal is happening — " She went on repeating almost the same phrases.

For the ear alone her words made little sense, but looking into her face and listening to her at the same time, I had the impression that she was following a line of thought entirely clear and logical to her. So I sat still, not interrupting, and after a while her thoughts came a little nearer. "Why was he in such a hurry this morning? Why?" she insisted, but not wanting an answer. "This terrible hurry! Unbearable! All I asked him before I left, all I asked was if he'd like to see the wonderful things we'd bought. 'No!' he said. 'What I want,' he said, 'is to walk into that house when it's ready, and stay there. Anything that happens between then and now is disturbing to me, and the sooner you have it ready, the better.' "

She was sitting as if listening to his words again, reading a special significance into them. As she weighed them over and over in her mind, she slowly relaxed and grew calmer. "Of course you have no way of knowing," she went on at last, much more rational now, "that what Béla as a rule expresses with his few casual words is always something concentrated, something that emerges from masses of ideas, something that stands for what he has thought out with care and precision. It has taken me almost twenty years to come to this conclusion, and to come to understand it, little by little — and his hurry now is bewildering to me. You should have seen the way he was throwing his papers in his suitcase last night." With each word she came more into focus; drinking her coffee now, she was almost herself again. "I must try to understand what is causing this feverish tempo, why he was so abrupt this morning, and merely said the first thing that came into his mind."

"I called the apartment when you were so long in coming," I told her. "I promised Béla to call him as soon as you got here."

She stood up instantly, heading for the telephone booth. After a short time, she came out again, smiling radiantly. "He told me not to spend too much money," she called out, even before she reached the table. "He tells me that every single time, before I start out. This morning, he didn't tell me, as if it didn't matter to him one way or another any more. But he warned me most emphatically now — 'Don't spend too much money!' he told me. Let's go," she said, gathering her belongings from the chair. "I hope we haven't missed too much."

We didn't miss too much. In fact, it was this time that we found the big work table for Bartók. But the whole day for me remained under the cloud of what had happened that morning, and even when I was at home alone I still could not escape from thinking about Ditta with deep uneasiness, unable to forget the strangeness of seeing her like that — as if she were standing at the edge of a cliff, or on the bank of a fast-flowing deep river.

But there was no repetition of the panic of that morning during the days that followed. The very next day it was she who waited for me and seized my arm with all her usual warmth and animation. Happy in my relief, I felt her excitement taking hold of me too.

"Do you realize that the apartment is almost complete?" I said to her. "If we are as successful as usual, this may be our very last day! It's like coming to the end of a journey, isn't it? I wonder if you will miss it as much as I will."

"I will miss it a lot," she replied, "but one thing is sure, Béla won't. He will be glad to shut the door on our Mexican gourds and the rest of it. He's anticipating moving into the new apartment with such concentration that Forest Hills no longer exists for him any more. That's why I'm so happy we've accomplished so much in so short a time."

At last we had everything — even more than everything! For the essentials were considerably loaded down with the by-products due to that peculiar system of auctioning — the grouping together of random objects in lots so that often to get one desired piece it may be necessary to buy them all.

Ditta and I were to unpack, for instance, barrels presumably filled with china but bearing the exciting and provocative label "contents, if any, unknown," their bottomless depths yielding more than enough cups, plates and platters to fill those spacious shelves in the kitchen cupboard which Bartók had hoped would remain empty for his own use. From other barrels we dug out a fantastic assortment of items: alarm clocks, candlesticks, ash trays, Christmas tree trimmings, even a goldfish bowl, and many other things that we did not have time either to sort out or identify. So eventually most of them found their way into Péter's room along with an overflow of larger objects which seemed to have no immediate use but which we felt might somehow find their places later on.

The imposing bulk of five radios (six dollars for the lot) seemed to fall into this category, although this lot held much more excitement since we did not yet know whether any of the radios might still retain the spark of life. Actually we found two that worked with some encouragement, but the real surprise of this collection was a hand-wound victrola of aged vintage and eccentric shape, complete with half a dozen cracked and worn records. It gave out a feeble quaver, and we could not decide whether it was the records that were responsible for the touching effect of its remote voice or whether it was the instrument itself. This machine, cleaned and oiled with special affection, was placed in an important corner of the living room near a pleasantly faded blue sofa and an equally faded comfortable red armchair.

Sometimes we found the by-products more rewarding than the objects we had bought for a specific purpose. For example, a large painted table which we had thought just right for Bartók to work on was so ungainly that we stowed it away in Péter's room, while a pair of red velvet Empire chairs, thrown in for good measure, after minor repairs on their golden frames and a vigorous shampoo of their grimy upholstery, blossomed richly before our admiring eyes. When placed in the sun-parlor music room, they gave its narrow awkwardness the grandeur of another era.

As we divided our purchases so that each room received its full share, we kept wondering about the people who had owned these things before. Who were they? And why had they deserted their belongings? What extraordinary adversities had made them toss aside the little white lamp, its shade so new and clean, or the oval dressing table with its ruffle perfectly intact, and combs and copper hairpins still in its drawers?

And when the very things we now arranged with such care would in the fullness of time again be discarded and again rescued from the shadowy depths of a Bronx warehouse, would the new owner pause a moment to wonder why, just as we did?

Finally the day came when the apartment was ready for Bartók to walk in and stay. The windows were hung with freshly laundered curtains and the walls of every room were bright with new white paint. True, the furniture we had so painstakingly oiled and polished had already lapsed back into much of its original dullness; but even so, the various pieces, as they stood in their appointed places on the softly faded rugs, seemed to have a harmonious relationship with one another, like the members of a large, hard-working family who had come together after a long separation to take part in some important and solemn event.

Ditta and I sat down for a few minutes to admire the effect before settling a last few details. "How lovely everything seems," Ditta said, "especially now that I look at it through Béla's own eyes. I'm sure, too, that he'll find it a good place to work in, for it has the remote and sheltered atmosphere he loves."

"As for myself," she went on, folding her hands in her lap in a mood of quiet and repose, "in a way I feel as though I had lived through all this before; and yet at the same time I know that often in the future I will remember how I sat here waiting, and then perhaps these few minutes will seem even more real than they do now."

After a while in her own room, Ditta stood leaning against a table and stared at the noonday blaze of sunshine.

"So lovely!" I said.

But she did not answer, standing motionless as though hypnotized by the light. "Which means," she said, after so long a pause that I scarcely connected her answer with my chance remark, "that you don't approve of my accepting this room for myself." It was obvious that I failed to understand. "You think it was selfish of me — and that I should have insisted on Béla taking it . . ." To make the implication clear beyond any shadow of a doubt, she added, "For he was the one — not I — for whom you have done all this." Having struck with all her force, she turned away again, retreating deep within the pain that this impulse had cost her.

My only desire was to make it clear that this was not the case. "But I don't understand what you mean by 'having done all this.' What have I done except to have a wonderful time day after day with you?" I leaned toward her, determined to show her how far wrong she was. "Didn't we, Ditta? Didn't we have a wonderful time, exciting, happy? Don't take those days away from us! I'm only sorry that they are all over."

She did not answer, but I had caught her attention, and her face softened and her head inclined slightly toward me.

"Even if this *had* been an ordeal instead of the pure pleasure it was, even if it had meant some hardship for me — and it really didn't! — it would have all been for you, and perhaps through you for Béla too, but first of all for you."

She gave me a fleeting smile, and I knew that she believed me now. In no time she was herself again, so quickly indeed that I was unable to adjust to the rapid pace of her changing mood, and remained deeply disturbed, while she on the other hand became actually gay and light as if she had rid herself of some disturbing weight.

As she moved around restlessly, she noticed the empty fish-bowl in a corner of the room.

"Why don't we do something about this?" She turned to me. "Do you remember that little pet shop near the subway station? I think we have just time enough to get some goldfish there for Béla. Why didn't we think of it before?"

Still unrecovered from the shock I had just received, I was unable to share her enthusiasm as freely as I almost always did, and she was puzzled and annoyed that I did not respond to her refreshed spirits.

And in spite of the fact that I followed her instantly when she was ready to go, as we were running down the hill she was conscious that my mood did not quite keep pace with our feet. "How glad I am I thought of the fish — Béla will be beyond himself with joy," she said, applying the magic formula which had never failed to revive even the weariest moments of the last busy weeks. "How carefully he will feed them, you'll see, strictly according to directions," she said, trying to talk me back into a lighter mood, "actually counting the little morsels as he scatters them in the bowl — not a grain less, not a grain more."

But I was unable to feel at all lighthearted — not that I was hurt or resentful, but I couldn't free myself from my train of thought: nothing could be more natural than this suspicion that was probably always lurking in the back of her mind. How many people must have tried to reach Bartók through her — using her as a mere steppingstone! Why shouldn't she be distrustful of me at times? Our friendship was still so young — why wouldn't she have an occasional apprehension about my sincerity? Her doubts had evaporated quickly, in truth she was glad to believe me, and was trying to tell me this now in her own way.

We found the pet shop and selected the goldfish, big ones, small ones, bright gold and red, and transparent gray ones for contrast. And we didn't forget the food, either. On the way home, we helped ourselves to some forsythia branches that had just burst into bloom. Back in the apartment again, we deposited our treasures in Bartók's room and had just enough time to put the water and the fish into the bowl before we saw Bartók slowly walking up the hill. As he had often told Ditta he would like to spend his first few moments in the new place all by himself, we hurried out the back door and wandered down among the young poplars below the house. Then we slowly walked up to the street, and went all the way to the empty lots and back again. Sitting down on the front steps, we waited for an invitation to enter. But as none seemed to come, Ditta finally decided to go in.

As she opened the door, I heard the eerie voice of the victrola from its infinite distance whispering "Yes Sir, She's My Baby." For a moment, I thought of Bartók unerringly attracted to the old machine, sitting oblivious of all else in the quiet order that had been made for him, and was almost startled when Ditta came back to the door at once and asked me in.

"You can stop it now, Ditta," I heard Bartók call out from the other side of the house. His voice was warm and vigorous. "Be careful," he warned. "That machine is delicate, but it works fine if it's properly handled." Then I saw the shabby old library table we had pushed out of the way into Péter's room jammed in the doorway of Bartók's bedroom. After discovering the victrola, he must have made straight for the one spot in the house that was not prepared for him. Looking in, I saw that Péter's room had indeed felt the full impact of Bartók's arrival and seemed to have been attacked by a tornado. Boxes and barrels that had been carefully and tightly stowed away had burst open, and Bartók was turning over the wild disorder of their contents.

"But what is all this?" he asked, astounded. "Why all these radios and things?" Picking up an alarm clock, he wound it and set it with precision. "Where do they come from? Do they really belong to us? Why have you hidden all the best things away, like presents before Christmas?" His questions followed each other so fast that we had no time to answer, and anyway by now the alarm clock had responded with a loud clamor to his manipulations. "It runs!" he said, hastily turning it off. "Perhaps it goes a little slowly — but we'll see," and he glanced at his watch and sat down, looking around at the upheaval. "It occurs to me," he said, "that we should leave this for Péter, just as it is. It would be better than a birthday for him to find all this stuff here!"

"But Béla," Ditta objected, "where could we put a bed for him? There isn't a square foot left."

"If I know Péter," Bartók answered, "he'd be happiest sleeping on top of a radio."

And he was on his feet again, looking at the box he had been sitting on. "What's in here?" he asked, and I was surprised to find that even a single box still remained unopened. He found it filled with books and started to take them out, one by one. "Now just look at this!" he said, pulling out a ragged First Primer. "Why did I never think of getting one of these for myself? If you want to understand a country, it's important to know what are the first words, phrases, and rhymes that the children learn. Though even that isn't basic enough," he went on, as he slipped the book into his pocket and started out the door. "One should really go back to the very beginning, to what they hear even before their eyes are open."

I stepped aside to let him pass, and he turned toward his own room, and asked us to help him with the heavy table that was blocking the doorway. "Why are you trying to get this awful old thing into your room, Béla?" Ditta asked. "Didn't you notice the nice one that's already in there?"

"This one is bigger," he said, surprised that an explanation was necessary.

So Ditta and I began where we thought we had left off, and helped to destroy the carefully planned order of his room. The table that already stood by the wall was squeezed against the bed, while Bartók, noticing that the table of his choice could be extended, pulled it open so that supplementary leaves of imitation mahogany rose into place, making an unpleasant contrast with the rest, which had been painted black.

Satisfied now that the table filled the room from wall to wall, his attention turned to the colorful embroideries we had tacked up to brighten the sunless room. "But these are Hungarian," he said. "And they are old, too. Where did you get them?"

Ditta nodded toward me.

He took one of the pieces from the wall and examined it by the window. "But it's been washed," he remarked with disappointment. "What a shame! The smell has been washed right out of it! If only you hadn't, I could tell exactly where it came from, trace it, perhaps, to its very village. Now it's all gone."

"It was really dirty," I said.

"Dirty indeed! Must everything be sacrificed for cleanliness? Surely it would have been enough if you had just shaken it out the window a little." He turned to look thoughtfully at another larger piece we had put on the bed for a cover. It was made of homespun linen, richly embroidered in a red that had faded with the years, its whiteness gleaming with starch. "Things like this should be treated as relics and preserved with reverence. What you call dirt is the mark of their history. Still, even with their flavor diluted, I'm glad to have them here."

Putting down the embroidery, he caught sight of the goldfish and leaned over the bed, watching the bright figures with pleasure. This time he had no reservations, he merely asked if the fish had been fed, and upon being assured that they had not, took up the box of food, read the directions and counted out, morsel by morsel, the number of grains appropriate to the number of fish in the bowl. Then with a last satisfied look at his room, he went out again to the hall.

He stopped in the living room doorway, silent for a moment. Then he said, "It's a surprise to find so many things here — it's so different from what I expected that it doesn't seem quite real to me."

"What did you think it would be like, Béla?" Ditta asked. "I'd love to know."

He went over to the red chair near the victrola. "Well," he answered, "I imagined it as more like the first time we saw it, only the walls painted white and the floors swept clean — almost bare except for a table or two and a few chairs, not much else really. That was the picture that formed in my mind, and lingered. It's almost painful to part with it."

"Of course. Yes, I understand," Ditta said.

He must have noticed the shadow of disappointment on her face, for he went on quickly, "But this thing alone," indicating the wide-open victrola, "more than makes up for the loss of the simpler image I had made for myself of these rooms." He closed the machine carefully. "It will be most useful for transcribing the Parry Collection. I can bring records home with me sometimes, and listen to them here in complete comfort." He looked at the floor. The sheen of the gray carpet seemed to suggest a further, less pleasurable thought. "There's another thing: I hardly dare think about it. How have you managed to do all this with only three hundred dollars to spend?" He looked around, uneasy and apprehensive. "I do hope it's all paid for."

Ditta smiled then, altogether comforted. "Why Béla," she said, "of course it's all paid for! There's even some money left over. I have all the bills, marked 'paid'! I saved every one of them — and can show them to you any time you like!"

Bartók seemed relieved and his face brightened again. "Well, then, with that worry off my mind, the whole thing looks even better!" With a new sense of possession, he went into the dining room, sitting down at that round table we had bought first, and looked out of the window at the darkening sky.

"Good," he said. "It's going to rain." Watching the clouds hanging low over the motionless pale green branches of the trees, he continued, "Those clouds are really thick and heavy — no doubt there is a storm brewing up there that will reach us any minute now." Only after I looked at his face and saw on it that intense anticipation of the rain, did it occur to me that he was looking forward to the sensation of being sheltered and protected by the roof and walls of his new home. This fleeting sense of security had to be enlarged and made explicitly real to himself by every available means, for he knew only too well that this sense of safety was made of a fabric thinner than mist, and just as perishable.

Almost as if hypnotized, we sat there waiting for the rain to come, but instead, it seemed to be getting lighter. Bartók ran his fingers back and forth across the smooth surface of the table.

"You know," he said, "it's truly miraculous the way you two women have managed to furnish this place for so little and in such a short time; yet the very ease with which you've done it strikes me as somehow immoral."

Ditta looked up startled, her face uncertain, as if wondering what would come now.

"Over and over again," he went on, "in my wanderings, I saw the struggle of the people in their poor villages to provide themselves with even the barest necessities — a table, a few chairs, a bed. That was about all the furniture they ever had, and often they made it themselves in their few moments of spare time, painstakingly, piece by piece — sometimes it took years. Their possessions were meager enough, God knows, but what human reality they had compared with this houseful of things acquired almost overnight." He looked around with a little smile. "I hope I'm right in believing that everything here is made by machine — otherwise I might not be able to accept it with a clear conscience at all."

Ditta, obviously not wishing to move any farther out on this thin ice, said, "But you haven't seen the pianos, Béla!" She got up and walked quickly to the sun porch.

He followed her to the music room, which looked even

smaller than before with the grand piano on one side under the windows and the spinet against the wall. Bartók's eyes were immediately caught by the gold and red glow of the two Empire chairs. "For the audience, I presume — how elegant! Just the right number for a packed house, too!" Sitting down at the grand piano, he leaned on the closed keyboard, turned his head toward me and said, "I'd like to play something for you if you'll tell me what you want to hear."

Overwhelmed by a violent attack of my old diffidence, I sank into one of the chairs and managed to say, "Oh, anything — thank you — anything at all. Whatever you please."

But Bartók still waited, and neither moved nor spoke. Finally Ditta broke the long silence. "Something of Bartók, perhaps?" she murmured, trying to help me out.

"Oh, yes, please! By all means!" I said quickly.

"But exactly what?" Bartók insisted, resting his hands on the keys as he waited for an answer. "Give me your choice."

There was another silence, and I realized that I was not going to be spared the ordeal of deciding.

"Allegro barbaro." I said the first thing that came into my mind.

"Why Allegro barbaro?" He looked at me sternly, leaving no doubt that mine was a particularly unfortunate request. "Do you think it's such an outstanding composition?"

"Why, of course."

"You do?" he asked. "Or could it be — " his eyes became penetrating — "that you chose it because that's the only piece of mine you can name?"

"Oh no, not at all! I know many others, too, but I happen to like this one."

"Whom did you hear it played by?"

"Maybe I just read it for myself," I answered finally. "We haven't had a chance to listen to very much of your music here, at least I haven't. But then I'm not a musician, really."

"How can you be a teacher of piano without being a musician?"

"I started out to be a musician," I told him reluctantly, "and I suppose I still am one in a way, only — well, I haven't been aware of what's been happening in the musical world lately because it isn't really my main interest."

"Oh, it isn't? What is, then?"

"Books," I said, and when it was too late to take the confession back, I blushed in embarrassment.

"Oh, *li-te-ra-tu-ra!*" he pronounced, giving each syllable separate emphasis. "So I am addressing a member of the educated classes, then?"

It was no defense to retort how extraordinarily well educated he was, because that wasn't what he really meant, of course. In fact I had no defense of any kind, ever, against his bantering way of assigning me attitudes I did not hold, as now when he assailed, using me as a whipping boy, the hollow imitation culture that had been a dead weight for so long upon the Hungarian gentry. His own creative force was fanatically opposed to that stagnant, almost impenetrable atmosphere that lay over the entire scene, inherited and perpetuated by all those who were too lazy and inert to break through it — "drugged by gypsy music," as he so often said. Bartók was not as much concerned with the simple and honest failure of those people to comprehend his own musical idiom as he was with their stubborn resistance to any spontaneous new expression — even when this innovation was springing so naturally from native roots.

Much later, after many similar scenes, I was able to reason out the particular motives for this kind of humorous personal accusation, but now I could only sit still in the Empire chair, hopelessly confused.

"All right then," he said flatly, "here is *Allegro barbaro*. But I want you to understand that it represents a period I left behind me long ago, so if you find it somewhat mechanical, remember that I warned you."

This was a remark from his own private world of fine distinctions, where each solution of a creative problem was a progressive gain over the last one of even a day before. But this distinction, however, failed to register in me as he brought the piano to life with a fire that seemed to kindle the entire house into a blaze of rhythm, consuming away all the excitements and tensions of the day. Bartók, playing his own music, was a demonstration of the absolute values in which and for which he lived.

At other times I was able to remember this experience, and remind myself that the very intensity that was such an alive force in his music presented itself in every other layer of his life and set him far apart from everyone else I knew. It was his genius and his misfortune that he was incapable of triviality in even the most trivial circumstances. This was a discovery that held me completely as I was listening to him play the *Allegro barbaro* that afternoon.

It was only when I became aware of Ditta standing in the doorway with a bouquet of red roses in her hand that I realized he had stopped playing. Then, behind her, I saw the old Italian landlord.

"I come to give you a welcome," he said to Bartók with a broad smile.

"And he brought the roses, too," Ditta added.

Bartók got up and shook hands warmly. "Thank you very much," he said, asking him to sit down.

"Beautiful music!" exclaimed the old man, putting his hand admiringly on the back of the other Empire chair. "Italy loves beautiful music!"

"I'm glad you enjoyed it," Bartók said politely. "I must confess, however, that my music did not always meet with approval in Italy. On one occasion both my wife and myself were whistled off the stage by the beautiful-music-loving Italians."

"Italy loves beautiful music!" the old man repeated imperturbably, not understanding or not caring to understand Bartók's remark. "I go now," he got up. "I only come to wish you good luck here, you and your beautiful wife!" Still smiling expansively, he shook hands with Bartók again, and Ditta saw him to the door.

"Why did you say that, Béla?" Ditta asked as she came back to the sun porch. "You know perfectly well that most of the time your music was very much appreciated in Italy. You told him only part of the truth. You always say yourself that's no truth at all."

"When I saw him standing in the door," Bartók said, "I thought he'd rushed upstairs to complain about the noise. It's lucky for us he really is a beautiful-music-loving Italian. Anyway, what I said didn't make much difference to him one way or the other."

In the kitchen a few minutes later, Bartók watched Ditta prepare the first meal to be eaten in the new apartment. "What a magnificent bird!" he exclaimed as Ditta finally took a large roasting chicken from the refrigerator. "Don't tell me that's another of your auction prizes!"

"Why, of course," Ditta answered blandly. "We went to a cold-storage warehouse, too." For a moment he didn't know whether to believe her or not, but when I began to laugh, Ditta couldn't keep her face straight and he had no more doubts as to the respectability of the chicken.

"Now how did this find its way here?" he asked, looking at a huge wooden spoon we had discovered in one of the barrels and which now hung on the kitchen wall by the stove. He smiled as if meeting an old friend. "It has been a long time since I've seen a spoon like this," he said, taking it from its hook and grasping its smooth, sturdy handle. "Just the thing for stirring goulash in a huge caldron at harvest time, or on some other great occasion — like a gypsy wedding. But no. No, that's all wrong — not gypsies. They have no use for a tool like this. They hardly ever boil their food. It's too slow to suit their temperament. A quick roast over a roaring fire — pigs that die suddenly and no one knows how — a chicken that just happens to fly into their hands, that is their tradition — they have no other way."

"Supper is ready," said Ditta. "Shall we eat on the porch?"

"Yes, it must be nice out there in the twilight," he answered. Then with some regret in his voice, "It didn't rain after all."

So we sat around a small table on the porch eating silently as the semidarkness closed in around us. Bartók seemed withdrawn and far away as he absent-mindedly piled the chicken bones on one side of his plate. Then all at once he looked up.

"Did I ever tell you, Ditta, the story of the chicken bones and the gypsy girl?"

"No, I don't think you ever did," she answered.

"Well, then," he said, and started slowly in a low voice, very subdued. "It was in Romania, in my very young days, maybe the first time I had ever been there." He was taking us again into one of his well-remembered landscapes. "A hot midsummer day, around noontime, I was eating my lunch in the cluttered yard of a run-down little inn on the outskirts of a small town at the very edge of a forest. It wasn't much of an inn, but it was a resting place for occasional travelers and their horses, too. I remember a makeshift table and the deep well in front of it with a wooden bucket hanging over it on a rusty chain. But the yard was completely deserted and I was eating there alone. Only a little cat came to make friends with me, rubbing herself against my legs and purring loudly. She was not after food, she merely wanted my companionship, for when I put down a plate of chicken bones for her, she just sniffed at it politely and then walked away.

"Suddenly I saw a young gypsy girl coming out of the woods as silently as a shadow. Almost before I could realize what was happening, she scurried right up to the spot where I was sitting and with quick brown hands snatched the chicken bones from the plate and darted back into the woods.

"Without thinking at all, I jumped up at once and ran after her as fast as I could. It was a compulsion, an urgent desire to comfort her, to tell her something or to give her something. Even as I was running I was disturbed and filled with sadness, for I feared she might think I was chasing her to punish her for stealing the bones, and I knew that no matter how fast I ran, I could never catch up with her, and I would never be able to reassure her and take away from her face that look of a frightened animal.

"I remember walking back slowly among the tall trees, and it was only then that I noticed how rough the ground was under my feet, and overrun everywhere by the creeping twisted roots of trees. There must have been a flood there once that washed away the topsoil, leaving those old naked roots clutching desperately at the barren earth that remained. And as I picked my way slowly through this maze, fat flies followed me, buzzing continually around my head."

His story was finished, and he put down his napkin, got up, and went into the dark house.

Ditta and I lingered on the porch looking at the last twilight as it faded from the sky. The exceptionally warm and bright early spring day had turned suddenly into cold dark evening.

"Now he is torturing himself because we fixed up everything

too well," she said quietly. "I suppose it haunted Béla all this time that he never caught up with that girl. Asking me if he had ever told me the story! Most likely he never even breathed it to himself before."

Bartók called to us urgently from within. "Where does one turn on the lights in this place?"

"Béla, I'm coming," Ditta answered, as she hurried in. One by one she clicked on lights in every room throughout the whole apartment. The sudden brightness seemed to emphasize how worn the old furniture was, how faded the upholstery and the rugs, giving the impression of a place that had been lived in for a long time.

Later, as I was walking down the hill, exhausted and dazed by the long day that had been filled with so many varied scenes and different moods, the last picture came back to me more vividly than all the rest — Bartók standing under the bright light of the new bulbs, among those pieces of furniture that were tired and battered and old, their worldly value used up long ago, standing there reluctant, hesitant to accept these possessions gathered "immorally" "overnight," without having put into the acquiring of them the earnest prolonged effort that would by his values have made them rightfully his own.

This new picture was to become even more haunting than my earlier image of him on the sloping street of Buda — again that amazing aloneness, that inability to blend into his surroundings. Was there any place at all where he really felt at home? Perhaps in the simple houses of peasants with whom he so much more closely identified himself than with his own comfortable class?

I was beginning to understand how little there was one could do for him, for the crushing consequence of his integrity would never allow him to merge with anything, even temporarily, that he did not fully believe in.

How completely Ditta and I had misunderstood his need, which had nothing to do with properly decorated rooms. He would have found ever so much more reality in the apartment as he saw it at first, with a few chairs and tables added. For him, all those strange unfamiliar acquisitions were somewhat like the "isolated miracle" he had never trusted, in contrast to that slow development and continuity, which had to embrace a natural beginning moving toward its own inevitable end.

If only we had been as inspired by his true desire for a frugal simplicity as we had been carried away by our own interpretation of what would suggest for him the feeling of being at home! And that brought on a further, more disturbing thought. Did he in the last analysis really want to feel at home at this time, did he want such obvious signs of permanent settling in, of staying on here for ever?

How I wished we could go back and start all over again from that day when those bare and simple rooms gave him exactly as much shelter and sense of security as he at that moment desired to fill his need.

7

DURING THE FIRST few weeks the Bartóks spent in their new apartment, everything worked smoothly to make them feel that they had finally found the hoped-for place where they could exist in their own way, sheltered and undisturbed. The spring weather brought flowers and fresh leaves to the gardens and trees of the neighborhood. Once when I went to see them, Bartók took me into the dining room to show me how the climbing roses had found their way into the house through the windows, and were spreading themselves up the walls toward the ceiling.

"It would be fine," he said, as I stood there admiringly, "but we can't close the window any more and the nights are damp and cool still." I got up on a chair and carefully pushed the stalks back through the window, bending them awkwardly in my attempt to make them stay upright. Bartók watched apprehensively. "I hope you know what you are doing and haven't caused irreparable damage to the entire plant." When I got down, he looked out and then with the utmost care closed the window against the leaves.

Like the spring itself, the old Italian landlord outdid himself to please his new tenants. "He brings flowers every day," Ditta said, pointing to vases about the room, filled with the fresh, faint colors of spring gardens. "And the other day he put new shades on our bedroom windows although we hadn't even noticed that they were missing."

"Indeed, he's so nice," said Bartók, "that I don't have the heart to ask him to use his radio a little more discreetly. He almost blasts us out of the house with his 'O Sole Mio.'" But he said it smilingly without complaining. It was all part of the new and promising scene.

The entire place hardly bore any resemblance to the one we had so painstakingly arranged, it was created by now according to their own image. Every nook and cranny bloomed with evidence of the work for which it was intended, books and music grew in small piles everywhere, an ink bottle sprouted a pen on the dining room table, and freshly written pages of music were drying, spread out in the sun like white clothes on the grass.

"I'm doing some copying for Béla," Ditta said, "but of course only a temporary copy, for it isn't really good enough. Just until he finds a professional. No, he's not composing," she laughed. "I know that's what you were thinking — but that will come, too, in its own turn. He's not in such a hurry now."

And this was the time, too, when Bartók's work at Columbia began, and that meant that another basic need was taken care of.

But more than that, Bartók was greatly pleased that finally he could begin to work on the Parry Collection, for his desire to transcribe this material dated from the time he first learned of its existence, and his appreciation of this achievement came from deep understanding. He mentioned often what a fortunate coincidence it was that Milman Parry, an Englishman, and his assistant Albert Lord went to Yugoslavia in 1933 and 1934 and brought back such a miraculously com-

plete collection of folk poetry that it stands alone in its field.
And what great fortune it was that this should have happened
at the twelfth hour, hardly a year before the signs of deterioration began to appear in this folk tradition that had been kept
alive for thousands of years, and in its memory went back as
far, perhaps, as the Homeric poems. The tremendous sensitivity that led Parry there just at the time before this heritage
began its way into oblivion was in itself a miracle.

The spring ripened, the days grew warmer, the fresh green
trees became dusty city trees, and a host of noisy, lively children took over the streets after school hours. Bartók did not
seem to notice, though at times his joy in the new place must
have become a little dusty too.

One afternoon I was expecting Ditta in my apartment, and
as I answered the doorbell I was taken aback when I saw that
Bartók was with her. Ditta sensed my confusion and said
quickly, "We brought you all kinds of presents." She was
gay, her eyes transparent blue, her face sunburned. Bartók
was holding something on a plate covered with a napkin, and
Ditta had a large envelope tucked under her arm. She opened
the envelope and took out a yellowed manuscript, "Fifteen
Hungarian Peasant Songs," besides an inscribed photograph of
each of them. Ditta put the manuscript in my hands. "From
Béla to you," she told me. "Now take good care of it, it's the
original." Bartók put the plate on the hall table, lifted the
napkin and unveiled a cake. "If you find out who wrote the
manuscript and who baked the cake, you can have both together with the photographs," said Ditta. But as I didn't say
anything, she answered for me. "Béla did both."

"Ditta helped me with one of them," Bartók said with his
usual scrupulous adherence to fact. "Can you tell which one?
I would try each carefully before giving an answer."

That was the only time — in those four years — that I felt unrestrained, happy, and close to both of them.

"What a nice place," Bartók said, following me as I carried my treasures into the living room. He walked about in the big rooms of the old brownstone house, noticing that from the windows he could see a strip of the Hudson River and a green fragment of the Jersey shore. After a while he turned to look at my undistinguished furniture. "Have these things originated from the same source as ours?"

"Not these," I said. "I learned that trick much later when I was fixing up my Vermont house."

"Vermont — that's near Canada, isn't it?" he asked.

"I'm about fifty miles from the border."

"Must be quite high up in the mountains." He wanted to know all about it, and I was only too eager to talk about the big white house on the hilltop and show photographs of it too. I had had the place only two years, and my joy in it was still fresh.

We were interrupted by my gray Persian cat, Lulu, who was usually put out of circulation when Ditta came to see me. Although Ditta never actually said anything, I had noticed how hard she tried to overcome her fear of my demonstrative cat. Taking full advantage of her liberty, Lulu walked around happily now and rubbed herself against Bartók's leg. She walked back and forth, purring loudly, as she pressed herself passionately against him, pushing her head right into his stroking hands. It was her standard performance for the benefit of a male visitor, but Bartók took it as a demonstration of feline discrimination in his favor and never failed after that visit to inquire about Lulu.

And the Vermont house too became more and more a topic of conversation as the city grew hotter and grayer with the approach of summer, and it was altogether natural that I should come to ask Ditta, tentatively, whether she or perhaps even both of them would like to spend some weeks there with me.

"That sounds like a wonderful solution," she said thoughtfully. "We are hoping to take at least a few weeks' vacation away from the city."

Before we knew it, it had become a definite plan that they would both come up and spend at least a month in the house in Vermont. Later on a date was set, and many details were discussed.

"Béla, of course, won't come," Ditta told me at one point, "unless we can pay our share of the expenses. That's Béla's way, and he is very consistent about these matters."

And finally, very meticulously, he arrived at a figure that was just right for both of us.

In the middle of June, a few days before I myself was to leave the humid hot city for Vermont, Ditta said wistfully, "I wish I could come up with you, and stay a few days."

"But by all means, why not? That would be wonderful! I'd feel so much better if you looked at the place before Bartók gets there. Maybe I described it too glowingly. Maybe it isn't half as nice as I think."

"Why this house might have come out of one of Béla's own dreams!" said Ditta as the place came into view, long before we drove up to the door. Her fresh response to the house echoed my own feeling about it. White and tall, it stood solitary on the hilltop, built in the form of a cross with its four wings set on a broad terrace surrounded by open fields and deep woods, a panorama of mountain ridges stretching around it in a semicircle as far as the eye could see.

As we came into the center hall of the house, Ditta paused a moment. "But why didn't you tell us how beautiful it is?

Those pictures gave me no idea at all!" And she began to run from room to room. "It's big enough to get lost in." She laughed. "How Béla will love these huge rooms — and the way the view seems to follow you wherever you go." She tried to see everything at once. "Those fireplaces, built right to the ceiling! Béla adores open fires — real ones like this. He loves all natural things. I can't wait for you to see how he is when he is in the country. He is his real self. All you have to know about Béla is that he loves everything that's real."

One morning a few days later, Ditta asked me if she might choose a room for him. "I wish you would," I said, and together we found the room that would exactly suit him. It had its own fireplace, a small piano, and windows that opened on three sides. It looked out on a series of mountain ridges fading from dark green through blue to pink, and the far-off squares of contrasting green fields were spotted with the small dots of grazing cows. The deep quiet of the room was broken by an occasional faint tinkle of distant cowbells.

"We'll have to put some heavy curtains on these windows and doors, to muffle all sounds," Ditta remarked.

"But it is so completely still and peaceful!" I said.

"You don't know Béla's ears," she laughed. "The things he can hear! At home, a whole row of rooms away from the kitchen, he could tell whether Zsuzsi, our housekeeper, was cutting the noodles into long thin strips, or little squares."

"It will be easy enough to find some old draperies in the attic," I said.

"And a large table," she added.

"Don't I know!"

We found a table in the library that could be expanded to banquet size, and to our delight we discovered all the leaves for it in the barn.

Only one shadow was cast upon our happy preparations, the

long thin shadow of Matthew, neighboring farmer and honor-
ary caretaker of my house since the day I bought it and even
before, for I had inherited him from the previous owner.
Matthew grumbled and muttered as we helped him carry the
table to the chosen room.

"Dragging the harvest table to the best bedroom in the
house — three women gone crazy is more than one man can
fight against." The third woman was Martha, the young
housekeeper who had been installed on Matthew's recommen-
dation. It particularly incensed him that Martha had caught
our enthusiasm and had plunged so eagerly into the work of
preparation. In all our previous differences, Matthew had been
able to count on her approval and support against my "city
ways," and to find her siding against him over the coming invasion was more than he could suffer in silence. "Them tables
was made for outdoor celebrations like the Fourth of July.
They were made by sensible people who used things for what
they were made for."

"Why, what is he saying?" Ditta asked anxiously, unable
to comprehend his Vermont brand of English. "Is he angry
about anything?"

"Oh no, not at all," I reassured her. "He's only telling us
that this table is called a harvest table."

"But it's a lovely name!" said Ditta. "Please be sure that
you remember to mention it to Béla."

Matthew continued his muted disapproval throughout the
week. He stood by shaking his head as we dug up patches of
witch grass in the field above the house and put in sunflower
plants in its place, for it had occurred to Ditta that Bartók
would be glad to find his favorite flower growing. Grudgingly,
he lent a hand as we hung the draperies in Bartók's room, but
his patience was brought to the breaking point by the fire-red
geraniums that we put in the window boxes. He pretended he

wasn't there when we decked out the upper balcony with arm-
chairs and awnings and small tables. And finally when I unearthed a discarded birdbath from the barn and carried that
as well to the balcony, it was the last straw.

"Of all the city-crazy things — even my old grandmother
wouldn't have done a thing like that." Ditta looked at him
questioningly. "She was crazy, good and proper, and proved it
too by dying in the nut-house in Waterbury." Waterbury and
Matthew's grandmother crept more and more into his dark
mutterings during the course of the week. But Ditta's visit
was quickly coming to an end.

Early in our last day, Ditta and I were walking down the
long well-shaded stretch of the hill that led to the village.

"Of course, it never occurred to you to spend any time or
thought on a room for me," Ditta said. Her remark fell on me
without warning, as suddenly as a summer storm. I said nothing for a moment, hoping that by some mriacle these words
would evaporate so quickly that they would leave no trace
at all.

But she spoke again. "Oh no, that wasn't important to you.
It never is to anyone."

"A room for you!" I said finally. "Why the entire house is
at your disposal. You can have anything you want."

"But one room, just for me, chosen with only half as much
thoughtfulness as the one for Béla, where my bed would be
sheltered from the wind and still look out on the loveliest
view. The floors heavily carpeted, and the door curtained."

By now I was used to these recurring disturbances of Ditta's,
and though her accusations were seemingly unreasonable, I
could usually find — indeed had to find — that I was guilty of
neglect in some vague passive way, as in this case when I had
failed to give her reassurance as to her importance in the picture, unaware as I was of her need of it, with our friendship so
thoroughly established.

Though Ditta herself had always set the tone of our concentration on Bartók, she probably would have welcomed at least some fraction of that same kind of attention focused upon her, with the same intensity. The reason why I had failed to see this, perhaps, was because, except for these occasional outbursts of resentment that passed as fast as they came, she existed on a responsible even level, her judgment keen and accurate, her understanding deep and so infallibly right that I was unable, at this time, to take into account these momentary "moods" of disharmony and their full implications.

However, when they came, as now, the one thing I was sure of was that a single false note on my part would prolong the scene and make it worse.

"A room for you?" I said. "Why all along I took it for granted — and didn't we talk about it many times?" (as indeed we had) "that you would have the room opening on the balcony with the full view of the mountains I like the best — and the walls blue and white, your own favorite colors — and for a bath you will have the birdbath right there so handy, and what could be better suited?"

This last brought a faint smile to her face.

"Oh, that Matthew," she said, laughing, later on that afternoon when we were busily rearranging the blue and white room.

In the evening, as we sat on the upper balcony, the open country stretching wide around us in the twilight, Ditta said, looking toward the blue hills, "You know, before I came to this country, I imagined it all dark. Tall buildings, smoking factories, no sky, no birds, no sun." The light of the setting sun was changing the mountaintops from blue to purple. "Although Béla told me many times about the great spaces of open country, about the virgin forests that were larger than the whole of Hungary, the mountains, oceans, beaches, the palm trees, the lakes, still, I just had to say to myself 'America' and it became dark again. But ever since I got off the boat, I found it all brightness and space and light, everywhere."

The fireflies were now sparkling in the fields. "Look how many of them there are!" Ditta exclaimed. "I wonder if you can remember at all how rare they were at home — we never saw more than one or two at a time." She pressed my hand. "How exciting and beautiful this is, how Béla will love it, I can't wait for him to be here and see it all. I wish he could have come with us, and then I wouldn't have to go away from here for a long time."

The day before Ditta was to return with Bartók, in the midst of all the last-minute preparations, all at once I realized that I had not seen my cat Lulu for a day or two. I suddenly began to worry about her, especially since she was expecting her kittens any moment now, and I thought guiltily that she must have felt neglected in the bustling house and gone off to bear them alone somewhere.

It was not until evening that I was able to question Matthew. He was only too ready with his answer. "Maybe the poor creature was smart enough to beat it and have her kittens in peace. She's had fair warning, the way you've been carrying on here. Cats are a lot smarter than some people I could mention, and Lulu knew when to get out from under — that gives me an idea, maybe I'd better do the same."

I was well aware of Matthew's stubborn opposition to change in any form. Nothing could prove it more plainly than the wretched state of his own slowly collapsing farm. The cluttered porch of his sinking house exhibited the same articles, on the same spots, year after year, unaltered within my remembrance. The only thing he ever changed was the calendar, and that too was hung on the same rusty nail, the new year covering the old. Matthew's resentment of Bartók, who, besides being a name he heard too often, was also a symbol of upheaval, was so intense that I feared he actually might carry out his threat of leaving. Since even in peacetime there was a great shortage of manpower in our part of Vermont, in this first year of the war it was impossible to find any male help at all. "Don't desert us when we need you most," I pleaded. "What would we do without you?" And although his answer was only a grunt, it was a reassuring one.

Later in the evening as we were sitting at the kitchen table drinking our after-dinner coffee, my growing uneasiness led me to mention Lulu again. "Please look for her, Matthew, you're the only one who could find her for me. No one knows this hill the way you do."

"Don't worry, I'll find her," he promised me, his old warmth returning. But it disappeared abruptly again when I reminded him that we would have to be at the station early the next morning to meet the Bartóks on the six o'clock train.

"I suppose next you'll want me to phone the governor to have a delegation with a brass band to receive them," he said sourly.

"Oh, no, Matthew, I'll be satisfied if we don't keep them waiting at the station." For one tense moment, I thought he might refuse me completely, but to my great relief, he contented himself with a grumble or two as he went out the door.

8

THE EARLY MORNING was cold. Heavy mist drizzled through the gray air and a thick fog obscured the mountains. Inside the house, warm fires blazed and newly cut flowers bloomed in their vases, and the dining room table was set with great care for breakfast. But in spite of the glow of the interior, the enveloping gloom outside held the upper hand, pressing heavily against the windowpanes as if demanding entrance.

It was scarcely light when Matthew drove up to the door, and as I climbed into the car and sat down beside him, I sensed that his mood had not softened during the night.

"Looks like we're in for it," he said, scrutinizing the sky with malicious interest. "Once fog is settled down on us this way, it's not likely to burn off for a long stretch." Pleased by the weather's refusal to cooperate, he could not resist making the most of my disappointment. "Don't you wish you could climb up there and sweep the clouds away?"

"Did you look for Lulu?" I interrupted him.

"Yes ma'am, I did, in all the places I could think of."

"In the sugar house too?"

"Yes, there too, inside and out, under the heavy beams, and even in the hollow maple tree that stands in back of it. I just couldn't see a sign of her; no matter where I looked. No telling what might have happened to her. Let's hope the crows don't find her before we do," he added ominously.

We drove the rest of the way in silence.

As soon as the train pulled in, I saw Ditta with a worried smile on her face, waving to us. Bartók was standing behind her, seemingly unaware of our presence, and looking paler than I had ever seen him before. Refusing my help, he carried his heavy suitcase to the car alone.

"His papers and things," Ditta explained to me in whispers, and continued, "Oh I'm so worried about him! He didn't sleep all night — and I am afraid he is seriously ill."

As the train departed with a shriek and Matthew collected the rest of the luggage, Bartók took refuge in the car. Leaning back heavily against the cushions, he looked like a ghostly image of himself. It was as though his face were now molded from some unknown substance, transparent and cold. He sat there alone, eyes closed, enveloped in deep sadness.

As the car was slowly climbing the steep hill, Ditta turned to him. "Look, Béla, please look! This is Agota's land already! All these deep woods on both sides of the road." Her lively voice tried to penetrate his gloomy reserve, and obediently he opened his eyes and glanced at the gleaming birches and the heavy silent pines, then, without comment, closed them again. Even the sight of the big white house looming up on the hilltop above us failed to arouse his interest. If Bartók had ever dreamed about a house like this, as Ditta suggested the first time she saw it, he certainly showed no sign of recognition now. He followed me through the rooms with unseeing eyes, and retired into his own without delay.

"How disappointed you must be," said Ditta, as we sat down to breakfast together. "Of course, I realize that all this wasn't done just for me," she continued, glancing at the carefully arranged table, her eyes coming to rest on the bright heap of wild roses at the center. "I like flowers, too," and her voice was taking on the cold touchy edge that I feared so much by now. "But I find it hard to enjoy them, knowing they were meant for Béla and not for me." Tired and hurt, she sat looking down at her plate and said nothing more.

I looked at her silently and stubbornly, in my dismay and disappointment of the moment, lacking the impulse to battle against this misinterpretation of my feelings.

But after a while, ashamed of my inability to respond, I got up and gave her a warm hug of welcome as if she had just arrived. The tension left her face instantly.

"Pay no attention to me," she said. "I can't help feeling like this sometimes when Béla and I go places together, it seems to me that I just happen to be along too."

"Surely not with me, Ditta."

"No, it's hardly ever like that with you."

Then she continued, in a rapid flow of words. "What's really troubling me now is much more important. You don't know how sick he is! It came so suddenly just a few days ago, I've hardly had time to realize it myself. First he complained of a pain in his shoulder, next he could hardly move his arm at all. He was so frightened, I never saw him like that before. What he seemed to be most afraid of was to be sick so far away from home, in this strange country. And of course he worries that he might not be able to give any more concerts. But worst of all is this apathy that came after his panic. You saw it just now — nothing seems to have any reality to him any more. You know how eager he has been for such a long time to make this trip, but at the last minute I had to plead with him to come at all. And I am not sure that it was the right thing, maybe it's not fair to you, actually."

"Of course it was the right thing to do, even more so if he is not well. This is the right place for him — just wait and see how quickly he will get better here."

These seemed to be the words she wanted to hear, and to believe, and by the time we finished breakfast, the atmosphere had cleared.

The sun came out too, in spite of Matthew's predictions, slowly burning its way through the fog. The mountain ridges appeared again, sharply etched against the blue sky.

"Our sunflower plants!" Ditta exclaimed, suddenly remembering. "Did they survive? Let's go and see!"

We ran out of the house and across the field, and found that the plants were still alive. Ditta admired the weak stems and the pale leaves.

"I hope they'll hurry up and grow."

Birds were zigzagging through the shining air, and the fields were covered with wild flowers.

"Of course it was the right thing to come. Béla can't help but get better here," Ditta said, lying down in the long grass, and she stretched out happily in the warm sunshine.

In the late afternoon, since there had been no sign of life from Bartók's room all day, Ditta went up to see if he was still asleep. She came down again quickly with the good news that he had slept all day, was feeling better, and was hungry too.

While we were preparing a tray of food, I saw Ditta fill a deep bowl with pine cones that were drying in the kitchen, and I looked at her questioningly. "He loves surprises on his tray," she said, selecting a variety of shapes, colors and sizes. "These will amuse him."

When she brought back the tray of empty dishes, she sat down at the kitchen table with a sigh of relief. "He ate everything but the pine cones! You ought to see him playing with them, and planning to find the mother tree of each kind. I'm sure he will, too."

"I'm really so glad, Ditta," I said.

"So am I," she answered, leaning back contentedly on the hard kitchen chair. "He's delighted with his room; and as for the view, he says he can't get enough of it. Why, he even showed me that what I thought was one huge mountaintop was really a series of different ridges blended together by the smoky mist. And you'll be pleased to know, I'm sure, that he asked about Lulu. He was so sorry to hear that she's lost."

Lulu! In spite of the tensions and anxieties of this day, she had been constantly in the back of my mind. Ditta's words gave me a fresh urge to look for her again. Together we painstakingly ransacked the barn, peering into the cluttered horse stalls, exploring the hayloft with its dusty piles of hay, calling out all the time a collection of Hungarian endearments such as no New England cat had ever heard before. But our calls remained unanswered.

"How can one possibly know where to look for a cat in a place as big and wild as this and so alive with danger?" Ditta asked hopelessly, as we walked back to the house empty-handed after our long wanderings.

It must have been around midnight when Ditta came into my room and awakened me. "Béla just knocked on my door and told me he heard the faint crying of a cat. He thinks it's coming from over there." She pointed toward the deep woods.

We both listened intently at my wide open window, but in the muted hum of the night we could distinguish no sound like the cry of a cat. Disappointed, I turned away from the window.

"Don't worry," Ditta said, "if he hears it, it's there. We'd better not waste any more time. Let's see if we can find her."

As we were leaving the house, Martha ran after us with a flashlight, though she knew I always carried one in my coat

pocket. Obviously she didn't want to miss any of the excitement. Quickly the three of us crossed the field, pausing at the
far end where a straight line of darkness marked the entrance
to the woods. "It's fearfully beautiful," Ditta said, holding
on to my hand. We stood there listening for a long time, but
heard nothing to guide us farther. Disappointed, we walked
back to the house.

Bartók's voice called down to us as soon as we came inside,
and we all went upstairs and stood at his door. He was sitting
up in bed with bright wide-awake eyes.

"We went right up to the edge of the woods," Ditta told
him, "and even there we couldn't hear it."

"Well, of course," said Bartók. "You can only hear as well
as you listen. Three deaf women wandering in the dark forest,
what an inefficient rescue party for that poor cat!" His voice
was resonant now, and as we lingered at his door, all I could
think of was the transformation that had taken place in him.
The face that had resembled a death mask in the early morning
was now alive and lit up from within.

"I said you were all deaf," he went on. "Don't you hear it?"

But we could only shake our heads, though we strained our
ears as hard as we could.

"Right now I can hear it," he said, with closed eyes. "It's
coming at regular intervals as though she needed time to rest
before her next cry."

"But what can we do?" I asked helplessly.

"Well," he said then, "since the deaf cannot lead the deaf,
why don't I get up and see what I can do?"

"Do you think you should, Béla?"

"What else is there to do?" he answered. "You don't want
that cat's life weighing on my conscience for ever, do you?"

He was eager to go now, sitting up straight in his bed, his
exhilaration mounting fast. A search through the dark woods

seemed to be exactly the right venture for his renewed and surging vigor.

"All right then, let's go," said Ditta happily, elated by the miraculous transformation that had occurred in the course of one day. "We'll wait for you at the foot of the stairs."

In a few minutes Bartók appeared, wearing a heavy brown flannel robe, and a faded woolen scarf was tied around his head. Even in this strange attire, he did not look in the least ridiculous — all the strength and harmonious form of his face was concentrated now in the one narrow strip that remained uncovered and accentuated by the scarf.

Pausing in the doorway, he looked out into the darkness. "I wish I had a walking stick," he said.

"Wait, I'll get you one," I told him, and from the hall closet I quickly produced a heavy cane with a broadly curved handle.

"Hmm, I like this," he said, leaning on it experimentally as we left the house.

With quick strides Bartók, in the beam of Martha's flashlight, forged ahead of us toward the dark outline of the woods. But all at once he stopped and stood still.

"Don't tell me you can't hear it now," he said, as soon as we had caught up with him.

This time we did hear it: it was scarcely a sound, no more than a slight tremolo at the edge of the wind, and without his intense suggestion we never would have known it was there. No longer in any doubt that it came from Lulu, I ran ahead eagerly. But Bartók's voice called after me.

"No, not that way! You'd better wait. I'm coming."

As soon as he reached me, he stopped and stood quietly again for a moment, listening alertly, then turned off the smooth path and disappeared among the dark trees.

"This way, this way," we heard him call with assurance, in his deep clear voice, and we hurried after him.

"We are very near to it now, she must be in one of these trees." He stopped under a tall maple.

Wildly excited, we pointed our flashlights up into the tree and the beams darted among the thick branches until suddenly through the leaves they rested on Lulu, pressed into one of the highest forks of the venerable tree, her silvery gray fur like upcurling smoke in the night. We all stood looking up at her, still not quite believing this extraordinary performance that had led us to her without a single valuable moment wasted.

"What are you going to do next?" Bartók's question cut into our jubilation. "That tree must be at least five stories high, if not more. How will you ever get her down?"

"With Matthew's big ladder!" said Martha. "I'll go back to the house and phone him. We'll bring it as fast as we can." She was gone in an instant, running through the shadowy underbrush with incredible swiftness.

"Lulu got what she deserved this time," said Bartók, staring up at the tree. "No doubt she was looking for nesting birds."

"Oh, no! She never goes after birds," I protested.

"Rather a risky trip for the view, don't you think? Next you'll be trying to convince me that she was seeking the heights of solitude! With that I would sympathize if I could believe it. But I'm sure this is only another case of the same old pattern repeating itself. Even after thousands of years of domestication and pampering, they are still not willing to give up the hunt. Just like people, they want everything. One can't help feeling satisfaction when one sees this greed ending in self-destruction."

"Béla, don't talk as if Lulu were already dead!" interrupted Ditta. "Surely we can get her down somehow."

"Yes, most likely, but she won't be any wiser for the experience, of that I am sure."

He sat down on the trunk of a fallen tree, and Ditta and I sat down beside him.

"This could be anywhere in the Carpathian mountains or in the lower Alps, though it smells more like the woods in Transylvania," he said, deeply inhaling the clear night air. He spoke slowly, thoughtfully, as though actually comparing his impressions of those faraway but well-remembered places with the sharp reality of his present surroundings.

"This old birch must have been dead for a long time," said Bartók after a silence, moving his hand over its smooth dry surface. "Under the thin bark I can hear regiments of invading bugs, grinding, eating, scurrying, drilling their way through layer after layer of this white body, gnawing out its very heart."

He got up and wandered deeper into the woods.

"Isn't it wonderful," said Ditta, after we could no longer hear his light tread on the dry leaves. "Only yesterday he was so hopeless, in a misery of pain and fear, and now already this countryside has brought him out of his terrible lonely world. Do you feel it too, how bursting with life he is?"

An impatient wail came from Lulu, and we called up to her encouragingly.

When Bartók returned he handed me a small branch. "Do you know what kind of evergreen this is? I've never felt such small smooth needles before."

"Hemlock," I said.

"Indeed. What other kinds of trees do you have here?"

"Maples, mostly elms, a lot of birches, oaks, and all kinds of pines," I replied.

He sat down again, and leaning forward, dug his hands into the pine needles at his feet. "Must be knee deep — the accumulation of centuries, I suppose." As he spoke his voice was resonant even at its quietest. "I don't imagine that you two women would care much to have your floors covered with this kind of carpet, but you can be sure that it took more time and more work to make than even the most precious of hand-woven rugs. Sun, rain, frost and snow and wind beating down incessantly on these trees above us, as the seasons rapidly turned, the leaves and needles falling, dying, making room for ever for the numberless new ones that were born in their places — these elemental things — and don't forget the bugs and birds and worms, too, helping the process along in their own ways, for they all have taken part in the creation of this pungent-smelling carpet composed of equal amounts of life and death."

As we listened to him there in the summer night this first time, his words unfolded before me a mysterious abundant existence until then unknown to me. And by the end of the summer this recurrent theme of his had become so familiar that I myself began to hear those hidden sounds, that hidden movement beneath all surfaces, dead or alive.

At last we heard heavy tramping steps and the sound of animated voices. Martha and Matthew appeared, carefully maneuvering a long ladder between the trees. "Where's the fire?" Matthew called. "I don't hear the alarm!"

We all got up and tried to help as Matthew, fussing and fuming, placed the ladder in position. Long as it was, it scarcely reached halfway into the tree. Running lightly up its rungs, Martha left us no time for dismay. From the top of the ladder she pulled herself from branch to branch with the rhythm and agility of a young leopard. "Her Indian blood," I whispered admiringly.

"What Indian blood?" Bartók asked, his interest instantly aroused.

"She's Indian on her mother's side," I explained. "In fact her grandmother is a full-blooded Indian, she lives somewhere around here in the back hills, doesn't she, Matthew?"

"That old witch!" he snorted in confirmation.

"I can reach her!" Martha called down to us excitedly. "She's sure held tight. I can hardly get her free."

We stood silently, holding our breaths as the branches swayed and creaked. "I got her now!" Martha shouted triumphantly.

I started up the ladder to meet her as she cautiously began her descent. Finally I held Lulu in my arms. She was exhausted, cold, barely breathing. When we reached the ground, Bartók touched her gently. "She's so limp — is she alive?"

"She is," I said, and added, as we started toward the house, "How will I ever thank you?" But it seemed as if he had not heard me.

Back in the living room Matthew was building a fire while Bartók stood by, watching him closely.

Wrapped in an old sweater, Lulu rested quietly in my arms. Ditta reached out a hand, as if to stroke her, but not quite daring to come in contact with the soft fur that was so warm and charged. "I'm glad you are here, Lulu," she said with affection. "Someday you will be able to tell your grandchildren that your life was saved by a famous composer."

"Oh, no, not her grandchildren," said Bartók, "more likely it will take several dozen generations of her kind before my name will mean something here."

Martha came in from the kitchen and ostentatiously offered Lulu a dish of warm milk. But Lulu did not accept it. Shaking herself free from her warm covering, she stretched feebly and walked toward the fire, her feet unsteady under her swollen weight.

"Why, nobody told me that she was in a delicate condition," said Bartók, lightly passing his hand over her disheveled fur. Lulu moved closer to him, purring loudly, and began washing herself. Her sides still showed the imprint of the branches which had held her captive in the treetop.

"Well, now you have your cat back again, but it seems to me she is somewhat warped!" Bartók said. His tone was joking, but full of tenderness. "All you can wish for now," he turned to me, "is that her kittens won't come out looking like four-legged pancakes."

"Béla, what a horrible idea!" said Ditta, laughing in spite of herself. I laughed too, but Bartók's face was serious.

Matthew's face was even more so, actually grim, as he stood by the fire he had built, silently watching Bartók. He had no possible key to the secret of the mysterious power of this fragile man, so unassuming in his brown flannel robe, with the faded scarf now fallen loosely around his neck, and the soft white hair left ruffled by the night wind. Why should these three women be so much under his spell, making such a fuss over his slightest whim? No one knew better than Matthew how unswervingly Martha at other times did things in her own way, and how obstinately I refused to be discouraged from my senseless city ways — and I think Matthew also was by no means unaware of the sharp edges beneath Ditta's quicksilver surface gaiety — yet here we were, all three of us, hovering over Bartók, blended into one unit of meekness, completely at his disposal.

Martha brought in a pot of tea and a tray piled high with sandwiches. We all ate hungrily, sitting around the fire in silence.

"But did you ever have a pet hen?" asked Bartók suddenly, speaking now in his clear precise English, addressing all of us. "I had one, a long time ago, at home in Buda."

"Oh, that lovely hen!" said Ditta wistfully.

"One summer," Bartók continued slowly, "someone gave us a brood of little yellow baby chickens. There must have been about a dozen of them. They used to wander around our table whenever we ate outside in our garden, waiting for morsels of food, I suppose."

"Of course they were," broke in Ditta, "since you were always feeding them at the table."

"Soon I noticed," Bartók went on, "that one baby chick seemed to be taking a most flattering interest in me. It was as though she had singled me out to be her special benefactor."

"Not without good reason!" added Ditta, who seemed to have an irrepressible urge to take her part in this story.

"As soon as she could make use of her wings, she would flutter clumsily to my lap and sit there confidently expecting the scraps of food that were handed to her from time to time. Later she took to accompanying me on my walks in the garden, running after me on her fast little feet."

"And this is all true," said Ditta, looking at us with serious eyes.

"During the winter," Bartók went on, "they were kept somewhere in the cellar, weren't they, Ditta?"

"Yes, they had a nice warm place down there."

"When spring came, they appeared again, full-grown and uniformly elegant in their smooth white feathers. It would have been a hopeless task for me, no matter how hard I tried, to distinguish my special hen from all the others. But she, however, had no trouble at all recognizing me, and insisted on the immediate restoration of all her personal rights and privileges."

Smiling faintly, he paused for a while, and as he stared absently into the fire, his thoughts seemed to be drawn far away from us, back into the intricate passages of another life.

"Those chickens!" said Ditta softly. "How Péter loved to play with them." Her face told of the many other memories this story was touching upon.

"And do you remember," said Bartók, smiling at Ditta, "that when we were in Italy the next summer we received a telegram from Zsuzsi?" ("Our housekeeper," explained Ditta politely.) "It must have been a message of importance, for heaven alone knows Zsuzsi was never given to sending telegrams lightly, but the only part I can recall now was the postscript, which read: 'Your Excellency's hen is enjoying the best of health.'"

Half sadly, half gaily, they both laughed.

"Whatever happened to those chickens? Surely we couldn't have eaten them?" Bartók asked apprehensively.

"We did, though!" answered Ditta guiltily. "All but your hen, of course. We had her for a long time."

"But what became of her at the end?" insisted Bartók stubbornly.

"I can't remember," Ditta said. "I just can't remember at all."

"That hen," said Bartók slowly, "and so many other things . . ."

He got up abruptly and walked around the room. Pausing at a window, he stood looking out into the night, an erect and solitary figure. After a long while he turned toward us again. "Darkness and trees and a big sky — it's all so deceiving — it could be almost anywhere." Quietly he left the room.

As long as I knew him, he never made any mention of the events of his first night in Vermont (although the next morning, Ditta told me, his first thought was for Lulu). As time went by I grew accustomed to the fact that he never carried the mood of one day into the next. Each day was a new beginning: one had to get acquainted with him all over again.

9

A FEW DAYS LATER I discovered Lulu in the back of
the deep closet near Bartók's room where she had many times
before given birth to her kittens. Fearful that he might find
the whole event disturbing, I decided to move her to another
closet in a remote part of the house. As I was coaxing her into
a basket, I became aware that Bartók had opened his door, and
was standing there silently observing us.

"What on earth are you doing with that cat?" he asked,
looking so stern that I was immediately on the defensive.

"Moving her away from here," I said.

"And for what reason — if I may ask?"

"She's planning to have her kittens here in this closet, and
I was afraid you might not like having them so near."

"Let me have her, please," he said curtly, taking Lulu away
from me and placing her in the basket. Getting down on his
hands and knees, he gently maneuvered her back into the
darkest corner of the closet.

"And you had better leave her there," he said, as he crawled
out, "alone and in peace."

Except for this momentary concern with Lulu's welfare,
Bartók gave no other indication of remembering the part he

had played in her rescue from the treetop on his first night in Vermont. Indeed, when he had appeared the next day, it had seemed almost impossible to believe that his animated concern of the night before had really happened. He had relapsed into his mood of apathy, as aloof and isolated from his surroundings as on the morning of his arrival. His face had again taken on the immobility of a marble statue, but a statue with eyes that were restlessly alive, and ever on the alert to repulse any sign of human communication that might demand recognition and response.

He never came downstairs before lunchtime, and then he would enter the dining room in the manner of a sleepwalker and seat himself facing the windows that opened toward the surrounding fields. There he would sit in silence, preoccupied, until a small occurrence or chance remark would rouse him out of his trance unexpectedly.

As once, when Martha placed a small basket of bread on the table before him. His face came alive with a slow disgust.

"How many different kinds of tasteless sponges do you parade in this house under the name of bread?" he asked, turning to her as she hovered about his chair.

"Oh, you don't care for it? I'm so sorry," she apologized. "Would you like me to bake you some bread myself?"

The apology and the suggested remedy were equally surprising from this wildly independent young woman who became altogether unmanageable at my slightest hint of criticism.

"Or maybe it would be even better if I brought you some of my granny's bread," she went on, remembering with uncanny instinct how interested Bartók had been in the remark about her Indian grandmother. "I think you would like that, because she bakes it in a Dutch oven."

"Indian bread from a Dutch oven?" Bartók said with a smile. "Hmm, quite a combination. But what is a Dutch oven?"

"Oh, don't you know? It's a kind of oven built right into the wall, and it's made of bricks, and instead of baking your bread on a metal rack the way you do in a gas oven like the one we have in this house, you put it right on the hot bricks."

"Why, of course," Bartók said, "that is the real way, the only way to make bread." He turned to me as Martha went back to the kitchen. "How is it that you don't have such an important thing as a Dutch oven in this house?"

"Well," I said, "this is a comparatively new house, built by a man who was reacting against the typical Vermont farm-houses with their cramped little rooms, close ceilings, tiny windows — built, you might say, in defiance."

"In defiance!" Bartók caught the word as though it were a ball I had tossed him. "Only a fool would build in defiance of the past. What is new and significant always must be grafted to old roots, the truly vital roots that are chosen with great care from the ones that merely survive. And what a slow and delicate process it is to distinguish radical vitality from the wastes of mere survival, but that is the only way to achieve progress — instead of disaster, as in this case of an omitted Dutch oven!" He paused a moment, then added, "There are also committed disasters. That electric machine, or generator, or whatever you call the thing that keeps on thundering all night like an angry Vesuvius — I suppose that was put there in defiance too?"

"No, not out of defiance, out of necessity. We were prom-ised electricity from the town a long time ago, but as nothing happened I had to put in that machine. And I'm glad I did. For when the war came, we suffered another postponement of the service."

"Suffering is just the word for it," he said.

"Now you don't want to tell us, Béla," Ditta said, "that you really find the machine as disturbing as that. My room is much nearer to it than yours, and all I can hear is a little humming that's hardly even there."

"It disturbs *me*," Bartók said to her sternly, and after a pause he continued in a milder voice, "It does something to the night, it upsets its balance, injects a foreign element into it, distorting the vibrant rhythm and harmony of the summer darkness. With that constant rumbling in my ears, I find it impossible to follow even the most simple line of thought. I have abandoned entirely the idea of working here, that is, of doing real work, the work I'd planned to do. Luckily I have enough other things to keep me busy." He got up from the table and nodded stiffly, as a departing gesture, which, however, impressed me more as an emphatic underlining of the complaints he had just enumerated.

After he had left the room, Ditta looked at me, slowly shaking her head in sympathy, and then suddenly burst into laughter.

"Your face!" she cried, "your face!" Her shoulders shook uncontrollably and tears came into her eyes. "If you could only see yourself. The way you look — it's just the way I have felt so often." And as her laughter subsided, she said, "But that's how it goes. With Béla you can never tell. So please don't take it so much to heart. It's not you, you must know, or your house either, it's this eternal quest of his for ideal working conditions, and I want you to know that even at home he has never found them for long. It was always like this — so many times and so many places, struggling constantly against interruption, but in the end he always managed to adjust himself, somehow, unwillingly and not without much pain for all concerned. It will be the same here too, just wait and see."

That afternoon I came upon Ditta and Bartók in the living room bending over some papers spread out on a small table in front of them. As I was turning away, Bartók caught sight of me.

"Come in and have a look at these English translations of Hungarian folk songs that were just sent to me," he said, and as I joined them, he handed me some of the papers. "What do you think of them?" he asked. But I hardly had a glance at them before he took them back again and threw them on the table.

"They are not really worth looking at," he said. "Just as I would have expected — hopeless." But still he sat down and kept turning over the pages, shaking his head slowly from time to time as he ran his eyes over the lines.

"Word for word, the meanings are accurately conveyed, and the rhythmical pattern is faithfully followed too, at least outwardly. But altogether what a total failure! Yet how could one hope to transplant these wild flowers of our native land into foreign soil and expect them to live? Reading these translations is like walking through a frozen garden, or, to be more precise, like being invited into a blooming garden, only to find in place of alive flowers the name of each one scribbled on the soil with white chalk."

"Isn't it fortunate then that instead of words you write music that needs no translation," I said.

"Not quite so fortunate as you think," he replied. "Music too creeps out of one's native soil with a national flavor of its own. A passage that rouses poignant echoes in the native memory of one's own people can hardly be expected to have the same effect on the listeners of another nation. In them it might well arouse an entirely different set of feelings. And there you have it — no matter how you choose to describe this phenomenon, some sort of translation already has taken place. As for actual folk song melodies, the same thing happens to a far greater degree and in a much more obvious way. Isn't it true that however charmed or touched you may be by a folk song of foreign origin, your reaction to it is relatively objective? How different from the host of subjective feelings you experience on hearing a folk song of your own country — its idiom has been growing in you during your entire life. Perhaps this is the reason," he said, as he got up and gathered his papers together, "why certain composers deeply rooted in their national idiom — like Kodály Zoltán, for example, who steeped himself in the language of his native folk songs — perhaps have to wait longer than others before they find appreciation outside their own lands."

As the door closed behind Bartók, Ditta said, "Yes, Kodály! So often when Béla talks about Kodály, he is really talking about himself too, in a way. No wonder, since they started out collecting songs together a long, long time ago, as far back as 1905, and their work was deeply interwoven although each of them used this material they had discovered together in his own individual way. And their friendship has always remained strong and vital, Kodály being one of the very few Béla really calls a friend. For by now you have certainly noticed that in spite of his deep concern for certain groups like the American Indians, he hardly ever reacts warmly toward people as individuals. Talking about the past, how naturally his affection flows toward things — a tree, a pet hen, or a corner in some far-off village — but seldom if ever toward one person." She sighed. "And Béla talks about the difficulties of translation! The whole of our life together I have tried to translate what people regard as the impenetrable impersonality of his behavior."

"Impenetrable?" I said. "He has never struck me as impenetrable. Unapproachable, yes. If he bothers to express himself at all, he is unusually frank. It's true he never does or says the things that people expect, but on the other hand those are the very things that people use in order to hide their real selves. Bartók is defenselessly exposing himself, with every word he utters."

"I'm so glad to hear you say that!" Ditta said. "It still amazes me how he is completely without any conception of what an everyday conversation is." She paused for a minute. "And think of all the explanations I have to make to the people who take personal offense at his impersonal conversation!"

"I wonder if it really helps to explain?" I asked. "Bartók is like his music, he cannot be translated, he has to be learned."

She laughed. "One of his friends once complained to me that Bartók never in all his life had bothered to ask him how he felt when they met from time to time. When I called Béla's attention to this, he was so surprised and looked at me with such a childlike earnest expression and remarked, 'Why, nobody told me he was sick!' that I realized all over again how ridiculous it was to try to change him into something that he was not."

Next morning Ditta found me in the hall closet sitting near Lulu's basket, admiring the new family of kittens that had arrived during the night.

"I've seen them already," she surprised me by saying, as she crouched down beside me. "Béla called me in," she went on, "in the middle of the night, soon after they were born. I couldn't believe it," she laughed, "for when it comes to birth and such things, Béla usually prefers to be a thousand miles away. As a matter of fact, the first thing he did was to reassure me that there was nothing unpleasant to see. He said that the kittens were immaculately clean and so was the mother, and that everything was in the best of order. If Lulu hadn't already won his affection, she certainly would have done it now by what Béla calls the 'efficiency of her motherhood.'"

We sat there and watched the kittens for a long time.

"You have no idea how fascinated Béla was by those tiny creatures. One in particular delighted him by the vigorous way it nuzzled against its mother's side, lifting up its head strongly in what Béla called the full triumph of a new life."

At lunch that day, Martha came into the dining room carrying something tied up in brown paper. As soon as she was certain that Bartók's eyes were upon her, she undid the package with ceremony and brought forth a large piece of dark bread which she placed on Bartók's plate. It looked hard, heavy, and dry. "That's all my granny could send now," she said importantly, "but next time she'll bake a whole loaf for you."

"Thank you very much," Bartók answered with unusual warmth, breaking off a small piece with considerable difficulty. "It smells very good," he said, sniffing it cautiously, "and tastes good too," he continued, chewing the bread slowly and with pleasure. "In fact there is only one thing that could be said against it," he added with his compulsion toward accuracy. "It hasn't got enough holes in it." As he looked up at Martha, and realized how his remark had offended her, he quickly added, "But it was certainly most kind of your grandmother to let me have some of her bread. She must be a very fine woman. It would interest me very much," he said, eating the bread exclusively and paying no attention to the rest of the food on the table, "to know what tribe of Indians she belonged to."

Martha was lost for an answer, but only for a second. "Oh, she comes from the state of Maine," she told him glibly.

"But what tribe?" Bartók insisted. "What tribe? Don't you even know the tribe she came from? Didn't you ever try to find out? Have you no interest in your origins?"

Martha remembered that something in the kitchen required her immediate attention, and when she came back a few minutes later, she spoke to Bartók with her usual self-assurance.

"I am so sorry that I really can't remember the name of my grandmother's tribe, but perhaps it would help you to figure it out, sir, if I called your attention to the fact that her favorite color is green. The truth is that she has such a liking for it she paints everything in her house green. Why," she went on, encouraged by the deepening seriousness of Bartók's attention, "do you know that when my daddy gave her a real nice icebox last Christmas, sparkling white and practically new, the first thing she did was to paint it green." Bartók continued to stare silently as Martha hurried on. "So doesn't it stand to reason that green must be the color of her tribe? Oh, you know what I mean." She became aware, too late, of the shocked look on Bartók's face and tried to coax him to accept her theory by adding further extemporaneous evidence. "The same way football teams have a color of their own, nowadays . . ." Her voice trailed off lamely into an indistinct mutter as she saw the rigid judgment in Bartók's face. But even the forbidding tilt of his head could not prevent her from making one more attempt to retrieve her prestige.

"Well," she said, almost defiantly, "I thought for someone who knows so much about these things, this might be a sort of clue to know about green being her favorite color." For a moment she faced him, and Bartók, with a great effort, said nothing. But the effort was only too apparent. Martha's confidence wavered, and as she walked to the door, it crumbled entirely. She looked back at him, and finding his face as stern as before, she shrugged her shoulders and with an uncertain smile on her face, disappeared — vanquished, for the first time in my experience.

Mealtimes with Bartók, even without such dramatic moments, seldom passed off smoothly. His appetite was small and uncompromising. He would hesitate so long before tasting his food that it always reminded me of a bather trying to summon up courage to ease himself into cold water.

Once when he caught me watching this procedure, I remarked, "You must have so accurate a conception of how each food is going to taste that you hesitate to try it for fear it won't live up to your expectations."

"Don't be so expressive this early in the day," he said, smiling faintly. "Instead, tell me if you know how to make potato dumplings filled with prune jam."

Somewhat taken aback, I was about to say no, when I saw Ditta nod significantly.

"Yes," I said, but with a good deal of misgiving. "Would you like to have it tonight?"

"Tonight!" he exclaimed, thoroughly shocked. "But I don't want it tonight! That wouldn't leave me nearly enough time to get into the right mood for it. Let me think now — today is Monday, isn't it? Well, let's say you make it for Thursday evening. That should allow exactly enough time to reach a mood of maximum appreciation . . ."

In spite of these inevitable daily incidents, Bartók quickly established his working routine in the house, a routine that for a long time seldom varied. The light in his room was burning throughout the night, right into the heavy grayness of the misty dawn. His breakfast was eaten in bed at midmorning. And if he came down for lunch, and we were lucky enough to pass this sober midday meal pleasantly, as soon as his last bite was eaten, he got up and left the table so abruptly that at times I did not realize that he was gone until I looked at his chair and found it empty. He stayed behind the closed doors of his room the whole of the long afternoon, bending over the harvest table covered by now with small heaps of papers from one end to the other. Those bits of white paper, each with its few neat lines of notes, how often I watch him spread them out and gather them together again wherever he happened to be, bending over them on tables big or small, dealing them over his blanket in bed (even sometimes balancing them on his sharp knees), but sorting them always with the same concentration as his eyes swept over the rows, picking out a slip here, a slip there, stacking the remainder in new piles only to spread them out again. And so he would work on with unfailing patience, like a fortuneteller, bending in concentrated silence over the intricate rows, trying to fathom the future from a shuffled and reshuffled pack of cards.

One day I went up to his room with Ditta to help carry his afternoon coffee. Unexpectedly we were invited to join him. For a little while he worked on in silence, then stopped to reach for his coffee and gave us his attention. Always curious about these papers that were forever spread out around him, I now mustered up enough courage to ask him what they were.

"This happens to be my Romanian folk song collection," he answered. "I am arranging it for eventual publication. Though I am giving every spare minute to it, I am far behind my schedule — I won't put it aside for anything but original work of my own. Not that there is any danger of my abandoning it now," he added, looking at me meaningfully. "There's no possibility of doing that sort of work *here*, and it's really a pity." He looked around the room with a small smile of regret. "You no doubt placed this 'pianino' in my room in the hope that I would come forth with no less than a masterpiece, even another *Allegro barbaro*." He looked at me with a humorous grimace. "One thing, and only one did you guess right — I do use a piano when I am composing. One is not supposed to, of course, it isn't really proper. One composes at a desk. Well, that's not my way, I compose somewhere between the desk and keyboard." He finished his coffee and continued to look about him. "Really this is an ideal arrangement — this spacious table so near the keyboard." He shoved his empty cup toward the tray. "Too bad so many other things are needed besides." He spoke slowly now, not smiling any more. "Peace, and quiet, and calm." He turned again to the slips on the table.

Afterwards, sitting on the upper balcony we had decorated only a few weeks before so hopefully, Ditta shook her head despondently. "And how he looked forward to this vacation in the country. All this long disturbed year in New York he was dreaming about a place just like this — a house hidden on a deserted hilltop, a forest of trees around it, and the silent mountainsides. And now that he is here — " She turned to look at the hills as if listening to their silence. "Of course if the calm and quiet were a thousand times deeper, it still would not help him to solve his problems. Problems which are enlarged and multiplied by the sudden return of his sickness."

"Return of his sickness? Why do you call it a return?"

"It only appears to be a new sickness to him because it has struck him under such thoroughly new conditions. For him it is an entirely new problem, to be sick in a new land, where he has neither time nor place to hide away. He is no stranger to sickness. Although he was able to sustain the most rigorous working routine and endure under the hardest conditions, just the same sickness has hovered over him all his life. But up to now, whenever it chose to strike he accepted it calmly, relaxed under it resignedly, almost willingly. It always carried him back to his childhood, right back into his mother's house. Whatever his suffering might be, he found in it a deep security, an underlying contentment. He hid himself in the soft dark depth of his bed and let the world outside disappear completely while the sickness passed over him. And as it slowly slackened its grip, he would sit up in bed, dazed and pale, with paper and pencil, working away almost in a coma of concentration through misty feverish nights and days, unaware of anything that lay beyond his room."

I looked at her for a while, huddled within her own sad thoughts. I suggested a walk. She got up instantly and followed me. But as we walked along our favorite path, she continued in the same vein. "But now it's an impossibility for Béla to make the strange and cold outside world disappear. For it makes a steady and hard demand on him. It requires his constant vigilance. And so he must apply an entirely different strategy. Now it is the sickness that must be made to disappear. The sickness must be willed away, denied — he is using all his strength to fight against it, his meager physical strength and his immense spiritual will." She stopped as though overcome by discouragement. "How do I know?" she went on, looking at me as if I had questioned her. "When I asked him this morning, for instance, how he had slept, he said, 'Not very well. I had to keep awake, for the pain in my shoulder has some secret will of its own to return as soon as I fall asleep, and if I sleep for a while, it has its own way of taking such a deep hold that it requires days of concentration to make it disappear again.'"

10

PALE AND TIRED, Bartók continued to wander around the house, sometimes before lunch, sometimes in the late afternoon. He explored from cellar to attic trying to familiarize himself with every little unimportant object. The most unexpected things would rouse his curiosity. Once he came upon a small clouded mirror in a crudely carved frame. He dusted it off carefully and hung it in his room.

"Almost exactly like those old glasses I used to see in peasant houses," he remarked, "a small blind mirror, just like this, only there weren't thirty-six other shiny ones besides as there are here. Only that one mirror in the clean room, and no one in the house knew his face any other way than as it was reflected, cloudy and uncertain, from the depth of the damaged glass." He always talked about the houses of peasants as one would talk about one's own childhood home.

After he had thoroughly explored the house, one day he wandered out to the barn. He hurried back almost instantly and faced me with the abrupt question, "How can you tolerate such a horrible disorder in that barn of yours? I have never seen anything like it in all my life! What a sinful waste it is, that jumbled heap of useful things. What an immoral waste! And besides, how can you exist in the proximity of such a chaos? It is beyond me to comprehend."

"I have nothing to do with the barn," I answered quickly. "It is entirely Matthew's territory."

"Is it, really? But it is your place and therefore your responsibility." His anger was controlled, but there.

He continued more mildly, reflectively, "How can you bear to let all those beautiful things rot away out there without giving them a chance to fulfill their usefulness?"

I suddenly realized that those beautiful and useful things were the stable equipment and other remnants left by the previous owner, which had always been to me the accepted and completely useless interior of the barn. I had neither horse nor carriage to use it, and no farmer within miles would have wasted gasoline to drive up the hill for the stuff. Bartók of course saw it all through the eyes of those poor peasants he had known in so many odd corners of the world.

"Those harnesses alone," he said, shaking his head, "what treasures to be cherished." Even as he fixed me with his accusing eyes, I could see that he was looking through me half a world away into Central Europe. "Have you no awareness of the time spent keeping ragged old harnesses in working order, restoring them to life practically every day anew, dried-up broken leather cured with bacon grease, sewed together again and a hundred times again? There is a special technique just in hanging them up, spreading them out just the right way, to save them as long as possible from complete decay . . ." He stopped in the middle of his sentence as if he suddenly realized how useless it was to tell me about these things, and saying no more he walked away.

And he himself took care of his own possessions just exactly like that. I never knew anyone who was so completely without wastefulness. The tiniest bits of pencil, an eraser too small to hold, a rusty old paper clip — all were carefully saved in the hope that somehow, sometime, they might grow back into usefulness again. The same meticulous care was given to his clothes. His tweed country outfit with its knickerbockers was twenty years old if a day, he informed me, when I asked him if it had just been purchased for his Vermont trip. "Buy new clothes!" The very idea irritated him. "I have enough to last me a lifetime even if I live to be ninety."

He could simply not understand when Ditta suggested one day that the next time they went to town she would buy a pair of shorts for him, so the sunshine could have a chance to brown his pale legs.

"I have plenty of shorts," he said, dismissing the suggestion.

"But Béla," Ditta explained, laughing and blushing at the same time, "I don't mean the kind of shorts one wears underneath, I mean the other kind that are worn on the outside."

"I don't see any difference between the two," Bartók insisted.

Ditta tried again. "The shorts you are talking about are worn underneath the shorts I am talking about."

"Oh, is that all!" Bartók said with relief. "Next time I set out for a walk, I shall put on two pairs of my own shorts. That should prove satisfactory, I hope, to all concerned."

The barn with its cemetery of "useful" things was not forgotten by him, although he did not mention it for a while. Any strong impression remained filed away in his memory as intense and pristine as it had been that first moment when it reached him.

One late afternoon as Ditta and I set out to walk to Matthew's house for something or other, Bartók decided to come with us. As we neared Matthew's farm, Bartók turned to me and asked, "What on earth has happened here?" He was staring at the open fields around a rickety tool shed, all strewn over with rusty farm equipment. A tractor standing on its head showed what was left of three broken wheels; the mutilated skeleton of a car clung flat to the ground, wheelless and windowless; a circular saw bent jagged and a twisted lawn mower toppled among intricate bits and pieces of discarded mechanisms the use of which was no longer imaginable.

"But how did all this come to be here, like a continuation of your own barn?" he asked, astonished.

I was so used to the sight of Matthew's fields that I did not immediately understand the connection between my unused harnesses and Matthew's junk pile.

"Oh, those," I said, catching the implication, and wondering how I could ever explain to Bartók that Matthew was a mechanic by temperament rather than a farmer, and tried endlessly to lighten the gruesome burden of daily chores with any mechanical equipment he could find or concoct from junk, forever repairing one broken instrument with another and casting each repeated failure aside in disgusted frustration to gather rust until it finally sank into elemental disintegration.

But even as I was shaping my answer, we reached Matthew's collapsing barn, and I saw distaste turn to horror on Bartók's face. He stopped suddenly to stare at the pitiful scene. The big barn had settled into the ground except for one end, which still stood precariously on its foundation as if on tiptoe. Unpainted boards leaned this way and that, with dark gaps between; they looked incapable of supporting the rotting shingles of a humped roof where moss gathered in such profusion that the whole structure seemed to totter with its green weight. Bartók's attention moved from the barn to the horses standing aimlessly near the doorway, and beyond to where a few cows, all bones and dirt, grazed in a field, and two fresh snow-white calves were lying in the tall grass.

"You mean to tell me," Bartók said, without taking his eyes off this macabre pastoral, "you mean to tell me," and his voice was choked with emotion, "that these wretched animals, these poor helpless beasts are housed in that barn through the cold winter?" His compassion seemed all but unbearable. "Take one look at those poor beasts, those winter-wounded bodies. The summer sunshine is never long enough to smooth and heal their ravaged hides before the merciless cold is on them again. And now I will be forced to think of them," he said in wild resentment, "every day this coming winter, every day I will feel through my own body the horror and torment of their existence, never knowing the hour when their icy hovel will finally collapse on them some bitter windy day."

"But look, Matthew's own house is not much better," I pointed out, trying to divert his attention from the barn.

"I'm not concerned about that," he said, refusing to turn his eyes toward the house. "Whatever his condition, he deserves worse. He has two strong hands and all the timber of the world besides. This place could be transformed into a paradise, instead of this . . . this . . . this sinking knee-deep in suffering and death." He turned abruptly homeward with such rapid strides that Ditta and I had to run to catch up with him.

And here it was again — I could not explain to him the special frustration of Vermont farmers in their unequal fight against nature. Yes, I am sad to this day that I could not tell Bartók all about Matthew, this best of neighbors and friends, whose only fault was that he was no real farmer in a land where even to be a real farmer was not enough. He had worked on the railroad in his younger days, and when the big farm had come to him, it had come like a landslide, and though he had resigned himself to it, he was helpless to resist its force. But his helping hand stretched to others over the entire hill, even to us summer people who would have been all but lost without him on that strange mountainside. Matthew was the soul of the hill: he knew every inch of the land, every disputed borderline, every rusty old water pipe that ran under the wild ground, every spring that could be persuaded to give water, every fertile spot, every fruit tree that bore a little better fruit than another — he gave his knowledge, his time generously, teaching us the way of existence on this land of his which meant only struggle and failure for him.

But Bartók would not listen to any defense of Matthew or allow Matthew to do anything, even indirectly, for him after that. Matthew had occasionally carried logs to his fireplace, but Bartók forbade me to let him do it again. Not that I had to tell Matthew to keep out of Bartok's way; he in his turn harbored ill feeling for Bartók, a silent lump of heavy grudge, partly because his sensitivity was hurt by Bartók's disregard, and partly because he had been sorely irritated from the beginning at Bartók's becoming the sole concern of our household. However, Matthew maintained his status against these odds. Always moving with assurance and ease through the house, he would often bring flowers and berries neatly arranged on green leaves to Ditta, and pay her gallant compliments. Evenings when we drank our traditional cup of after-dinner coffee with him and Martha in the kitchen, he told more intricate stories about the hill than ever before in his desire to prove himself to Ditta, and through Ditta to Bartók. He conjured up the old life of the hillside as it had been when the people who lived in the house "really belonged to them." He made us hear sleigh bells as the neighbors gathered from miles away at the church on snowy Sunday mornings; he showed us the same church burning with wild flames in the stillness of a white winter night. A stranger in the house could only have guessed that Bartók's presence was a disturbing factor for

Matthew by his abrupt departures that always preceded the sound of his descending steps on the staircase.

Martha, on the other hand, fought a desperate battle to regain Bartók's respect, forfeited by her indiscreet attempt to link her grandmother's Indian tribe with football teams. Since it would only have kept the unpleasant incident alive to bring more bread from her granny, she gave herself wholeheartedly to breadmaking on her own — but with more ambition than success.

One afternoon as she was trying the latest of her many foolproof recipes, Bartók wandered into the kitchen and stopped, his interest aroused by her busy beating of dough in a bowl.

"What in the world are you doing?" Bartók asked, his usual impersonality concealed for a moment by his intense curiosity.

"Making bread," she answered, proud and assured now that she had gained his attention.

"Bread?" Bartók asked. "Making bread? Is that the way you make bread?"

Although it was a noncommittal inquiry, Martha was keen enough to sense some trouble and look up for further explanation. When none came, she turned uneasily toward me as though asking, "What is wrong now?" But I couldn't guess, either. I only knew that according to his immovable standards something was amiss.

"So that's how you make bread," he said, stepping nearer the table. "In a cold porcelain bowl, with a cold metal spoon, right in the middle of the afternoon. Small wonder that your concoctions have no resemblance to anything that could rightfully bear the name of bread." He looked toward me with disapproval, and then back into the bowl. We both waited for the explanation which we knew would come sooner or later, and we did not have to wait long.

"To begin with," he said, emphasizing each of his words, "it should be done *at dawn* — at dawn when there is still some remaining darkness of the night to mingle with the light of the new day, and in a kitchen that is not as cold with porcelain and enamel as a hospital. Yes, in the half-dark and half-light of a kitchen that has the clinging aroma of old warmth, and in a deep, long, wooden trough, wooden and not porcelain, wood," he emphasized, "a material so much nearer to the substance of our bodies. The trough must be deep and long enough to hold the heaping mound of flour on one side, and on the other the dark pool of fermenting, brewing, moving, alive mixture with its germ of yeast — and always a morsel of yesterday's dough crumbled into it to link the unbroken chain of hundreds of years of breadmaking — then kneaded into a swelling, rising, softly breathing heap, not by a metal tool but by the hands of a woman to impart that flood of life-giving warmth to our daily bread."

He wasn't looking at either of us now but leaning against a chair, his back to the wall, his eyes half closed, having told all that he wanted to tell. Looking at his calm face, the last of his slowly spoken words still in my ears, I knew that he had forgotten Martha's breadmaking — that it had brought to mind a stronger image, a composite picture formed by many repeated scenes watched by the all-seeing eyes of a child, the many slightly varied details fixed now into a firm recollection lit by a faint ray from the distant past. "Thank you very much," he said in his everyday voice. "Thank you, but please don't bother to make bread for me any more."

When I mentioned to Ditta how we had been "caught" by Bartók making bread in the wrong way and at the wrong time of day, she showed no surprise. "Oh yes," she said, "we always had to make bread early in the morning in our house. That's how it was done in his mother's house, and of course for him that was the only way." Then she added, looking at me closely, "There is nothing strange about that." And when I said nothing more, she decided that I had not meant to criticize Bartók, and relaxed into her usual conversational manner.

"Don't forget," she continued as if, after all, Bartók did need some word of defense, "what a very sick child he was, afflicted with a most unpleasant skin condition that started even before his earliest memories, perhaps with one of his first vaccinations, according to the story his mother used to tell us so many times. The family doctor was supposed to have used some vaccine obtained from a neighbor who had kept it so long that it must have been spoiled, although that's only a guess, of course. Nobody ever knew whether the vaccine was really to blame, but, at any rate, Béla became infected and it was the beginning of a long siege of suffering that lasted more than six years. Imagine, six years!"

And she looked at me, almost hypnotizing me into seeing every smallest unit of that long time tick away.

"Years, months, weeks, days — his entire face and body covered with sores, not one single spot on him clear enough to receive a kiss from his mother. His mother! The only person in his world, with him always, taking care of him, determined to make him well at any cost, neglecting the rest of the family. He really trusted only his mother, the only one who would not show disgust at his appearance — everyone else he suspected. He suffered a constant agony of fear of being looked on with disgust, perhaps because he himself felt so repelled by his own face. He never dared to look into a mirror, he hated the sight of himself, and used to lie awake at night, dreaming — he told me this once — dreaming how it would be if he could cast away his horrible skin and greet his mother in the morning pure and white as fresh snow. But when the sores actually did disappear, as happened occasionally for short periods, he suffered an even more unbearable fear — that they would appear again. It filled him with such foreboding that his nights were even longer as he waited for them to come again — and of course they came. Then there was his fear of being seen by a stranger! He hardly ever left the house. He regarded children of his own age as his worst enemies and his terror of them became an obsession, his fear of their ridicule remaining with him long after the disease had disappeared. He never played with other children — I don't think he knows to this day what play means."

She paused.

"He never used his childhood — as childhood is given us to use. His mother alone loomed over those years, high and strong, a pillar for him to hide behind, sheltering him from the outside world he dreaded so much. She herself taught him, at home, his first letters, his first notes. Yes, she was his teacher too — for many long years, even after she had nursed him back to health. His desire to please his mother was then and remained one of the strongest passions of his life. Do you understand really the effect this unfortunate beginning had on him? To understand him even a little bit one has to know all. I hope you know that this is the reason why I tell you so many seemingly unimportant details. I feel that if I tell you anything, everything must be told. I cannot escape, you see, Béla's training — for him only the entire truth is the real truth, every tiny detail is important to the whole; you see, that is what the truth is made of, in life and in art too. That's why I tell you all these things as they come into my mind, to make sure that I give you a complete picture."

In response to some deep need, Ditta had to talk about him. As I remember those long and lovely summer days now, we talked about nothing else but him. It did not seem a bit strange at the time, it was the most natural, the only natural thing. Ditta talked, and I listened. There was in her whole lonely being this great need compelling her to try to go over every little part of the ground Bartók had covered throughout his life. I wonder if Ditta ever knew what she sought, and I am not even sure she was aware of looking for it, but there was unmistakably something she hoped to come upon. If only she tried hard enough, something left somewhere behind him, something disregarded, forgotten even, might by chance or persistence be found and would provide a key to their entire life together.

In the course of such a painstaking search, it was inevitable that Ditta should give a scrupulously exact and brightly lit account of each recollection, weighing each word with care to make sure that nothing untrue creep into the memory. Once, describing some small incident, using her special instinctive method of analysis, she stopped suddenly, looking at me with an uncertain smile, and said, "No, I don't think I am telling you the truth — it is not Béla I am describing now, but my own feelings about him. One cannot be careful enough."

So as the days went by an inner view of Bartók took shape in my mind, a picture that was not merely a double exposure, but instead a manifold of exposures blending into one, growing deeper in each of its dimensions.

Talking always of him, Ditta and I walked the shaded roads of the mountainside or turned into the far-stretching fields, stopping by a raspberry bush, or under an apple tree, resting in the burning warmth of the sunshine. At times Ditta's serious-ness melted away completely and gave place to her childlike gaiety, and her laughter rang out to the hills that echoed it back. Or she sang in her bird voice in a rhythmically humorous manner that was her own adaptation of Bartók's singing style, full of the joy of picking and tasting the red sunwarmed sweet berries, or the small tasteless apples that the trees offered in such abundance.

While Bartók was sitting alone behind his closed and curtained door, bending over the harvest table, and in the silence of the room working on his Romanian collection, I could follow him in my mind through all his years from a sick childhood filled with an eagerness to please his mother and make her admire his early experiments on the piano, those lovely little melodies that delighted her so much, and those unlovely ones that delighted her not at all and which she discouraged with all her authority, but more often than not in vain. Then as Ditta's reminiscences sent darting points of light into the past, I began to see him in those long early years of struggle, straining himself to the utmost as he sought to save from the hours taken from him by the necessary task of earning his living time enough to carry on the work he was possessed to do with such compelling passion; the pianist whose rare gifts were already widely recognized; the young composer forging his way toward a goal of still unknown dimensions. Fighting against the indifference, antagonism, or the outright ridicule of his own people, he was intensely involved in the battle for the understanding that seemed so long in coming, finding joy and satisfaction in penetrating ever more deeply into his own world.

But whenever I came unexpectedly face to face with Bartók, all other pictures disappeared, and I found myself back on that darkening narrow street of Buda where I had my first glimpse of him, his aloofness so complete that he might have been existing in another dimension. If he spoke to me when I was not expecting it, I felt always a faint shock of surprise. "Oh, you again," he would call as I passed his door on tiptoe as usual. "You always make me feel there is a burglar in the house," he told me on one such occasion. "Can't you walk just normally?"

"I can't," I answered, looking into his face, and it was literally true. "I really can't. Something won't let me. I wish I could fly whenever I have to go by your door."

"I wish you could too," he readily agreed. "Although the flap of your wings would no doubt irritate me exactly the same way. All rhythm has its natural law — this kind of restraint is nothing else but a mockery."

From then on I tried to walk as it came, with as much freedom as I could produce, but he recognized my step in spite of my new style. "Oh, it's you making the whole house shake again." I heard the resigned irritation in his voice as I hurried away.

"I hate to disturb him," I told Ditta with despair, "but I have to pass his door to go to my own room, and whatever way I walk it irritates him."

"It's not that, really," she tried to console me. "He's just surprised — he's startled out of that deep concentration of his, finding that there is a household of people around him, busy with their own lives."

One evening as I braved the walk past his door, it opened, but to my relief it was Ditta in the doorway.

"Come in, come," she said gaily. "Béla wants to show you something."

It was my cat Lulu lying on the huge four-poster with Bartók stretched out full length in beautiful repose. Yes, my cat Lulu, inspired by the respect in which Bartók's room was held, had decided to move her entire family into this privileged sanctum.

"The kittens are over there in the closet," Bartók explained. "She carried them in here one by one, holding them gently in her mouth, stepping so cautiously and with so much control, that although her hindquarters swayed from side to side, the kitten dangling from her mouth remained steady. One by one she deposited them in the closet, in the meantime talking to them in a language amazing intelligible. They moved in here only two or three days ago but I can safely say that by now I understand her language fairly well. To talk her tongue, however, might take a little longer. It is a purely guttural sound," he explained seriously, "and though there are only two or three basic patterns, there are variations for each depending on the response or cooperation she receives. The warning sound is particularly interesting, it grows into panic intensity if the kittens fail to obey her. The calling theme is the simplest, just two tones, the second an octave higher than the first, softer or louder but always the same," and he made that familiar sound so accurately that a sleepy kitten slowly emerged from the closet, taking a few shaky steps forward on her weak little legs.

"I didn't mean to disturb her sleep," he said, proud of his success but sorry at the same time, "but at least I proved it to you how good I am!" He got out of bed to put the helpless kitten back into the closet. "I can call many birds too," he added as he came back. "If I should find myself in the jungle à la Kipling's Mowgli, my quick ear for language might even save my life." He stretched out in the bed and settled the pillows and blankets around him. "And how much more exciting it would prove than learning the Berlitz method. 'What time of the day is it, sir? Please pass the bread, madam.' Instead I would merely say to an approaching lion, 'Please spare me, I have great respect for you and your free life and it gives me no end of pleasure to live in such unspoiled society.' " He leaned back on his pillows silent and content.

"Do you know the story of 'The Cat That Walked by Himself'?" I asked him after a while. "It's by Kipling."

"Kipling?" he asked suspiciously. "But it's not in the *Jungle Books*."

"No, in the *Just So Stories*."

"I never read those," he said, "never even heard of them. Are you sure there is a book called that?"

I only nodded.

"Tell it to us, Agota," Ditta asked, always ready for a story. But only after Bartók expressed a desire to hear it did I begin the story of the cat. They both followed it with interest right to the end.

"So lovely," Ditta said.

"Thank you." Bartók looked at me pleasantly. "It is a very fine story, and I enjoyed it very much."

A few days later, Bartók stopped me on the stairs.

"About that cat story," he began, and waited. "I found it among your books. I read it last night." There was another pause. "Your interpretation of it was rather superficial. You blurred those crisp clear outlines, put too much sugar in it, too. Kipling isn't really sweet — bittersweet if anything. Telling a story, one cannot be accurate enough, just as interpreting a piece of music. Only what the page in front of you has to offer — no more and no less. Better read it again. Take a second look." And he continued on down the stairs.

That's how it went — he could be lighthearted, he could be gay, but the games had hard and fast rules. And as soon as a game bordered in the slightest degree on reality, playing was over, and he stood guard again with his sharp weapons — absolute accuracy, absolute order.

11

ONE DAY as we were sitting down to lunch, Bartók called
our attention to a woman descending the narrow pathway
above the house. This narrow path from the back hills, hidden by long grass and never used by outsiders, was the last
direction in which I would have looked for an unfamiliar
figure, a strange figure dressed all in black, not young but not
old either, and wearing a hat! A hat trimmed with roses. Who
could it be?

"Don't you know her?" Bartók asked, as she turned into the
short road that led to the back entrance, the door to the
kitchen.

"Never saw her before," I answered, as I hurried out to meet
her.

Martha opened the door to her, and the woman introduced
herself. Her name was Mrs. Gonzales — my next door neighbor, she said, that is my back next door neighbor, living somewhere at the tail end of my acreage, where I had been only
once. I had often heard about my Spanish neighbors, and
whenever I did, I remembered that exciting day when I was
shown the borderlines of my property for the first time. Instead of crossing my land, we had driven all around the mountain and then walked up the other side, a complicated approach

along a narrow road more like a cow path, inaccessible to cars. I remembered now that before we reached my borderline I had seen a small cottage, looking even smaller than its size, perhaps, because it was standing in the middle of a huge cleared field. It was late in the fall, the yellowness of the fields was frosted over with a white coat, and my eyes wandered from one field to the next above it, noticing how the faded green grass showed through the transparent white cover.

I asked Mrs. Gonzales to come in and have lunch with us, but she declined.

"I stay here, if you don't mind," she spoke haltingly in broken English, exhausted by her strenuous walk, her dark forehead spotted with drops of perspiration, her faded black dress and old red-rose-trimmed hat covered with dust as were her heavy black shoes. By the time I had made her sit down, Bartók had appeared in the kitchen too. He remained standing in the open doorway without taking his eyes off the visitor.

"I come," Mrs. Gonzales said without any preliminaries, "to tell you my husband say you should buy our place. My husband sick — very sick," she pointed to her chest and shook her head, "can't work no more." She paused a moment, then continued with renewed strength. "Our farm is nice — it's good — lots of good land, clear land — right next to yours. Yours no good. No good, my husband say. Maybe sometime it was good. No good any more. You buy our land, my husband say — he can't work no more."

As soon as I recovered from the shock of my surprise, I said slowly, "I am sorry," not knowing how to say anything else. "I'm sorry," I said again, feeling a deep uneasiness. "I cannot buy another place, but I do appreciate your offering it to me." Seeing the dismay in her face, I went on, "Even this place is too much. I know that my fields are neglected, but where can I find anyone to mow them for me?"

"Everyone would want to cut our land," she broke in, "the best hay, clean fields, big barn — twenty years my husband worked every day."

"I know it's beautiful," I answered, hardly able to find my voice, "I know it is."

"No fancy house like this," she went on, hopefully, completely disregarding my negative answer.

She came as a messenger from her husband and she was determined to succeed, to make me accept her offer as much for my own good as hers. "It's the land that counts," she came at me again, "the land! Our land clean like floor, clean animals, healthy, everything good."

"How long would it stay good if I had it?" I said in desperation. "Wouldn't it be a shame to let it grow up into wild fields like my own? You see, Mrs. Gonzales, I have more than I can take care of already with just the house and the garden around it."

"My husband said you should buy it," she repeated, again ignoring all I had said. "Everybody will give you help. Those fields are easy — a child could cut it. Your fields gone too far, as good as dead."

I had been slow to realize that a battle was in progress between us — between her determination and my helplessness. It was sad that I could have done nothing even had I been seized by a sudden desire to own her magic land. I looked into her nice tired face, rough, dry, sunburned, and into her small very bright eyes intently fixed on mine.

I offered her some refreshment, but she refused. There she sat on the chair with compressed lips — she had to make good, she couldn't afford to lose. I understood what it meant. It wasn't easy — the back farm, the sick husband, and the war making it impossible to get anyone even for an hour's work. But for me to express these feelings would have been useless.

Nothing short of accepting her offer would have helped her at all.

I was so intensely involved in this struggle forced on me by my purposeful visitor that I had completely forgotten Bartók standing in the doorway. But he had stepped forward now and was regarding the woman as intently as she was regarding me.

"I can't see why you don't consider this offer," Bartók said, even before I had a chance to make an introduction. Mrs. Gonzales looked up at him gratefully, even smiling a little.

"But how could I?" I looked at Bartók in despair, realizing as I introduced them that now I had two strong-minded people against me instead of one.

"You sell your land," said Mrs. Gonzales, her attack accelerated by gaining unexpected support. She spoke as if she had found the final solution, and as if taking my acceptance for granted she went on to discuss a few last details.

"Sell your place — stones, tree roots, ledges. What you want it for anyway? Fancy house, that's all, nothing else. You'll be happier to have our place."

I stood dumfounded.

"Don't you understand what she is saying?" Bartók turned to me impatiently, emphasizing each word. "Why don't you listen to her at least? She is offering you good land to replace your bad land."

Quite frantic then, I am afraid I lost my head. "It's insane," I burst out, much more violently than I had intended. "A place in the back hills, no road to it but a cow path, a tiny little house standing alone, no neighbors for miles, no electricity, not even a phone. What could I do with it all by myself? Don't I have trouble enough with this civilized place?"

Mrs. Gonzales sat up straight on the very edge of her chair, hardly touching it. My cruel description of her house had wounded her. There was complete silence.

At this nightmarish moment an unexpected voice from the world of reality spoke casually. "I thought you loved this big comfortable house, Béla." I don't know how long Ditta had been standing in the doorway. "You have told me many times how much you enjoy these huge rooms and all the windows."

"Didn't you hear that the land is no good?" Bartók stopped her abruptly.

"But I think those fields are lovely," Ditta persisted. "What's wrong with them?"

"What's wrong?" Bartók said. "Everything."

Mrs. Gonzales had stood up in the meantime. My outburst had hit her, it seemed, where it hurt most. She must have heard the same criticism many times before. Without any further discussion, she made her farewells and left. Although defeated, she was still calm, friendly and dignified.

After she had gone, Bartók did not return to his untouched meal. Sad and thoughtful, he closed himself into his own room.

Mrs. Gonzales' visit was not mentioned until a few days later when Martha, coming into the living room with the afternoon tea, brought the news which I had already heard to my sorrow, that one of the kittens had been crushed to death under an ironing board that had collapsed in the kitchen. As she was indulging herself unrestrainedly in the sordid details, I exchanged one horrified glance with Ditta and made an attempt to silence her. "Keeping it untold won't help," Bartók said. "It's all part of the carelessness, the lack of planning, the lack of foresight. Now I suppose you are going to tell me that the unsteady ironing board in this 'civilized' house is part of the lack of manpower in Vermont." Angrily he went out toward the kitchen and, a moment later, returned with the two remaining kittens in his arms. "I will take care of these from now on," he said.

Ditta reached toward them, her hand lingering lovingly above the small fluffy heads, but she drew it back without actually touching them. I felt her desire to stroke them, and how she couldn't work up the courage to do so. I felt her love for them, and her strange fear.

I had seen her conflict many times. "Though I'm really better with cats than with dogs," she had told me on another occasion. "We kept a little dog for Péter when he was little, he wanted it so much. Nobody knew how hard it was for me — but Péter's delight more than made up for it." I suddenly remembered all that now as she suggested to Bartók that they might take the kittens back home to New York with them.

"Let's wait and see," Bartók said evasively, though obviously pleased with the idea. "I don't like quick decisions." However, he put a kitten on each shoulder as though declaring them officially his own, and then turned to me, speaking pointedly. "But your fields remain your own responsibility, and you should try to find a way to take care of them. How can you carry it on your conscience? So many acres of land lying around you wasted."

He was calm now, so I hoped I might be able to explain to him how things were with the land in Vermont.

"My fields are only a very small part of entire counties that are turning to wilderness again. Half Vermont — probably more — has not been worked in the last fifty years, a lot of it not since the Civil War. This land is not easy to work. It doesn't give enough in return. Farms are constantly being abandoned, and then picked up by helpless summer people such as I, keeping a little garden at best and forgetting what lies beyond it."

"You seem to be satisfied about it," he answered. "You have it figured out and you sound as if all were as it should be. Thousands and thousands of acres of land lying idle, unproductive — all those places that once were cleared by tremendous sacrifices, hard work and industry. Can't you visualize the ruin of it — being unproductive is like being dead." He sounded as disturbed as if all those fields had died in front of his eyes.

"I don't understand all this, Béla," Ditta said. "On other vacations I never heard you talk like this. You used to take parks and gardens and mountainsides for granted without making it an issue that they weren't bearing potatoes. I keep on wondering what is so special about this place that upsets you so?"

"Do I have to explain that this is primarily farm land? It's only a summer place because it's not functioning according to its nature. It constantly pains me to see this deterioration."

"But there is unlimited good land ready to farm in this country," I argued. "It's not as thickly populated as Europe — there is land to choose from here. Some people choose to work on more rewarding land than these stony hills — that's only natural. There is nothing wrong with that."

"Nothing, if you are willing to accept it. But now that I have become acquainted with this part of the world, I feel that it's worth working for. It's not statistics for me any more, as it seems to be for you. It's more like encountering a friend in need of help. Besides, the easiest way to forget one's own responsibility is to talk about what's happening in other people's gardens. You would do better if you'd find a way to cultivate your own — I for one would respect you more for that than for reciting lessons in history and economics which you are not thoroughly acquainted with."

Bartók didn't come down to dinner that evening, and as

soon as Ditta entered the dining room, I realized that she wasn't herself. She ate in silence, saying nothing of her own accord, and answering me with no more than an absent-minded yes or no, and nothing at all after a while.

Dinner over, I made another futile attempt to reach her, suggesting a short walk. She answered no, without any hesitation, and for the first time that evening she lifted up her face to look at me. I was suddenly hit by her strained, anguished expression and the tired hopelessness of her eyes.

"Oh, yes, a happy little walk," she laughed woodenly, "among these beautiful hills that are giving Béla so much joy and delight. No, thank you very much."

But after she said goodnight, her hand on the doorknob, she hesitated still. "But I know that it's not the countryside that's to blame, the conflict is within him, and I'm afraid it is incurable now."

I sat for a while staring into the pale flames of the candles on the table. It was still twilight — it took for ever for the dark to come to our hilltop — and I went out to the open evening to wander around alone, first in the garden then on toward the large field above the house. There was a narrow path winding through the long grass and as I followed it it led me up the hillside to the solid dark line of the trees. At last I sat in the tangled grass to look down at the house now far below.

Bartók's room was brightly lit, Ditta's room had a subdued light, and the faint glow from the dining room reminded me that I had left the candles burning. The kitchen windows blazed at me; Martha was washing the dishes, I thought, and Matthew was helping her, or even more likely they were having coffee at the yellow table, puzzled that Ditta and I had not come to sit with them as usual. All at once I was homesick for that happy half-hour shared by the four of us. What innocent culprits we all were, together with the house, and the fields that had gone so wildly astray, and the whole Vermont landscape for that matter! Why did Bartók find it so disturbing? He had come here only for a few weeks of relaxation, and the fields looked lovely as they were, overgrown with tall wildflowers, sumacs here and there, and thistles. They were not sick fields, as he called them, but just on the verge of a new beginning, of growing back into woods once more.

Sitting there in the summer twilight, I tried to find a reason why these green meadows that were such a delight to the rest of us gave no peace to him. Useless, dead — what harsh words. Was there any connection between those words and his own condition? If these fields were full of corn or wheat for his eyes to gaze upon, would that really soothe and satisfy him? Or would he in some reverse and even more painful connection compare the fruitfulnes of the fields to his own illness and uncertain energy?

And yet, for all his private shadows, those neglected fields gave him endless pleasure in the days that followed. At first he did not venture far from the house, merely following our short private road to where it met the deserted dirt road that connected us with the outside world, and there he would stop a while, looking at the long line of mountains, to turn back again and follow the path in the other direction to where the trees grew in tangled wilderness. This small stretch of land he seemed to learn by heart, there was hardly a tree on the way he did not touch or a single bush he did not rest his eyes upon, as if he wanted his surroundings to touch him with deliberate slowness, to penetrate him by degrees, so that neither the smallest flower nor a single blade of grass would pass by him unnoticed.

12

W<small>HEN ONE AFTERNOON</small> he appeared dressed in his old-fashioned knickerbockers, walking stick in hand, and invited Ditta and me to take an excursion with him, I naturally took it for granted that my presence would be a help in showing the way, and could hardly wait to take him to my favorite places in the woods. But as soon as we were out of the house, Bartók took the lead, walking with the purposeful strides of one who had covered every inch of ground before.

"This is not the right way to the path," I called after him, but he gave no sign of hearing me. At the end of the field he crashed through the bordering trees and the maze of treacherous underbrush that separated one field from the other. He jumped the stone wall with agility and was halfway across the large field before Ditta had hesitantly picked her way over the barrier of slipping stones, holding on to my hand with a tight grip and timidly inquiring whether there might not be snakes hidden among the rocks. Vainly we tried to catch up with Bartók as he crossed the steep third field that swept upward toward thick forest. He paused at the border of birches and pines, but as soon as we caught up with him, he slipped through the prickly branches and held back the saplings, inviting us to follow in his footsteps. Like a heavy **door** closing

behind us, they sprang back into place, and we found ourselves in a tangled web of bushes kept in semidarkness by the
full arms of the trees. Bartók was studying the ground under
our feet.

"There must have been a path or road here one time or
another if we are at the spot I studied from the attic window.
That is what the treetops indicated to me. I don't know what
we may find here — maybe an old deserted road or just a
narrow path that a farmer used in those 'prehistoric' days when
farmers were farming their land." This last remark, of course,
was addressed to me, but without any trace of his previous
bitterness. "At that time," he went on, "when farmers were
cutting wood to build their houses and their barns and then
to keep them warm, and to fix up the old ones when it was
time for it, perhaps this was a logging trail running from one
end of the hill to the other." He stopped to look this way and
that among the mass of trees as if he had caught a glimpse of
what he sought.

"I can't really see it with my eyes, but I can sense the rhythm
from the bending away of the earth on both sides."

Ditta and I stopped as he began to walk back and forth,
looking hard at the ground. All at once he dropped to his
hands and knees scraping at the soil with deft fingers. "Look
here, look here!" he called triumphantly. "Look at these tiny
red toadstools growing in a straight line in this hollow on one
side of the road. And look here!" He crossed quickly over.
"Here are a few on the other side too, almost invisible lines,
but running parallel to each other. Doesn't that suggest to
you the left and right wheels of a cart?"

He got up, holding one of the blood-red toadstools in his
hand. "More depth, more dampness, more toadstools. Most
likely it's not scientific at all, but it's a theory." He looked at
the broken stem of the toadstool in his hand. "These things

are so delicate. I don't remember ever seeing anything like them before. I wonder if they grow any larger, or is this their full growth. Now why don't you two look around too, and see if you can't find a bigger one for me? How can you just stand there doing nothing?" His excitement was so acute that he couldn't understand why we did not share it with him. "Don't you have any curiosity at all?"

"Here, Béla, here are some big orange-colored ones. What about those?" Ditta called to him halfheartedly.

"Oh, those," Bartók said, shaking his head, "those you can find in any wood from one end of the world to the other. No distinction whatsoever." But still he bent down to them for a closer look. "There are two kinds of these, as you can see — one with the solid orange surface, and one with the scattered white spots on it." He broke off one with the white spots and turned it upside down. "Full of black bugs, as I expected. I have a strictly private theory about those spots. I suspect those busy black bugs are responsible for them." He smiled. "Too much ammonia in their little puddles."

As we went deeper into the woods, Bartók guided us along the invisible road. "Can't you feel the form of it, the balance of it?" he asked, whenever we wandered even a little to one side or the other of the way that only he could make out. I could neither see nor feel anything about it, except how important it was for Bartók, a matter of the utmost urgency that a road materialize out of the dark stretch of forest ahead, a road hidden in the tangled wild vegetation that made each of our steps precarious. And as we progressed, it became evident that we were following some kind of path here and there clearly defined, then lapsing into complete obscurity. Bartók walked ahead, treading lightly, with the tender caution he always displayed among growing living things, as if his feet hardly touched the ground, as if they had eyes to see each white head of the Indian pipes pushing through old leaves, and each small green shoot, "pointed and brave," as he described it, struggling to become a tree. "It will have a hard time at best fighting the elements, and it's safe to say, not much of a chance."

The road widened as we walked on, slowly climbing the hill. On our left were only pines, an age-old growth of forest, thick and tangled, an eerie green darkness lying between the heavy tree trunks. Bartók stopped, and when we caught up with him, he put his finger to his lips, to warn us not to break the deep unbroken silence of the place. We had hardly taken a few steps forward when Bartók stopped suddenly again. Ahead of us, in a hollow, the way was blocked with scattered white birches, huge old trees lying heavily on the ground as far as we could see, marking the earth with sharp white lines. It hardly seemed possible there could be so many fallen trunks lying side by side, crossing and recrossing each other in a chaotic web.

"Why, that's just like a cemetery!" Bartók said in amazement. "How did it happen — all these trees on the ground? What could have brought about such a catastrophe?" He walked far into the fallen forest, picking his way slowly between the tree trunks, turning from one to the other, almost as if he were unknowingly taking toll of the disaster. When, finally, he sat down on one of them, Ditta and I walked over and joined him.

"It must have been the hurricane," I said, "quite a while ago, a year before I bought this place, I think. I heard about it, but I never really saw it, for I never walked this way before."

"And what a terrible force it must have been," he said, as his hand moved along the crusty dried-up bark of a tree trunk. He inspected its long torso and the light green shoots growing

out of evenly spaced holes in semicircles around the free half
of the sunken trunk.

"Can you think of any reason why these small shoots should
grow like this as if someone had carefully measured the distance?"

He bent down to look at them, but did not answer.

"Someone did," he remarked.

"Oh?" said Ditta, surprised.

"Although not with a tape measure, if that's what you're
thinking. How then? With what? How?"

We looked blankly at the verdant shoots.

"Try to guess, at least. Use your brains," he urged us.
"Don't you have any imagination at all? What? What and
why? Don't you ever ask any questions? Don't you ever try
to find out? Do you just take everything for granted?"

A pause again, but no answer.

"Well, I'll give you another chance," he began all over
again. "If I should pull out those little plants, which of course
I'm not going to do, you could see that they are growing out
of perfectly round holes, very much the same as those you
yourself would dig in the ground to put a young plant into,
and each of them is the same size and depth, and just about
the same distance from one another." He spoke with exaggerated clarity, each word spoken slowly as if to give it a
chance to penetrate our minds. A puzzled smile appeared on
Ditta's face, but that was all. "One more hint," he said, "although I don't know why I bother with you at all. When I
look at those evenly placed holes, I hear a sound — ta-ta-ta —
ta-ta-ta — ta — ta-ta-ta — ta-ta-ta — ta." He repeated the
rhythm over and over again, monotonous as a dry wooden instrument hitting its single note with unflagging precision.

Ditta began to shake with repressed laughter, and as our
eyes met, we set each other off.

"I don't see anything to laugh about," Bartók said, "in the fact that you are unable to reason anything out. Don't tell me that you still don't know!"

"I really haven't got the slightest idea. Please tell me, Béla. Please," Ditta said. She was certainly more amused than curious, but we stopped laughing.

"I said, I hear a sound sharply echoing through the woods: ta-ta-ta — ta-ta-ta — ta." There it was, the same sound again. Only its accurate, sharp rhythmical pattern was exaggerated by his impatience — otherwise without a hairbreadth of change, and with intense seriousness. We didn't dare look at each other this time.

"We heard you, Béla," Ditta said, and she seemed really interested now. "We heard you, but we still don't know. Tell us, please." She looked up at him, childlike, as I had seen her so many times before, waiting for his answer.

"Woodpecker!" Bartók threw the word at her. "Woodpecker! What else could it be! A woodpecker drilled those holes." And then, abruptly calm, he was telling a story.

"While this tree was standing tall and upright and to all appearances sound, it was already eaten by deathly little bugs buzzing under each of its layers, by soft worms and hard bugs, yellow, brown and black, millions in the upright body of this one tree. No great conquest for a hurricane that could fell the healthiest giants of the forest. But healthy or sick, they all come down, and the bugs take over completely. In these holes here, earth and rain and food and soil have gathered, and now this dead trunk is decorated with life again. Now life begins here in its slow way, encroaching imperceptibly as did death before. The eternal cycle, a layer of death, a layer of life, alternately in the selfsame pattern, layer upon layer to the very core of the earth. Life invades these dead bodies, claiming them entirely for its own, and will cover every inch of them with glittering fresh green as the dead bodies sink away under the living weight, their existence fulfilled and completed."

After we tumbled over the trees that were blocking our way, the road stretched suddenly wide and clear ahead of us. We sank into the soft earth darkly cushioned with needles.

"For long years, this has obviously been untouched and unseen." Bartók's cheeks were red, his eyes shining. "Even birds are scarce here, it's too dark for them, I suppose."

Conscious of the hollow silence around us, we moved slowly, more and more closed in by the rising hillside on our right, while on our left huge white birches were stretching at a slant into mid-air, holding on tightly to the descending ground. The fluid sunshine was pouring in great pools through their leafy crowns to the dark ground below us as far as our eyes could see.

"It feels good to find such a well-deserved victory," Bartók remarked as he stopped suddenly feasting his eyes on the snow-white evenly stretched trunks.

"They had to reach the sun, and they did, although they have to stand forever on tiptoe to hold on to it." And as we continued on our way, all at once we walked into a shaft of sunshine lying brightly before us on the dark road, reflected from an open field we now saw closed away from us only by a rickety wooden fence, the hinges of its gate too rusty to open. Bartók jumped over quickly, leaving Ditta and me to crawl under.

"It's pasture land," Bartók said excitedly. "Please, really look around now, and for once take notice, for it's so clear to see that this is exactly the same formation as the other part of the hill. The only difference is that the first part was sweeping upward and this is descending. It is like the skeleton of the same body since this is stripped of almost all its old growth." We were standing on the crest of the hill, flooded by warm sunshine. "Like a pasture in the Alps. Look at those steep cliffs, those huge boulders circled by small nestling flowers."

Bartók stretched out on a smooth warm stone. There was a twisted and bent apple tree above his head, the ground beneath strewn with its shrunken fruit. He gathered the apples within his reach and made a little pile of them, then began to eat, absent-mindedly, gathering a few brown seeds in his palm, his eyes fixed on the view. The apples all eaten, he took up a stick, made holes in the ground and poured his collection of seeds into them, covering them neatly and patting down the earth with soft, even motions.

"The herd is not at home," he remarked with distinct regret. "But they were here yesterday." He pointed to the big dark droppings in the short grass. "Dung," he said, using the strongest of Hungarian words, the one I had never expected to hear spoken aloud, let alone articulated with so obvious a relish in its substantial rhythm. I tried to look unconcerned, but Bartók detected my embarrassment.

"It didn't occur to me that you might be offended, although I should have known.

"What a pity," he continued with sympathy, "not to be able to feel the strength and purity of real words, words that stand for the very thing they are expressing. How vulgar substitute words are, by suggesting that they cover something ugly or evil. These words were accepted naturally by people who lived in close connection with the earth. These words in their original strength emerged like plants from the fertile soil, with special power and beauty, and were used by people who worked, rested, and made love on this soil and called every part of their bodies by these direct and inevitable names, names they used with both gusto and tenderness. Those who try to change these words, covering over their real meaning, making cheap substitutions, are the ones who cast ugliness upon words and meanings alike."

He stopped for a moment, then spoke again more bitterly. "As far as I'm concerned, the most vulgar word in any language is 'unprintable.' That's the word that makes me wince, and how often I have had to suffer from this word in printed texts of beautiful folk songs, inevitably in the most beautiful ones, created in a mood of warm spiritual and physical tenderness, or in a deeply needed joyful humor to break the monotony of hard life. If you think you are able to listen in the right way, I am going to sing one of those unprintables."

He sang then a little song full of those startling words, pronouncing them as clearly and roundly, with such uncompromising force, that it seemed miraculous how rightly they blended into the melody, creating a beauty I could never hope to find again in a lifetime. The joyful rhythm, so accurately repeated as one verse followed another, rising and falling as naturally as one's own breath. When he finished there was a long silence between us.

"Is this bawdy to you?" he asked finally. "Unbeautiful? Unprintable? Is it only your withering roses that have pure sentiment?"

"Her withering roses?" Ditta asked, and I too looked at him questioningly.

"Yes. Although you sang outside the house," he said, "I heard you just the same, and I assure you that even the memory of that song makes me shudder. One thing I admit: the songs you always sing are of uniform quality, except that each one is even a little more horrible than the other. Oh, those dying autumn leaves swept by the howling winds; and oh those 'rocking waves on the surface of the Balaton.' And oh, that music so fittingly distasteful and untrue."

"You mean the other night while I was weeding the garden?" I murmured, sinking with shame. "I did it for the fun of it."

"Oh, no you didn't. It was a performance tremulous with emotion, and studded with false notes. Well, it's not your fault entirely, for those so-called songs have been manufactured year in and year out, and poured over the public in such steady streams that unless you are on guard against them you become immune to their ugliness. Every period has its share of false talents who are infected with glibness and who mix words together with a consistent banality, only equaled by the sickening notes — for you can't expect me to call it music. However, it is often called folk music, and these imitation folk songs parade under the name of Hungarian if they are concocted in Hungary, French if made in France, and so on. The truth is they have no national characteristics — only superficialities distorted into nationalistic caricatures."

He jumped to his feet and we followed him along the narrow path at the edge of the hill, separated from a sheer drop only by a fence of wild apple trees strung with a single strand of barbed wire. At every turn a new picture of the valley sprang into view, the cemetery with its scattered stones on green patches of ground, and well shaded by weeping willows, a group of small houses with children and dogs, calm cows scattered on the faraway fields. Since the road was constantly winding, each picture was visible for a moment only, hanging as motionless in space as pictures on a wall. We reached another wooden gate, new-looking compared to the first. It opened into a wide vista of hills stretching upward and rolling down on our left almost to the foot of the valley, immaculate and smooth as green velvet. A few harvested fields slowly turning yellow, enhanced the fresh green of the others.

"We are trespassing," said Bartók, and stopped, and we stopped with him. He stood still, his eyes savoring this landscape so unexpectedly clean and orderly.

A few hundred feet from us, halfway down the valley, was a big barn, its roof patched and repatched with tin and different hues of shingles, but sturdy and well preserved. No sooner did I see the little white house standing barrenly unadorned and unshaded in the middle of a field than I knew where we were. But Bartók said it first. "Why, this must be the place you have turned down." He made no other comment, but his voice had carried to me the untold and limitless implications. He started straight toward the house.

Mrs. Gonzales came out of the door almost as though she were expecting us, the surprise on her face mitigated by a friendly smile. Bartók got to her first and bowed so deeply over her hand that it reminded me of an incident he had once related to me. He had been invited to a formal evening by one of Hungary's richest and most aristocratic counts. "I went," he said, "because I had always wanted to see the inside of his palace and its old treasures. But as I arrived in the huge hall, holding my engraved invitation, and saw the long receiving line headed by the countess, and the ceremonious deep bow-ings and hand-kissings of the guests, my interest subsided. I was ready to leave when a sudden large group of arrivals arrested the attention of the guards. I threw away my invitation and slid under the red plush rope, and there I was, wandering to my heart's content without all that ridiculous nonsense."

Yet here on the threshold of a bare little cottage in Vermont, he voluntarily made the formal ceremonial gesture — and if he didn't kiss Mrs. Gonzales' hand, he all but did. She herself was just as smiling now, standing at her own doorway, as she had been unsmiling in my house, and gave me an extra smile as if to make me understand that she bore no grudge against me in her heart. In the square, neat kitchen, we sat down at a large linoleum-covered table. Like most country kitchens, it was the main room of the house, its walls whitewashed, the raw boards of its floor scrubbed golden clean.

"We came through the woods," Bartók said, following her with his voice as she moved about. He spoke with a liveliness and spontaneous flow, a conversational ease with which I was completely unfamiliar. Most of the time he tended to speak half to himself, breaking off in the middle of a sentence if he felt like it, lapsing into silence as if the spoken words were leading him halfway to his own domain where he wanted to be left completely alone. But now he seemed to have a desire to talk to Mrs. Gonzales with no reservations, to tell her all about his walk through the woods.

"No one comes through there no more. You lose your way easy," Mrs. Gonzales said warningly to him.

"Not I," answered Bartók. "I never lose my way in the woods. I can read the signs." He was boasting like a little boy.

"No signs, no more signs," said Mrs. Gonzales, misunderstanding him. "No good way, foxes too, many red foxes."

"I am indeed sorry we didn't see any," Bartók said. "I would have loved to catch one and bring it to you for a pet."

"No me — not for me," she laughed, and held out her hands. "Not for me. My husband skin no fox and trap no fox. Trap no creatures. Keep good dogs, that's all." As she said "dogs" I saw Ditta look quickly around the room in case one might be hiding in a dark corner.

"That's nice," Bartók said. "I'm glad to hear it. But you should go through the woods sometime. I would like to take you, and I'm sure you would like it."

"No, no old coach road for me. The woods are too thick, tear your clothes. I go through short cuts if I go, but I don't go much."

"Old coach road!" Bartók exclaimed, and jumped up in his excitement to face her. "Really, was that an old road? I knew it! I knew it must have been something like that."

"Long time ago, when the quarries were worked on the hill,

there was house there too — halfway house. Coaches, carriages, going, coming. Big road, short cut going to Canada."

"It's very interesting," Bartók looked at her. "I'm glad you
told me that."

"Now you eat something," Mrs. Gonzales said. She wiped
the oilcloth clean with a damp rag and then placed deep soup
plates on the table. She put out a big bowl of fresh butter, a
pitcher of buttermilk, and a plate of thick dark bread and corncake. Bartók sat down again and helped himself to one bowl
of buttermilk after another and ate big pieces of the corncake,
and the hard sourish bread thickly spread with butter. Mrs.
Gonzales never stopped coaxing us to eat more, and we did it
if for no other reason than to keep Bartók company. Not that
our politeness mattered — he seemed to be unaware that we
were sitting at the table, too.

"This is a wonderful treat," Bartók told Mrs. Gonzales. "I
don't remember ever eating anything so good. But it would
taste even better if you would sit down and eat with me." For
she was still standing, near the table, watching over us and
making sure that we had enough of everything.

"Thank you, but I eat with my husband when he comes
home, soon now. He'll be glad to see you here."

As indeed proved to be the case. When Mr. Gonzales finally
appeared in the doorway, we all stood up. He was a tall thin
man with very long arms, his face long too and deeply burned
by the sun, though its underlying pallor gleamed through the
dark skin like wax. His thick black hair was matted and damp
with sweat, yet when he saw us a pleased surprise lit up the
fatigue of his face. Mrs. Gonzales introduced him, and we all
shook hands, but instead of joining us at the table, he sank into
the broken-down black leather couch and said apologetically,
"I seem to be a little tired today."

Mrs. Gonzales carried a plate of food to him. "You eat, you
rest," she said warmly.

"Indeed you had better, you well deserve it," Bartók said, with such compassion that I looked up to make sure it was really he who was speaking. Pulling a chair from the table, he sat down by Mr. Gonzales. "You have the most beautifully kept place here I have seen for a long time."

"I am glad you like it," he answered, flushing with pleasure at this praise of the work into which he had poured his life.

"If you would only know what a great joy it is to me to see so perfect a place! You must be proud of it."

"Good clean land," Mr. Gonzales said modestly. "No stones or tree roots. They were dug out with my own hands." He put his food on a chair to hold up his hands to show them to us. They looked like red-brown stones, big and heavy, the fingers no less gnarled and knobby than the tree roots themselves.

"You deserve real praise, Mr. Gonzales," said Bartók, warmly pressing the hand that was resting limply on the chest of the sick man. "Few people have the distinction of having such beautiful things to speak for their hard effort. But you have the land to praise you. I can only wish you good luck to go on."

The intensity of Mr. Gonzales' joy at this overwhelming appreciation seemed to sap the last of his strength. As Bartók let his hand go, his head fell back, his eyes closed — he was in a deep sleep, breathing loud and hard, with open mouth and heaving chest. Bartók got up and stood for a moment looking down at the sleeping man.

"You see how sick he is," said Mrs. Gonzales. "He worked too much, too hard twenty years, every day — built the house himself, cut the trees for it too. He loves to work so much, he feels even sicker because he cannot work."

"I know," Bartók said. "I know."

"Come again, please," Mrs. Gonzales repeated to each of us

as we shook hands at the door. But she ran out before we reached the turn of the path to warn Bartók once more against the woods. "You go down the field right here." She was pointing toward the lane that dropped away over rolling green fields. "All the way down till you reach the road. No woods, please. Gets dark too early there."

Bartók smiled and nodded, leading the way down the lane she had indicated. Once he turned to look back. She was still standing there and raised her arm to point silently. His head slightly bowed, he hurried on his way, leaving us to follow some distance behind.

"I am so glad you finally saw him this way," Ditta said. "It did me good too. He is like this with those he admires, respects and trusts completely. What brings on this feeling in him is hard to tell. It's not people with prestige, money, not even great accomplishments. It's something I only vaguely sense and don't know how to put into words."

We were walking after Bartók as rapidly as we could, not to lag too far behind.

"But there was something else too," Ditta went on, thinking hard. "It's really just a thought. It's Mrs. Gonzales! She somehow reminded me of Béla's mother, or, maybe, it was his behavior toward her that reminded me of the relationship between him and his mother — that complete openness, that eagerness to please. I wonder if he realized it at all, or did he just let the feeling take hold of him and allow himself to sink into it completely?"

Was Bartók feeling any better these days? The long afternoon walks colored his cheeks, and wandering through the woods always lifted his spirit. His hands, his pockets were always full of his findings when he arrived home, and he made a display of all the things for us to see: a patch of moss, a kind he was not at all familiar with, or something very well known indeed, like the ladybug he brought in on the back of his hand one day. After we admired it, he stretched his arm through the open window. "Watch how perfectly she will take off. And listen to that slow happy buzzing sound she makes. See?" And his eyes followed it until it was gone.

When Ditta and I accompanied him on his walks, it was the same. He had a thousand ears and just as many eyes. "See this!" he would say, and "See that? Look at that tremendous lichen on that tall tree there. I never saw one as large as that in my life before. It is like the cross section of a huge open umbrella."

He stood there looking up at the tree so yearningly that I said, "Maybe I can climb up partway and get it down for you with a long stick."

He looked at me as if he did not believe he had heard me rightly. "Did you say you would get it down? Did you really mean it? Would you do anything like that? It would be like demolishing a whole city! Or more likely, a whole world. Can you imagine how many different kinds of insects built their different abodes in it? How many eggs are deposited in them? What shelter it provides for an indefinite number of living things from wind, from rain, from snow?" But he quickly forgave me as I was lucky enough to call his attention to something he would otherwise have missed. And when we sat down to rest, as always, there was singing.

Bartók would begin alone, his deep voice intoning the melody with precision and a tempo that would reveal the characteristic pace of motion, an entire way of life of the people who created it. After a while Ditta joined in with her clear soprano.

"And what about you?" Bartók would ask me. "Let's see how accurately you can sing a song like this! But first just listen to this one, and note what a compact musical thought is compressed into this little song. For me it is a miniature masterpiece, in its limited existence as perfect as any composition can be."

Bartók fell into a reflective mood as he went on. "Meeting with songs like this played an important part in giving me freedom and releasing me from the harness of the single rule of major and minor scales. When I first became acquainted with Debussy's music, and when I was able to separate myself from the magic of it, I found with amazement that his work too contained these pentatonic turns that played such an important role in my own music, and I realized that he undoubtedly was no stranger either to the East European folk song."

So it was during many afternoons of wandering through the woods singing and talking. Bartók seemed tireless these days and even on the way home his eyes were photographing and enlarging all the zigzagged details of the woods.

But when evening came, he once again sat huddled in his armchair near the blazing light of the open fire, and although the reflection of the red glow was shining on him, it did not seem to warm the pallid coldness nor relax the rigid outlines of his face. I can see him now sitting there, his right arm crossed over his chest, holding on to his left shoulder with a tight grip, while he seemed to be listening with closed eyes to the pain that was lurking in his body. Sinking deeper and deeper into sadness, he showed only hopelessness and despair, motionless as a statue into which its creator had poured unknown anguish. Filled with a sense of this agony, this suffering as of a stone, one could not reach out a helping hand, one could not offer the touch of mere human sympathy.

13

ONE NIGHT the electric generator that had remained a source of irritation to Bartók, mild or hopeless according to his mood, broke down, leaving the house in complete darkness. The breakdown was no surprise to me, since a small part had burned out weeks before and had been replaced by a temporary device because of wartime shortage. We had plenty of oil lamps in readiness to meet this emergency when finally it arrived. Not more than a few minutes after the house had been plunged into darkness, I knocked on Bartók's door with a lighted lamp in my hand. He answered my knock, but when I entered I found him with closed eyes, his head fallen back on his pillow, his face abandoned to sorrowful sleep. Even after he opened his eyes, he did not see me. But as I stood there with the burning lamp in my hand, his eyes suddenly focused on the light, his dejection changing into intense pleasure.

"*Petroleum lámpa!*" he exclaimed, as the oil lamp flooded the joy on his face with warm radiance. "When did you find that thing? Did you have it in the house all the time without even showing it to me? You've kept it hidden away while I struggled night after night against the terrible drum-beating of that machine! Don't you understand? This could have solved everything! But now, of course, it is too late."

He paused a moment, his eyes drawn again to the flame, steady in the silence. "I was sitting here working," he went on, "and all at once I felt the sound of night around me. I was listening to this and that — the life and death battle of sharply armed bugs, and I seemed to hear those little black spots one finds sometimes on the wrong side of leaves, coming to life so quietly, barely rustling the leaves they are born on — and all at once, I saw you with that lamp in your hand."

I was making room now for the lamp on the small table near his bed. He did not take his eyes from it for a minute, following it with a friendly smile as if meeting an old friend after a long time. "The wick needs trimming," he said, looking at it closely. "It isn't quite even. I will attend to that myself, I know how to take care of these things. I've worked long enough by such lamplight, and happily too. And remember, no more of that terrible machine for me from now on." He was sitting in the circle of the pale yellow light, his frame, narrow as a child's, inhaling slowly, deeply drinking in the humming buzzing summer night as if even the air tasted different without the drumming of the "infernal machine."

From that evening on, the lamp never left Bartók's room. It was taken care of by him tenderly and painstakingly. The lamp was always on his night table, its chimney sparkling, its wick straight and white, a respected, pampered object, an endless source of delight. Also, from that evening, the electric generator remained silent at night. Everything requiring its operation was turned off or disconnected. Except for a few flickering oil lamps, the entire house lay in darkness. Our discomfort was relieved only by the consolation that Bartók was working happily in the silence.

But even this joy did not remain intact for long. He soon discovered that the oil in his lamp would not last through the night, and a second lamp was needed. So a second lamp was taken to his room, but it did not meet with his approval; nor did any other, as one by one every lamp in the house was inspected. None compared with that first one picked at random. Though we were eventually driven to borrow lamps from the neighbors in an effort to find one that pleased him as much as the first, by now I knew that no other lamp could bring back that sudden joy of surprise, nor duplicate the unexpected magic that had brought to him for a fleeting second the very flavor of his past. For the only good he found in the present were the things that reminded him of the past, but these elusive images could be barely touched before they were melted away by the cold insistence of present reality. These poor fragile symbols were doomed to die almost before they had materialized, leaving behind them only the haunting memory that made his existence in the present even harder to bear.

One day when he was tending his lamp, his first lamp, his only lamp, for no second one remained in his room, he turned to me. "Now if you will only get for me a piece of bacon — but I mean a solid piece of it, not one of those paper-thin tasteless slices that you call bacon here. Then I could prepare a little supper for myself, toasting the bacon and a piece of bread over the chimney of my lamp as I used to do when I stayed in so many faraway country places. Oh yes, many times that used to be my evening meal and it was a good meal, too."

I brought the bacon, not in tasteless paper-thin slices, but in a great big hunk, just as he requested. Immensely pleased with it, he did not trust this heavy-brown-paper-wrapped package to the refrigerator in the kitchen, but kept it in his own room on the window sill. However, it wasn't long before the bacon disappeared, and since he never referred to it again I could only hope that the memories it awakened brought him a fragment of peace and joy.

Although the generator remained in silence and Bartók had

by now learned that his work at Columbia University was to be continued another six months at least, he showed exactly the same dejected attitude as before.

"Six months," he said, whenever the subject came up. "How can one settle down to do any work like that in six months? To be able to do one's work undisturbed, there must be the feeling that time is there as long as it is needed. Six months! It cuts into the sense of continuity. I seem to see a sharp, dark barrier ahead of me — here it ends — as if I were sentenced to death, and were being kept alive by six-month respites. It's hard enough to conduct the fight with time even without breaking it into small pieces like that; to arrest the lightning swiftness of it, to bore a hole at its very center and crawl into it silently, to attend to his own creation unconcerned by any other obstacles than his own limitations — that is all one man can do."

Those sentences spoken with such foreboding, with such dark impatience, gave us a flash of insight into the strong resentment he felt when so much as a minute of his time was threatened by outside intrusion.

A day or so later when we were finishing lunch, we heard a car pull up in the driveway. When Martha came in to announce that visitors were waiting to see Mr. Bartók in the living room, he put down his knife and fork instantly and sat up straight in his chair, looking around him with the helplessness of a cornered creature.

"Don't let them in!" he said to Martha in panic, and then turned to Ditta. "Please, tell them anything you like, just keep them away from here."

Ditta got up quickly and left the room. But when she came back in a few minutes, her face was gently pleading, her voice coaxing and soft. "Please, Béla, please see them, just for a short while. How can you possibly do otherwise? They've driven all the way from New York. Going and coming, it takes two days, and they came only to see you. Can't you give them just a little time?"

"I can't help it if they have two days to throw away. I haven't even a minute to waste." His voice was quiet and tense. But Ditta stood there looking at him pleadingly, and presently he got up to follow her, defeated, his face showing hopelessness and bewilderment. As she opened the door, Bartók stood hesitantly for a moment and his expression changed. It set suddenly into the unapproachable aloofness the outside world knew him by, into that classical mask that was ready for any public occasion, and which was generally mistaken for the sign of an essentially cold personality.

As the second part of August was approaching, a sudden change took place in the weather. The hazy languid air of long summer days turned to cool and clear crispness. The sky hung lower, the mountains seemed to move nearer, the green erect pines stood with their needles sharply edged in the transparently iridescent sunshine. A few yellow leaves appeared on the white birches, and here and there bright red ones burned on the maples. The outlines of mountains became clearly drawn, and winding paths, secrets of summertime, could be uncovered at a glance. The sudden change of the atmosphere brought about a great restlessness in Bartók. He appeared early in the mornings fully dressed, and began his tireless wanderings.

"That's how it comes," he said, "the end of summer; it's exactly the same in the Alps or in the Carpathian mountains, this exhilarated brilliance, this concentrated power of essence, the climax, the end."

He was on the move the whole day long. Thin and wan, his cheeks lay on the sharp outlines of his skull, his eyes burning large in their sockets, a constant inner vibration driving him, beyond his powers, to cover every inch of the countryside.

One evening he came home, leaning on his stick, dragging himself heavily, completely exhausted. He was silent during dinner while Ditta and I talked excitedly about a strong echo we had encountered that afternoon while passing a barn on our road.

"What do you call a strong echo?" Bartók finally asked.

"Why, it throws back each word, loud and clear," Ditta answered.

"How many times?"

"What do you mean — how many times?"

"Does the echo have its own echo?" he explained. "How many times does it answer you? Once, twice, three times?"

"Only once," Ditta admitted. "But very distinctly."

"So it's nothing like the echo of Tihany, which answers at least a dozen times," he said with satisfaction. "There is a phenomenon you don't run into every day." He turned toward me. "Did you ever hear the Echo of Tihany?" (*Tihanyi visz-hang*)

"No," I said, "but I've heard about it."

"Everybody's heard *about* it, of course! Can one grow up in America without hearing the name of Niagara Falls? You couldn't have grown up in Hungary without hearing of the *Tihanyivisz-hang*. Still, there is a great difference between hearing about something and actually experiencing it." He said no more during dinner but it was evident that he was entangled in the magic implications of that name.

As soon as the meal was over, he rose from the table and said, "Well, let's go and hear this famous echo you two discovered," and we started off into the twilight.

"What a cold landscape this is," he said, as we hurried along a road between the tall rows of dark pines. The swollen bulk of the mountains lay heavy in the distance, its outlines sharp and dark against the glow of the sky.

"It doesn't seem so cold to me," I answered.

"The soil is cold, stony, hollow, unyielding." He tapped the ground again and again like a blind man, sharply, with his stick. "Hear that sound, how hard it is? Stone upon stone. No life in the depth of it."

When we reached the bend in the road and the old deserted barn became visible a few hundred feet ahead of us in a hollow, he motioned us to stay where we were and come no nearer. He hurried on alone beginning to call, "Echo, echo!" as he went. He spoke softly as if trying to wake a sleeper, calling, "Echo, echo," and there was an extreme tenderness in the voice of the echo that called back to him. He spoke louder then, "Echo-o!" raising his voice at the end of the word as if leaving it open for the echo to finish. He called loud and soft, in all imaginable varieties of tone, the echo coming alive with a counterpoint of its own, giving him his voice again as the voice of a stranger.

By now he was beyond our sight in the darkness of the deep hollow around the barn. He began to call in Hungarian, "Visz-hang, visz-hang." His voice was deeper now, alive with expectancy as the old New England barn returned the Hungarian words with a passion that had not warmed its mother tongue. Then Bartók called out "Tihanyi visz-hang!" and repeated it over and over again until the joint cries rose desperately into the last light of the sky, so far away that the urgent voices could only grow more plaintive, aware that in such remoteness there could be no listening power capable of understanding nor inclined to offer help. It was completely dark now. Bartók and the echo kept on calling to each other in ever more hopeless appeal, the eerie hollowness of the echo magnifying the sadness of Bartók's voice to an unbearable despair.

However, when he joined us on the road after a while, he said casually, "Yes, it is quite a powerful echo as echoes go, in fact it's fairly good, although nothing really unusual." And no one spoke again as we slowly walked home under the clear August stars.

At just this time when Bartók's disposition was so vulnerably tuned to the slightest disturbance, I received a letter from friends saying that they were driving through my part of Vermont and would like to spend a few days with me. "The house is surely big enough to hold four more people without difficulty," Ditta said when I consulted her as usual about Bartók's probable reaction. I was inclined to agree with her, since both of the men were well-known concert managers in Europe and their wives were also occupied in the field of music. "It might even help him," Ditta said, "to talk things over with them, since they have the same problem of transferring their activities across the Atlantic." When the news was gently broken to Bartók, he made no remark and showed no reaction except perhaps for a shadow swiftly crossing his face that even his rigid control could not hide.

It would be impossible to trace the imperceptible stages of retreat into himself during the few days before the actual arrival of my friends, but by the time they came, Bartók was as completely withdrawn as a turtle closed into the walls of the house it has spent a hundred years growing. Far from talking his problems over with the visitors, he made any conversation at all impossible by instructing Ditta to say, as they were being introduced, how sorry he was that he could not speak or understand German. He had also asked her to explain that speaking French or English made him tired, so he had no choice but to remain silent. And silent he remained.

When occasionally he came down for dinner with the rest of us, he showed no awareness of the people around him except for one stiff bow of the head intended as a greeting, but always

given with the impersonality of a blind man uncertain whether
he might be bowing to a room full of people or to empty space.
Most of the time, however, he ate alone in his room, and always went in or out of the house by some secret device of his
own that kept him entirely invisible.

Only when he learned the time, to the exact hour, of the
projected departure of the visitors did he agree to join a farewell excursion. He presented himself at the appointed time,
and climbed into the visitors' comfortable car as though taking
his place in a public conveyance. Sitting in the open car,
watching an entirely new landscape rolling by in the fresh
sunshine of the clear crisp morning, although he did not break
his silence, his face relaxed into softer lines. He could not help
but respond to the quickly changing scene and the familiar
excitement appeared and made his face alert again.

We reached the point at which we were to leave the car and
walk with our picnic baskets to our destination, Cow Lake,
some two miles back in the hills. My friends examined the
terrain with growing misgivings, and when they saw the narrow
uneven cow path we were to follow, they seemed almost ready
to give up the whole adventure and go for a comfortable ride
instead. Bartók, however, ignoring their hesitation, with a
look of undisturbed joy plunged down the path ahead of us
all. We followed single file along the uneven track that was
tangled with heavy long grasses, the wake of our footsteps
oozing sticky dark mud behind us as we passed. On one side
of us lay a marshy land that must have been somehow related
to the lake we hoped to reach. But there was no lake in sight.
On the other side we were closed in by a steep rolling hill covered by young birches growing up from wildly scattered mossy
stones.

My friends complained more with every step about the
"dirty" road, and tried to persuade us to turn back before the

going became even harder. Finally when the wife of one of them, who seemed too heavy for the narrow road, took a sudden fall, it served as a good excuse to turn around. But they went back without us, for it was easy to see that Bartók was determined to carry through our original plan as he continued serenely to lead the way forward.

Their departure lifted a weight from us, making the rhythm of our walk free and lighthearted. Ditta and I, drawn into Bartók's deep silence, made no remark, and neither of us knew whether Bartók was even aware of what had taken place until all at once he looked around and said, "Did you see poor Mrs. Ship keel over?" (Translated from the German the name of the capsized lady actually did mean "ship.") And as if this remark had broken the mask which he had worn for the last week, Bartók became as spirited as someone just released from a long confinement. "There isn't much wrong with this road that I can see, it would be a joy barefoot, most satisfying to see the mud seeping through one's toes. It is very clean mud. Only that peculiar German spirit could abuse it as dirty."

"Why don't you take your shoes off then?" Ditta suggested.

"It's too late now," he said, "the path will be wide and dry in another moment."

As if by magic, the path did change into a wide smooth lane at the next turn, and a moment later the lake became visible, a large piece of shiny water lying quietly encircled by softly rolling mountainsides. Now that we were within sight of it, we hurried across the open fields, over the fresh dry grass that led down to the very edge of the water. And in the open expanse of beautiful landscape we found ourselves completely alone.

Bartók was delighted, and even more so when he discovered that we had the entire basket of lunch to ourselves, for our friends in their hurry had forgotten to take their share. We found a comfortable spot under a willow tree right at the water's edge.

"I must go swimming at once," Bartók said, "to work up a good appetite, for we must finish that basket of food in case your friends decide to come back for their share, choosing the horror of a filthy road rather than to go without their lunch. It would give me a special joy if they would risk all just to find at the end that the food is gone and the basket is empty."

"What makes you like this, Béla? You know that you were terribly impolite — and they're such nice people." But Ditta couldn't stop smiling, seeing Bartók so happy.

"Oh, yes, indeed," said Bartók, "but somehow I don't feel in the least conscience-stricken about it all." He laughed, and Ditta shook her head helplessly. "But before you go on with your scolding," Bartók continued, "remember that ages ago there was someone who used to tell our Péter, when he was a little boy, stories about another little boy called 'good Lacika' — stories for every possible occasion involving the highest moral principles. And one day when such a story had just been finished, the moral neatly pinned to its end, and that certain silence duly observed which allowed the beneficial substance to sink in, Péter unexpectedly broke the silence by saying, 'Now *I* will tell you a story about a good Lacika.' And he promptly began, 'Once upon a time there was a good Lacika — ' the same way all the stories started — 'and one day when a lot of guests came to dinner and they were all sitting around the dining room table, this good Lacika quickly climbed up to the top of the sideboard and wee-weed into everybody's soup. Yes, that's what he did.' And Péter didn't forget to tack on the moral either: 'because he was a good Lacika.' Well, I'm somewhat hindered by the departure of the guests and by there being no sideboard to climb onto; however, there are plenty of tall trees around us."

While he was swimming quietly at the edge of the deserted lake in the placid warmth of noon, Ditta, without taking her eyes off him, was talking to me in whispers. "Do you know who that 'someone' was who used to tell Péter the stories about good Lacika? Béla's own mother. And do you see how carefully he omitted her name, even from Péter's story? For Péter, as I well remember, began 'Now, Grandmother, I will tell you a story about good Lacika.' "

Bartók came out of the water, drawing long silver lines after him as he waded to shore. "And now for that basket of food," he said, stretching out on the green grass in the brightest sunshine.

"We've got everything ready right under the tree over there," Ditta told him, pointing to the display on a gay tablecloth.

"Oh, no, not there, not in the shade! We cannot waste a drop of this bright sunshine — there's not much left to waste any more. How careful one always is toward the end," he sighed.

We carried the food back to him right to where he was sitting, and he bit into the first sandwich that his hand found. But discovering a small basket of grapes, he promptly put the sandwich down and reached for the grapes instead. He took the small basket in his hand.

"All I want is this, for it's harvest time. Can you smell the full ripeness in the air?"

It was a drenched stillness — every blade of grass, every leaf on the trees flowed with ripe juices like wine — and there wasn't a breath of breeze. All was standing still, and the mountains, like a colorful cloth, stretched around the shiny glass of the lake.

"Yes, there isn't much time when all comes to such complete ripeness and somehow the end always comes so abruptly."

Béla Bartók as a young man, 1905. The living room furniture
was made for him (hand-carved) by a "szekely" peasant artisan.
G. D. Hackett

Béla Bartók in London,
1911. *G. D. Hackett*

Béla Bartók in 1912.
G. D. *Hackett*

Béla Bartók
as a young man,
with his mother.
G. D. *Hackett*

Béla Bartók about 1919. G. D. *Hackett*

Bartók and
his mother,
1929.

Ditta Bartók,
Buda, about 1929.

Bartók's oldest son, Béla,
holding Péter, 1932.

Péter Bartók
and Hungarian nurse
and housekeeper, 1932.

Béla Bartók at the piano, 1932. *Kellner Jeno*

Béla Bartók at home
in Buda, 1934.

Béla Bartók and his son
Péter playing the game of
Who Can Keep from Laughing
the Longest.

Bartók with his wife Ditta,
his mother, his sister Elsa, and
his son Péter, Hungary, 1935.

Béla Bartók, 1941.

The author outside the Riverdale apartment occupied by Bartók (3242 Cambridge Avenue, Bronx).

Béla Bartók at Riverton, Vermont, 1941.

Béla Bartók
at Riverton,
1941.

Ditta and Béla Bartók with the author, Riverton, 1941.

Béla Bartók, from the cover of a concert program. *G. D. Hackett*

He was eating the grapes slowly. "The trouble is, of course, that one is so wasteful up to the last. It doesn't help to know how quickly everything rushes toward its own destruction. We have to be reminded by many heavy blows, over and over again. Though you are made to realize by all the signs that the end is near, nature keeps playing deceitful games with you, and takes back all the warnings. Don't you be fooled by this last outburst of burning sunshine — it is only one minute of standstill." He put the basket of grapes down, barely touched. "This lake will be frozen to the bottom in no time, never fear." Then getting to his feet, he said, "Let's look over the terrain."

At the end of an open field, we came upon a small house, neat and bare, most likely for a long time unoccupied. Ditta and I walked up the few steps that led to a long narrow porch. While we peered into the darkness of small empty rooms, Bartók walked around to the back of the house, and called to us presently, "Come here and see what I've found!"

Standing in a sunny field in the middle of a patch of wild blackberry bushes, their tangled arms loaded down with over-ripe fruit, Bartók held out a handful of luscious berries to us as we pushed our way to him through creeping vines. "That's what I smelled all along," he remarked.

"You eat them, Béla," Ditta said. "We'll pick our own."

"Take it, take it, please," he urged her. "Bring a dish quickly and I'll pick you some more." We ran back for a dish from the lunch basket. "Just hand it to me," he called, "and I'll pick you all you want. Don't get entangled in those wild branches."

But we picked our way slowly toward him, right to the midst of the bushes, to the middle of the sun-drenched field where he was plucking the berries with clever fingers. "I won't leave a single one for the birds," he said. "They've had their chance for their harvest; it's our turn now. You never tasted anything so good. They're filled with the warm sun itself."

Our dish was soon full and while we walked back with it toward the house, he wandered deeper into the wilderness. We had hardly time to reach the porch and put our dish down before we heard his urgent call again, so urgent now that we feared that something had happened, and we ran back through the stinging vines as fast as we could.

As we came to the end of the bushes an entirely different landscape stretched ahead of us. In a wide field, a long line of unkempt apple trees offered bent branches studded with ripe red apples like so many overloaded Christmas trees. Underfoot in the long grass, a solid layer of half-rotten fruit was turning to cider in the full heat of the sun. Bartók, standing on tiptoe on a stone wall, reaching into a tree, was almost completely screened by the heavy branches. As we approached, he began to throw apples, one or two in our path to start with, and then all at once the apples came aimed right at us in a steady rhythmical shower. He seemed almost drunk with the overpowering fumes that rose from the ground with the pungency of fermenting wine. We dodged and hid and shouted. "Stop, Béla, stop!" Ditta called, laughing.

"Just a little manna from heaven," he called back, and the apples came in quicker tempo. When we ran away, he stopped throwing the apples, but as we came out from behind the trees to approach cautiously the rain of fruit began again. For a while he wouldn't let us come near at all, until all of a sudden he gave up the game and sat down abruptly on the stone wall, his cheeks flaming with sun and fatigue. He was eating an apple now, filling his pocket with more.

"If we could only gather it all and store it for the dark days — this abundance — for that is what it is for. How sad that everything got so mixed up, that we were turned out of the Garden, rejected, and have almost completely forgotten our heritage." As we walked slowly back toward the lake, the sky was darkened by a passing cloud. A breeze came up, touching the branches of the trees, rocking them gently back and forth, and we heard apples falling in a heavy shower like great drops of rain. But when we reached the lake, the sun was out again and the same breeze that had shaken the branches of the trees before now moved the face of the water, making wide rings over its smooth surface.

By the time we had changed into bathing suits behind a curtain of bushes, Bartók was already in the water. Ditta's feeling toward the solitary beautiful lake reminded me of her feeling toward animals, love mingled with fear, her fear a little stronger than her love. The joy she felt as she melted into the freshness of the water was spoiled by a sudden fear of a school of baby fish that followed her wherever she went — or so she said. No sooner had she begun to swim along the shallow edge than she staggered to her feet and rushed for the bank. Standing hesitantly at the edge, yearning to go in again, she took a few cautious steps into the water, hesitated, and once more ran out. Back on shore she explained that a great big frog had bitten her foot, and she could not possibly go into that lake again. Dressed in no time, she sat looking at the water, her feet carefully hidden in her wide skirt, waiting for us, smiling, greatly relieved at being out of danger.

When we were all dressed and our belongings packed, as I hung the lunch basket now weighted down with wet suits over my arm, and Ditta picked up the dish of wilted berries, it occurred to us for the first time that we were miles from home without any means of transportation. There was nothing to do but walk toward the highway and hope to find a telephone somewhere along the road. The sudden quietness that always followed Bartók's brighter moods had settled heavily over him — the brighter the mood, the deeper the stillness that followed. He walked a few steps ahead of us as though in a thick mist of his own silence. What a relief it was to see, as we approached the highway, the long green car waiting there, having come to our rescue. As we were greeted by our friends, I wondered whether Bartók felt the same pang of conscience that I did. But whether he did or not, he began to speak in his carefully controlled English, describing at great length the beauty of the lake we had found, the deserted house, the fields of berries and the abundance of fruit in the apple orchard.

"How is it, Professor Bartók," one of my friends asked him, "that you who visited Germany so many times are not familiar with our language at all?"

Bartók looked at him for a moment, and then said with great seriousness, "If there were a German language unrelated to the one which is spoken today and which is a party to such terrible deeds, a language preferably dated before Bismarck's time, I would be glad and proud to remember and speak it again. And in that case, it would never have occurred to me either," he added sincerely, "to withdraw the German texts from all the editions of my work."

14

AFTER THE VISITORS had departed, Bartók did not settle back into his well-established routine. Signs of the approaching fall absorbed him completely. The days were as warm as mid-summer, and crystal-clear. "But don't let that fool you," he repeated again and again. "The birds are not deceived. They are not delaying their plans for departure because of the lingering sunshine. See their growing excitement!" And as the days passed, he constantly drew our attention to their loud chattering as they zigzagged in the blue air, crossing and re-crossing the fields over our heads, flapping their wings rapidly, calling to each other significantly.

Sometimes he came home early from his walks just to make us come out with him again, when there was something that he was eager for us to see in the woods. He would have marked already whatever it was with a white string, perhaps nothing more than a few curled-up leaves on a birch tree, sheltering a sleeping bug, or a worm "who will appear next spring in the full splendor of a butterfly."

As he was dragging himself home one day on heavy feet, I wondered whether he might not be worse instead of better for his stay in the country. "I have pain in my leg," he told Ditta, when he noticed that she was watching his slow and difficult steps. When finally at home and rested, he said reassuringly, "This is really a change for the better. As long as I'm able to limp to the piano, I can still give a performance, perhaps even a good one. What really counts is my arms and they seem entirely free of pain. I could fly with them if I wanted to." And he stretched out his arms, waving them up and down with his wrists completely limp. He smiled, "You see, like wings, light as a feather." They were indeed light as feathers, so very thin now that his shoulder bones showed through his light shirt, sharp as arrows. Next day the pain was back in his shoulder again.

This was the day Ditta and I had planned to lure him to a folk dance and song festival in nearby Northfield. Although Bartók said a definite no-thank-you in the morning, repeating over and over that he had no intention of coming, we went on with our plan all day long, hoping to win him over at the last minute. After dinner, when it was nearly time to leave, he was sunk deep in a corner of the sofa near the fire, motionless, the flames illuminating his rigid features. "I think I had better stay home too," Ditta told him. "I'll feel much happier to stay with you."

"No, no," Bartók said as she sat down beside him, "I want you to go. I insist upon it. I expect to be in bed very shortly, and I want you to watch and listen, and describe it all accurately to me tomorrow."

However, Ditta neither watched nor listened, filled with apprehension. The only thing she could think about was getting home at the first possible moment. As we came up to our hilltop, we saw the house still lighted, and as we stopped in the driveway, we heard the sound of the big downstairs piano.

"Oh, the 'Outdoor' Suite," Ditta said. The sound, forceful and overwhelming, filled the night, a pure passionate singing sound, the wild freedom of its spirit guarded by his immense control. The music, unconstrained, seemed to come not only through the open windows but directly through the very walls of the house as though freed from any material impediment.

We did not go inside for some time after he finished playing, but when we opened the door to the living room, Bartók was still sitting at the piano. "Back so early?" he asked, looking around with a vivacity that was the last mood we had expected, leaning a casual elbow on the piano, calm, strong, and altogether composed.

"Béla, we heard you playing," Ditta said. "It was beautiful to listen to you out there. But why aren't you in bed?"

"In bed? Perhaps I would have been — but just as I was going up I had a sudden desire to read some music for a few minutes, and naturally I turned to this music cabinet here. You see?" He waved his arm, and we saw that the entire room was strewn with music, the cabinet standing in its darkish corner wide open and completely empty. "You never saw such an unsatisfactory heap of music," he went on, before we could say anything. "And would you like to know who is the composer who is represented by the most volumes? Thirteen of them all told and to be exact. Karl Czerny!" he said. "Yes, you did hear right, Ditta. I said Karl Czerny. But if you still find it unbelievable, come and see for yourself. I have arranged my findings into different groups, as an archaeologist might arrange his findings into little piles." He led Ditta to the neat stacks on the piano. "Karl Czerny — thirteen fat volumes of him. The rest of the composers are lagging far behind, represented by their most unrepresentative works: Brahms by his waltzes, Beethoven by some variations and contra-dances, of all things. And oh, by the way, I am represented too, although somewhat indirectly, by a volume of Bach-Bartók *Wohltemperierte Klavier* and the *Allegro barbaro* of course, besides the first book of *For Children*, the pirated edition naturally, full of mistakes."

"You *know* there is a wonderful collection of music upstairs," Ditta interrupted him, "with all ten volumes of the *Mikrokosmos*. I saw you just the other day looking at the Beethoven-Schnabel sonatas."

But he ignored this. "You didn't tell me anything about the dance," he said. "Did I miss much?"

"No, not really," Ditta shrugged. "But it was nice."

"Do you remember anything, to give me an idea? Can you dance any of the dances or sing any of the songs?"

"Maybe a little," Ditta said, and promptly took a position in the middle of the room. With arms raised high, she turned around a few times and began to sing with lukewarm gaiety, "Out of the igloo into the rain."

Bartók interrupted her at once. "Igloo? Why igloo? What do the American people have to do with igloo? I don't have to hear any more of it to know that it cannot be a real American folk song. And you?" He turned to me. "Do you remember anything, or is your mind too absorbed in these lofty passages of Karl Czerny to notice such earthy things? Those spiritual runs, those heart-rending repetitions for five fingers!"

I merely shook my head.

"In that case, I had better teach you a dance myself," he said.

"I don't know how to dance," I protested.

"That's no obstacle in this case. All you have to do is stay just where you are, rooted to the very spot. I'll take care of the rest of it. Your part in the dance is to disapprove of my part in the dance. This dance, you see, originated in the time when the terrible pretensions of the educated middle classes penetrated even into the villages, spreading their germs of false modesty, so that even the natural peasantry, its womenfolk, of course, could not help but be infected by the doctrine that to accept love naturally is both indecent and undignified. Love was created, it seems, for the benefit of man alone. The best a woman can do is to tolerate it with disapproval. Won't you play, Ditta, the little Romanian Dance, Number Two, please?"

Ditta began to play and Bartók began to dance all around me while I stood as I'd been told to, rooted to the very spot. First he paced out a wide circle to the slow measures, but as he increased his tempo, the circles became smaller. Round and round he went, beginning to push at me playfully till, right in front of me, he was taking two steps to the right, two steps to the left. Then making the full circle again, waving his arms, he came rapidly inward, pushing at me harder, challengingly. He was singing now with the piano, strange words I did not understand. I caught only glimpses of his face as he flashed by, and was amazed at the wild spirit that was showing there. He stamped his foot, closing in as the tempo grew faster and yet faster, in a rush of irresistible joy. Then all at once it was over. He was sitting on the sofa, leaning back, resting heavily with closed eyes.

I was still "rooted to the spot" as Ditta got up from the piano. "You were wonderful, Béla," she said. "In fact, you were so good I had a hard time keeping up with your wild tempo."

"My tempo was perhaps somewhat exaggerated," Bartók answered. "But it was my partner's fault, of course. I tried to arouse an active annoyance in her, but in vain." He opened his eyes again and looked at me. "You were no good. You neglected to take part, even passively. You were supposed to register objection and annoyance. That's why I had to speed up the tempo, trying for a reaction. The happier the man becomes, the more annoyed the woman is supposed to be. That was the effect I was trying for — but nothing came of it." He leaned back again on the cushions of the sofa, and went on. "I will never forget the pair who introduced this dance to me. The perfection of their performance! The quality of the performance, of course, should not influence the evaluation of a song, but the combination of a rare presentation and a rare song remains with one forever and is a great inspiration when the time comes to use such material creatively in one's own work. What matters most of all, though, is to penetrate into the pulsing life of the people themselves, to become imbued with their way of living, and to see their faces when they sing at their weddings, harvests and funerals, and from all these associations to distill and preserve something more significant than a song on record, something beyond music and words, an abstract essence that will remain a living force within you."

He spoke so freely and willingly that for once I didn't hesitate to question him.

"But how do you go about meeting the people?"

"Well, arriving in a strange little village, I go to the school teacher first if there is a school, or to the priest — there will surely be a priest even if there is no school — and explain what I am trying to do, asking them for information about the best singers in the neighborhood. The information they give me is almost always wrong, of course, but it gives me a lead to follow, a kind of introduction. It's easier to break the ice if I can come into a house and say, 'I heard you are the best singer around this place. Would you like to sing into my machine?' or something like that. For of course I never traveled without it.

"But meeting the people is not always the most complex problem, for at times it happens just the other way around. Appearing unexpectedly in one of these remote villages, often consisting of no more than a single crooked street, you and your mysterious-looking machine immediately become the object of overwhelming curiosity. At first you are scrutinized with suspicion, even fear, your equipment taken for some sort of surveying device to remeasure their little parcels of land in order to reduce them to a size even smaller than before.

"But when the news gets around that it is only songs that you want, there is a relieved laughter on all sides. No longer a potential menace, you all at once are regarded as something of a fool, perhaps the city version of the village idiot himself. Yes, even before you open your mouth, you have already been feared, respected, ridiculed, and laughed at.

"Then at last you begin to work — slowly, painstakingly, trying to gain the confidence of the villagers, to warm the songs out of the people who are so naturally distrustful of the city dweller and uncomfortable in his presence. To make them sing into that machine, which for all they know might explode right in their faces, you have to overcome their deep-rooted shyness, their fear of seeming ridiculous, and in some way break through the crust of long-forgotten experiences and emotions under which the oldest and purest songs often lie.

"It's not anything that can be hurried, but somehow it always happens sooner or later. An old man, an old woman will start singing in a quavering uncertain voice, and one song leads to another and soon the machine is forgotten, but what a treasure of harvest is stored within.

"What inexhaustible springs are released when the women take over the field! In my experience, the most interesting material almost always comes from them, for the songs of women are somber and seem to flow from deeply wounded hearts, while the songs of men more often reflect unquenchable gaiety and reckless humor.

"But there was one type of woman who above all others revealed the most valuable songs to me — the woman who had worked the fields all her life, sharing the work with her man, and forced the soil to yield the barest necessities. Her voice is impassionate and strong as her gawky body, wind-dried, sun-dried, bony, flat-chested and drab, in the ragged clothing of the poor. But what depth of human emotion in their deep-resigned voices, what reality, what truth."

He turned to me abruptly. "And rest assured that their songs are not in the effusive style of your withering roses. But in the unadorned compressed bareness of an entire life behind them." He broke off as if he wanted to think out the rest in silence.

"You are like a child," he said to me presently, "and just like to listen to stories and ask questions all the time. A child has an excuse for asking questions, he has no other way of learning. But you can read. You revealed to me that books are what you like — so why don't you read some of the material that has been written on this subject by myself and many others? You can find plenty if you are really interested, and not merely curious. Why don't you look into it yourself? You might very well share the opinion of some, that gathering and using folk song material means only putting down the given melodies, and then fabricating little pieces out of them in your spare time — but that is not the truth. Collecting gives you an opportunity to sink so deep into the source of your nation's musical treasure that you become part of it. You mingle with your heritage until it becomes, like the language itself, your very own. Writers, composers, poets alike, and of course painters too." He stopped for a moment, but he was not yet through.

"Chatting about these things," he continued, "is more confusing than enlightening. If you want to know the truth, you can get it only by studying the carefully organized and well-balanced material. When I answer the usual questions like yours, I allow myself the luxury of developing whatever details I feel like, perhaps completely irrelevant to the picture as a whole, and so what I say may be rather more obscuring than constructive. Therefore, if I've succeeded in giving you the wrong picture, that's what you deserve. If you really want to know, you will go to the sources and draw your own conclusion."

He really stopped now, with abrupt finality, as always, and there was no continuing the conversation. His reasons for answering any such questions as I had just asked seemed to spring from an altogether accidental desire of his own to think aloud, to develop a theme of his own choosing. I never had any illusion that I had been taken into his confidence. I realized that I was barely included in this conversation he was having with himself, and that my questions obviously became silly and irritating to him as soon as they failed to coincide with the direction of his own thoughts, and as soon as his own desire to speak these thoughts aloud came to an end. Furthermore, at the instant of this divergence, one became an intruder on his privacy, into which he withdrew with the finality of a banged door.

The days became cool, the nights really cold, and though earlier in the season Bartók had often spent the long mild evenings in the living room before a fire, he now discovered the upper balcony and sat there under the cold brightness of late August skies, sometimes until the stars faded into the penetrating chill of dawn. On one of those nights, the Northern Lights appeared — such a sudden surprise for him that he awakened Ditta, and she in her turn awakened me. We stood by him, shivering as the frost-white rays reached up to the apex of the sky. Bartók experienced it with an immense excitement, motionless, enrapt, until the spectacle began to ebb. Ditta and I slipped inside the house unnoticed, while Bartók remained in his chair, wrapped in his old brown flannel robe, and no doubt stayed until long after the last rays had vanished and the old stars had again taken their familiar places in a sober sky.

And so as the summer slowly turned toward fall, Bartók took in every phenomenon with almost painful, solitary delight. Yet when Ditta said to him one day, "There are so many things we have planned to do here, Béla," hoping to lure him out of his mood of almost complete isolation, he dismissed her suggestions without even discussing them.

"The trip to that mountain on the other side of our road, with the deserted house and the field of yellow wildflowers you told me about," Ditta persisted.

"Maybe it is best to let that go," he shrugged.

"But what about the visit to Martha's Indian grandmother?" she started hopefully another time. "Don't you remember, Béla, how wonderful it was when we went to that small village to visit Zsuzsi's family? It might be a little bit like that!"

"One thing is never like the other, especially when a world apart," Bartók answered.

"Then let's go, because it will be something entirely different."

"Why don't you go?" Bartók asked her finally. "I wish you would, except for the fact that Matthew would have to harness up those feeble horses of his to drag you up the mountainside. The very thought of it makes cold run up and down in my spine."

"But Matthew is always driving Martha up there," Ditta protested. "It wouldn't be a special trip for the horses."

Bartók silenced her with one glance. "It's sad enough if that's the way it's done," he remarked, "and I prefer to know nothing about the arrangements."

But we did take one more excursion together. Bartók's curiosity was aroused by signs he had noticed along the Montpelier road — "Visit Barre, the Granite Center of the World"

— and so we went to Barre on a lowering Saturday afternoon. It was a sunless day, so heavily overcast and threatening that I suggested turning back almost as soon as we had started. Bartók, however, insisted that there was no smell of rain in the air, that if it rained at all it would not be for another day. "It's too cold for rain," he said with finality, and we drove on.

I could see by his pallor that he wasn't feeling well; he was listless and showed none of his customary interest in the new landscape. While Ditta and I were getting permission in the office of The Rock-of-Ages to visit the quarries, Bartók remained seated in the car, though he got out promptly as soon as we returned.

Work had stopped for the weekend, and the place was quiet as we began our wanderings into this deserted landscape of stone. When we reached the first quarry Bartók stopped to examine the rope ladders, fragile as filaments against the cliffs dangling into the open cavities. He touched and pulled at the ropes twisting into the monoliths below, down to an endless chaotic geometry of mutilated planes. We wandered from shaft to shaft beside a small train of heavily loaded cars that sat on a long undulating track. Bartók stopped to lean against the rough-hewn surfaces of blocks ready for shipment, piled so tightly on the cars that they formed a huge meaningless barrier between one deserted region and another. Leafless dead trees stretched their bare arms covered inch-thick with white dust, as if snow-laden in the depth of winter.

Bartók seemed to have found a kinship between this nightmare of wounded nature and his own bottomless gloom; he walked on tirelessly, as if exploring the landscape to its ultimate and most hopeless desolation. By this time we were far beyond the quarries that were still being worked, and had reached a territory long ago exhausted and abandoned. At one point we could not see Bartók at all and Ditta called after him, but he did not answer. Hurrying apprehensively, we found him standing at the edge of a deep pit where old water lay heavy and smooth as marble, darkened almost to blackness by sharp cliffs that leaned out over it, shutting away the sky and any living reflection from its shineless, inert bulk.

We seemed to have arrived at a borderline. It was Bartók who suggested that we turn back.

Retracing our steps, we began to realize how far we had traveled into this unreal land. It was a long tiresome walk back to the car waiting outside of the office of The Rock-of-Ages. And just before we got there, the car already in sight, we heard suddenly the long wailing of a siren, a piercing voice of panic crying over our heads. As we ran toward the automobile, a man came out from the office and signaled us to stop. "It's an air raid practice," he explained. "The shelter is this way." He showed us with polite authority to a doorway that was to be our improvised air raid shelter, and then went back to his own office.

It wasn't actually a very long wait as we leaned against the wall of the building, but the sustained shriek of the siren kept on sharpening itself like a knife scraping across the stony land, and spread toward the horizon in a flock of echoes. Nothing else happened, no one joined us; it was getting dark now, and cold, and we just stood there, abandoned like stones against the wall, petrified by that great rush of naked screaming. Then, abruptly, it stopped and left us in a completely dead silence.

The man came out again, showed us politely to our car, remarking with what was intended to be humor, "Well, here we are, all still in one piece," and thanked us for our co-operation.

Bartók said nothing then nor on the way home, and it was not until we were sitting at dinner that I noticed that he was stricken by some powerful disturbance. There was a look of horror in his eyes as they stared unseeingly out of his pale face. For a moment I hoped it was the flickering candlelight that had painted the pattern of dark shadows under his eyes.

"What's wrong, Béla?" I heard Ditta ask him. "Was it the air raid drill? It was only a practice air raid, not a real one."

"For me it was a real one," he answered quietly, "real and terrible. All the stones of the quarry were falling, shaking houses, shattering windows, burying people and animals. A single stone, alone, wiped out civilizations — and that siren was deafening millions of people, piercing their hearts as they ran under the falling bombs, in the merciless crushing finality of destruction." He stopped, and put his napkin beside his plate.

"There *is* a war," he said, "the bombs are falling, this very minute, like the minute before, somewhere, always somewhere and there is no escaping from it any more."

The next morning he told us that he had decided to go back to New York that very day.

"But we could stay another week, Béla, please. These are the best days of all," Ditta pleaded with him, but she seemed to know that it was in vain.

"I want you to stay," Bartók told her, as she was hurrying upstairs to pack. "I want you to stay, just as long as you can." He was calm and resolved.

And she agreed to stay, because it was evident that Bartók preferred it this way. He wanted to go alone.

We were at the Riverton station again. It was late evening, about eleven o'clock, but almost light under the tremendous sky of August stars. Lost in its own darkness, the little station, no more than a wooden shed, stood midway along a railroad track that unwound from one set of hills only to wind itself back into the hills on a farther horizon. Bartók, dressed for the city, was sitting in the car, waiting for the train to come. In city clothes, he no longer belonged with us. "Are you sure the train will stop at this God-forsaken place?" he asked restlessly. And there was no reassuring him.

"Don't you want me to come with you, Béla?" Ditta asked for the third time.

"No, no. I want you to stay and have a good happy rest." From far off two bright ribbons were drawn across the darkness to the headlight of the train. "And don't forget those kittens, and be sure to bring them when you come home."

As we got out of the car in a hurry, we found ourselves desperately involved with Bartók's heavy suitcases. The three of us wrestled with them as the hum of the train grew into a roar. We were still tugging and pushing them across the platform as the train ground to a stop. How much easier it would have been if Matthew had been there to help! But Bartók had especially asked me not to let him drive us to the station.

15

AND THERE WAS still another face of Bartók's to carry in my memory now: the one behind the glass of the train window that seemed to be reflected from the surface of moving water, white, shadowy, and peering gravely into the dark outlines of vanishing landscapes.

During those long, clear, roomy days in Vermont, when the shadows around the Bartóks were still far away and only bordered the distance, the clouds reflecting on their faces could still be blown away by a gentle wind. But after they moved back to the city each day seemed to add another weight to the darkening force that was crowding closer and closer around them, and could no longer be dispelled.

The change on Ditta's face was to keep rhythm with Bartók's own, except when time began to move the two as if in contrary motion; and while Bartók's features were to become more tender, calm, and resigned, Ditta's face was destined to take on a frantic expression, her eyes to blaze with trapped and final helplessness. So I like to bring it back with her original smile upon it, the smile she was born with, as she so often used to say.

But we found ourselves far from smiling during the heavy

rain that came down in torrents after Bartók's departure. The gloom that had hung over him during the last days of his stay in Vermont was seeping out now from every corner of the house, as though he had left it behind for us to inherit. Ditta and I wandered from room to room as if driven by relentless sadness, embarrassed, separated by a wall of unhappiness, each of us following her own lonely way.

The sky was still dark with rain when we sat down to lunch the next day, well settled now in our morose silence.

"Remember when we were choosing his room for him?" Ditta asked, breaking sharply into the quietness. "When we planted the sunflowers and the birdbath on the balcony?"

These questions, I felt, did not need any answer, but all at once her shrill laughter made me lift my eyes from my plate. She was studying the dining room with slow interest, seeming to notice it for the first time.

"Where on earth did you get this dining room set?" In her voice was a mixture of irony, curiosity and antagonism.

"At a place very much like the one where we bought yours," I said carefully.

"But this is so elegant, this black glass on the table, pink rug, and peacock draperies." She waited a moment, and then she laughed again.

"Those auction sales of yours," she said, her laughter sharpening until it sent shivers through my body. "Those auction sales of yours. Were they really at all real?" Her voice fell to a deeper pitch as though she had something very important to communicate. "You know, finally I came to the turning point when it dawned on me that all those things we were buying together with such excitement and happiness were actually purchased by you beforehand, and your so-called auction sales were hoaxes, staged for my benefit alone."

"It would have required quite elaborate staging," I said,

laughing, anxious to soften if I could the edge of her hostility.

"It was too fantastic to be real. All those things piled up around us, mountains high, like money, silver, gold, all in a dream. It's yours if you care to pick it up. And then, of course, you wake up in your bed." She looked at me triumphantly.

"Except we didn't have to wake up," I said calmly.

"That's just it," her voice was even stronger than before. "I am not half so naïve or gullible as you think." She looked into my eyes with a penetrating stare, holding them, not letting them move away from hers. Her tone became beguiling. "I hope you're not surprised, for that is not the only thing I do not believe."

"What else, Ditta?" I looked back at her. "Please tell me what else."

"The entire thing," she said after a while. "Just about the whole thing."

"What whole thing?"

"The way the whole thing happened, from beginning to end. The way you turned up at the Baloghs' that evening, the way you became my friend, understanding me so completely."

For a moment I thought she had come to a resting point, but her voice was still rising.

"And then, of course, everything happened like magic. The Riverdale apartment and this house too, and the way you are always there when I need you most. My soul-mate by prescription." She raised her head high and sat straight up in her chair, unsmiling and ready to be challenged.

These strange wanderings of Ditta's that happened seemingly without reason from time to time were no longer entirely surprising to me, but they still gave me almost the same sensation of bewilderment I had felt on that very first occasion. As before, I was only terribly concerned about them, and never really hurt. For no matter with what sharp accuracy she sent her words into my heart, I could not help but feel that they pierced her own even before they reached mine. By now, at least, I sensed that these disturbances occurred, in a way logically, at those times when immediate problems seemed impossible to solve, and were crowding around her unresolved, even as new ones were already on their way toward her. No matter how far afield these side roads into unreality seemed to lead her, I felt they were somehow closely connected to a private and logical pattern, and she alone could follow that secret way into an escape world of her own, a tangled maze of roads and paths where she felt just as much at home as in the world she shared every day with others. Then, as soon as at least some of the heavy pressure was lifted, she was herself again, except for a vague, uncomfortable feeling that haunted her — a longing to be forgiven for some disturbing thing that was hidden in her memory. What it could have been, she had no way of remembering.

The next time I saw her that day, she was waving a letter in her hand.

"Just arrived from Béla," she cried lightheartedly as she ran toward me, and, as if our conversation of a few hours before had never taken place, she began reading it as soon as she reached me.

She must have read that letter many times by now, for she laughed even before her eyes could run over the lines, and as she read it out loud and I laughed she laughed again with me. Bartók's letter was seemingly cheerful enough, telling about his trip home and describing, step by step, the difficulties of serving himself a meal, how many times he had to open the refrigerator, and how many times it had to be closed again; lighting the gas, turning it off, and so on. It obviously had one purpose alone: not to speak of anything that really mattered, but to call forth a momentary smile. And for Ditta, at that particular moment it seemed to serve its purpose.

The rain went, the country was gleaming fresh and new around us. Early the next morning Ditta came into my room.

"I think at last I came to understand a lot of things last night," she said as she sat down on my bed. "We have no reason to reproach ourselves or worry about Béla's vacation here. It could not have been better anywhere else than it was in this house. If you are still brooding about some of the things he said, you had better try to see them in an entirely different way. Just think how fortunate Béla was to be able to find an outlet for the worry and sadness that was piled up in him, gathering, growing there for a long time. That through his mild grumblings and fumings he found a way of freeing himself from a lot of general dissatisfaction, allowing it to emerge to the surface. For the worst thing of all is for Béla to be un-complaining — then one has no way of knowing what is going on within him. Like that long time after his mother's death when he seemed to lose even his power of speech, his ability to show recognition of people and things. And it made me really feel good as I was thinking about the bright awareness he had here, the way the smallest thing became visible to him in such sharp focus. If you could only understand what it meant that he wasn't sparing us, for he is most particular and most exacting with those who are dearest to him. Besides, it showed how thoroughly at home he felt here. Béla's actions should always be interpreted in his own light. The way he worried about your neglected fields, taking them so much to heart, really meant that he loved every inch of them. You must understand how much good this vacation has done for him already."

Since I did not brighten up as quickly as she wanted me to, she tried another way.

"Just remember," she said, laughing, "just remember those few days when your friends were here. He didn't complain then, did he? He couldn't have been more silent, more withdrawn. Try to think about the way he was with you and the way he was with them. Then you will understand, and you will not fail to see what that difference meant, unless you insist on feeling like a stepchild. You know I can see through you."

She smiled then, and all at once laughed her free gay laughter. From then on her spirit rose, and stayed high throughout that lovely last remnant of summer. It seemed like a long time, but really it was no more than eight or nine days, slow, shining days falling into many separate parts, like those endless days remembered from childhood. Ditta's face brightened, calm and fresh with happiness, as we wandered among the tinged leaves of the trees burning wildly in the sunlit air that was warm and cool at the same time and intoxicatingly flavored with the long summer's ripening.

"I really believe that by the time we get back home again Béla's sickness will be gone," Ditta said at the end of a full and happy day. "It has happened like that other times. Sickness touching him with a strong firm grip and releasing him again. As swiftly gone as it came, leaving him healthier than ever before."

As soon as the sun grew cool she left the outside and spent long hours at the piano, playing it with enormous vitality.

"I never knew you to play like this," I told her one evening.

"Oh, you are not the only one," she answered me seriously. "If you only knew how the most unimportant musicians take on a patronizing air when it comes to my playing. As if my only claim to a relationship with the piano were merely that I am Bartók Béla's wife. But he would be the first one to deny that. He's a stranger to such compromises. If he didn't have a solid ground of faith in me he wouldn't even take the trouble to keep working with me, let alone appear with me on concert stages all over the world.

"Of course the fact that I am Bartók's wife and pupil at the same time offered me an endless opportunity to learn from him all that he is capable of giving. And that I held on to this opportunity and did not take it lightly is true. I have never ceased to be the pupil I was before I became his wife, and he has never stopped teaching me. Would he have done that if he didn't think it worth while? Twenty years, almost, and I know I have not failed him. Our playing together, you see, is a vital part of our marriage. One of the most important parts, perhaps. And if you only knew how many times he told me that I should keep on interpreting his music in its own true style. That I, Pásztory Ditta, must carry on in his tradition, to keep it pure and alive as long as I can."

We often ate our dinner in the warm kitchen, Martha and Matthew hovering over us, playing well-established pranks with each other, partly for our benefit and partly out of pure relief and sense of freedom. For the man who had to be respected whether one wished it or not, who had to be reached against one's own desire through some deed or hard task, was safely gone now, his thickly curtained room deserted and still.

It was so easy to make Ditta laugh. She admired generously the single flower or the small branch of colorful leaves Matthew would lay across her plate, and praised the freshly pressed apple cider, rusty-brown and pure-tasting, that he put on the table without fail for each evening meal.

"I feel so strong," Ditta said, stretching out full length one afternoon in the tall grass. Ripe, dark fall flowers were swaying around her in heavy purple and deep yellow.

"I mean strong not only in body, but strong all together, a full harmonious strength flowing through my entire being.

And I feel a way I have never felt before. I feel that I can bear responsibility now, and all my fears seem to be gone, and I feel that I can take my full share in whatever may come, no matter how trying, how hard, how terrible. Whatever it will be."

Our vacation was drawing to an end. We were to leave in a day or two. Packing and putting our clothes away, we seemed to enjoy the most boring occupations.

"May I leave my summer things in the drawer?" Ditta asked. "So I will find them here next summer. And some of Béla's things too?"

She hung the battered sun hat and the walking stick in the closet.

"And to think of it, that we have a house to go home to in Riverdale, and all the things we are planning to do this winter. You may laugh," she said, "but I feel the excitement of a child going back to school in the fall, and the joy of losing myself in work again. That's what a good vacation should really do, give one that fresh desire to work, and I'm sure that's how Béla feels too."

With cats, kittens and suitcases, we were at the Riverton station again, loaded down with a giant bunch of flowers Matthew had brought to Ditta and a small hemlock tree in a huge pot that we had dug up to take to Bartók. Besides, there was a loaf of bread for him from Martha and a keg of apple cider from Matthew. The conductor had to hold the train for us until Matthew and Martha had piled everything in our tiny roomette and we were done with the laughter, the many repeated goodbyes, shaking and waving of hands. "Happy journey! Come back. Come back soon!" they shouted after us as the train slowly pulled out. We took a last look back at the dark woods on the hillside that hid away the white house.

16

I HAD ONLY a glimpse of Bartók when we arrived at the Riverdale house in a loaded taxi. He came outside to welcome us briefly and to rescue the kittens from the commotion of unloading. It certainly did not seem to me that his vacation in Vermont had had any of the hoped-for good effects. The fading sunburn had left a yellowish pallor on his face, and except perhaps for his increased composure he looked very much as he had at the Riverton station on the evening of his departure.

Once our formal greetings had been exchanged, he said nothing more to me. The next day, however, he surprised me with a telephone call, speaking in a voice that sounded so serious for a moment I was frightened. But the reason for his call was soon made clear. Although at first he was pointedly delicate about it, he told me how worried he was that the kittens were not leaving any "traces" behind them, and expressed the hope I could suggest some course of action that would remedy the situation.

"Why, it's only a day," I said, trying to sound very natural, and promised to come right over to prepare a special box for them.

The next morning he telephoned again, first of all to let me know the box did not work and, furthermore, to tell me how altogether worthless my help had turned out to be and what different results he had expected from one who had brought up generations of kittens and supposedly loved them too.

"But cats or kittens are apt to be like that for a while when taken from one place to another. They have to get used to their new surroundings before they are able to function as they should," I told him.

I could picture him through the telephone, shaking his head with that certain dissatisfaction as was his way whenever someone disappointed him by a lack of knowledge in his own field. On the day he called to tell me that the traces of the kittens had finally been discovered, although he sounded much relieved he did not fail to point out that they were "not in that specially prepared box, either, but in the pot of the hemlock tree. More touching than one could have imagined possible," he added, and his voice was so admiring and warm that I suddenly realized I had never heard it that way before.

"Do you understand how logical, how beautiful, this is? That handful of their own home soil." He didn't speak for a while. "Now I am glad that you brought that tree to me, although I must say I considered it rather a waste to drag it away from its own forest, just to have it die here, far from its own home."

For a minute I had a desire to apologize. I meant to say how sorry I was that it hadn't occurred to me the hemlock tree might not be able to survive in the closed-in apartment, but I didn't say it after all. For how could I be constantly conscious in all my deeds of his lightning-swift awareness of the disturbance of the roots of growing things? And not only really rooted things, but all things should be left, he felt, just where they belonged.

"Whoever would have thought those small creatures capable of such subtle recognition?" he went on. "What an elemental instinct homesickness is. How overwhelming. What a strict law, which ought not to be lightly disturbed."

Arranging to have soil sent right from the garden in Vermont seemed to him to be the only solution. But before he worked out any plans, luckily the kittens adopted the soil I was lifting from the Italian's garden, right under his window. And while I am sure that Bartók was glad to be free from the burden of soil transplanting, it was at the same time a disappointment to him too, and he did not mention the incident any more.

Bartók became increasingly silent in this early fall of 1941. It was hard to tell exactly when it happened, but all at once he was so completely enveloped in remoteness that it was impossible to reach him. One could sit right next to him and even exchange a few remarks with him and still he would not hear a word. His eyes were not looking at the things around him. Even the way his hands rested on the head of one kitten or the other suggested the long distance he had gone away from the outer world. It was as though he had substitute eyes and ears to use for the outside, while his real ones were engaged on another plane of perception that was his alone.

"You don't know how frightening it is to watch him as he goes on with all his senses turned within," Ditta remarked one day.

"It reminds me of the way he was in Vermont when my friends were visiting," I suggested, and couldn't help a quick smile. "The way he came and went in that blind way of his, as if completely confident he was in possession of that fairy-story hat which made him invisible. And what's more, he seemed to be wearing it all the time, too."

"Oh, but that's not the same thing at all," Ditta said. "That kind of behavior is not a rarity with Béla — it's an everyday occurrence and I am very well used to it. He assumes it in many different situations and always when he is composing But this is something new again. He was stunned and silent for a long time after his mother's death, but still somehow he was with us, responding wordlessly, and aware of the life around him. Now, every day he seems to be a greater distance away and I can't even imagine where he is, because the strange calmness that has taken hold of him won't reveal anything to me."

Yes, drifting away and retreating beyond reach, Bartók was indeed unapproachable, although there were times when he made the state of his dark feelings felt, and as time went by his negative attitude toward his life quietly and slowly, without passion, revealed itself. Now from fragments of many different conversations one can put together in his own words his dejected mood; it might have been a long monologue, it was so uniform in feeling.

"Our life has settled into a definite pattern here." He was answering Ditta, who was pointing out to him how much better off they were this winter than the year before. "But as for my interpretation of it, it is not for the better but, on the contrary, for the worse. Now that our existence here has taken on a definite shape, it is more and more evident to me that we are navigating in a vacuum, completely sealed, and there is no hope left of finding our way out of it, toward a more real life."

Or another time. "We do have a roof over us. We have a place to stay, but still we can only exist unattached and unrelated. The work I am doing here means much more to me than just a job that provides us with what we need from day to day, it is really so close to my heart that I would like to adopt it for my own. If only it weren't so temporary that I can hardly even lay my hand on it, let alone lose myself in it. And as time is passing, I realize that the very small amount of work I might be able to put on paper couldn't possibly make any difference one way or the other."

And again another time: "I am not healthy — far from it — but I am not actually sick either. I am somewhere in between the two, dragging out my days and nights without strength or vitality, and all I can do is to wait. Perhaps I will get better or perhaps I will get worse, and which it will be I have no way of predicting.

"And as for my existence here as a music maker," he said, making a hopeless gesture with his hands, without a smile, "the few concert engagements I have now and then won't let me forget that I am still a pianist and not entirely obscure here. But what could speak more clearly of the unimportance of it all than that I have a long winter ahead of me, almost entirely without a scheduled concert of my work and no chance to make myself better known, better liked or understood. Drifting along without any weight of roots, and yet without the freedom to abandon myself to the four winds. Tied down by unfamiliar ties to strange streets — streets that I don't really know, but merely recognize."

But more important than all the rest and revealing his ever-present preoccupation was a helpless and desperate theme.

"A war is going on; the evil forces are gathering speed, rolling ahead without barrier toward those places I know so well that I can follow the course of each falling bomb, and witness the destruction in its wake as if with my own eyes. A war that could easily wipe out the world, or at best, leave it in complete ruins, burying the countries one by one, and my own among them. So in all likelihood, I will never set foot on my homeland again, and if by some unforeseen chance it comes about that I do get there somehow, it might be under such changed circumstances that I wouldn't belong there, nor anywhere else."

Dark, hopeless visions! War, danger, destruction. "How I wish he would complain about something personal once more," Ditta would say now and again. "Or show some preference, like, or dislike, instead of being pulled by an invisible rope into the midst of all the terrible happenings at home."

And we would both remember his eagerness to expand, to flow into the mainstream of life and not be pushed off alone into a backwater, and left behind. We could recall his urgent desire, only a year ago, for ideal working conditions, and his passionate vulnerable reactions to the slightest tremor that might make a difference in the shaping of his existence here under the new conditions. But all that was gone now. Now his strongest passion was to feel, through his own body, the experiences of the people on the other side of the world, of the men, the women, the children, animals, and even insects. He imagined a hundred times the burned-out dark forests and parched patches of deserted little gardens.

"I was wondering," he was looking at us with guarded eyes, "whether the torture of annihilation of a small remote part of the earth with all its inhabitants is less intense in suffering than the annihilation of the entire world. Is it less severe because it is restricted to a few people, a smaller piece of land, to only a handful of the green covering of the earth and its smallest insects trapped and buried deep in their zigzagged abodes?"

Enveloped in his hopelessness, refusing the slightest flicker of light to penetrate its midnight blackness, he was engaged with all his senses in the struggle going on across the ocean, pulled by the weight of his severed and smarting roots toward the distant, never-forgotten soil that was in such great danger now.

And this maze of roots, like so many live wires, held him

tight in a grip of pain. It seemed to be his only desire to abandon himself to this pain, without any wish to free himself from it, to lessen its grip, to soothe it, to heal it. Was he, with this suffering, trying to pay his debt to himself for not being in Europe and in the midst of it all? Did this constant anguish serve as the living link that kept him tied to that other self he had left behind, and was he seeking to witness through his own body all the agony of all the phases of the war, in order to allay his own deep and torturing remorse?

17

BUT IN SPITE OF these grave images that possessed Bartók of a world that was sinking away and dying in pain, in spite of the lurking sickness within his own body, and while he maintained that nothing mattered any more, he was at the same time pouring a feverish energy into his own work. His working hours lasted through the entire day and through the nights, except for those few hours when he slept. And even then, as Ditta told me, the scattered papers remained on his blanket, the sharpened pencil in his hand, and the light left on shining brightly into his face. Nevertheless, it remained most important to complete the Romanian folk song collection, to get it ready for publication without any waste of time. The work on the Parry Collection at Columbia was as intense as ever, though the worry over another six months coming to an end and the slow progress he was making, measured against the tremendous bulk of the collection waiting to be finished, was a constant source of irritation. He was continually apprehensive also that the material he received from Harvard would not come as quickly as he needed it, or that it wouldn't be the material he wanted most to work on. The Parry Collection mostly contained heroic ballads, and a small number of lyrical songs, which interested him much more.

"If I do some of the ballads and some of the lyrical songs, I will leave a badly balanced collection behind me. But since I am allowed such a short time to work on it, how much more unified my contribution would be if I could at least finish the lyrical songs."

What a striking contradiction between the energetic concentration he gave to his work and the hopelessness he showed in relation to everything else!

It was some time before I realized that he was slowly emerging and finding his way back from the impenetrable and distant place where he had lived during the beginning of the winter. Gradually he seemed to become aware again of his present surroundings and his extreme identification with what was happening on the other side of the ocean was losing intensity. Though at the time it happened he made no mention of Pearl Harbor and the active entrance of the United States into the war, this seems to me now to have been the turning point that brought Bartók back again. And after a little while he began to talk about it.

"Now that the strength of America has entered the war, one can't help but feel that the balance of the struggle all at once has become righted. Whatever the outcome, whether it is too late or not, it still makes one feel better to know that the countries won't disappear as easily as anthills. Yes, to be able to hope, even for one minute, although hopeless again in the next. At least a pause to allow one to straighten up and breathe freely once more. The mere fact that there is a chance."

A chance for the world, but not for himself. It was more or less an accepted fact by now that there was to be no more for Bartók than this static day-to-day existence, and the question Ditta had begun to ask herself on the long-ago afternoon in the 14th Street Childs restaurant, as we sat in our dark corner,

had been answered in the negative. The move to America
would never enable Bartók to work creatively, and his cruel
uprooting was indeed proving to be in vain. It had also become
more deeply understood that Bartók himself had probably
never hoped leaving Europe would solve his problem, had not
ever expected to be able to continue where he had left off, but
had been aware from the beginning that he would be caught
between two revolving millstones. Nevertheless he had chosen
to leave, driven not only by hatred of Nazism, but fleeing at
the same time from those many members of his own class who
had so readily accepted it. From the moment of his departure, he had foreseen and had become resigned to the fate
which he knew could not be altered one way or the other. The
only thing he had not realized in advance, perhaps, was the
accumulation of small, sober, step-by-step obstacles that were
to trip him up. These pebbles were the unexpected hardships.

I noticed at about this time in the winter a slight change in
Bartók's appearance — perhaps because I did not see him for
a week or so when he was in Canada changing his visitor's
status into that of a future citizen. I saw him a few days after
he returned, and it struck me that the harmony of his features
had suffered a slight transformation under the pallor of the
skin, and that his figure too, as he moved from room to room,
seemed to have lost some of its purposeful bearing. Ditta too
must have been aware of this change, but, as always when
something was hard for her to accept, she first had to reassure
herself it wasn't really so before she talked about it to me.

"Béla is looking well these days, don't you think?" she asked
me one evening as we stood at the dining room window looking out into the darkness of the empty street.

I did not say anything and we stood there silently for a
while.

"I was expecting him home from Columbia hours ago. He was never quite this late before. Is it really as frozen-cold and windy outside as it seems to be?" Then with a quick change of pace she turned to me and smiled. "I must tell you something, though I hardly dare to speak about it. There is a good chance that perhaps Péter will be coming sometime very soon." She gave me a searching look. "You do believe it, don't you? It does not seem impossible to you?" She spoke even faster now. "Béla says that everything is being done to get him over here quickly. Plans have been in progress for quite a long time now, but we had to wait for Béla's first papers. There is good reason to believe it will happen without much delay."

She was talking with assurance, perhaps even quoting Bartók's own words. A little later, however, her own apprehension broke through to the surface again.

"It seems almost impossible that he, alone, a single straw from a burning haystack, could come out of it unharmed, and traveling through so many countries at war, and across the ocean too."

We did not see or hear Bartók arriving until he stood in the door with his hat and coat still on and his briefcase in his hand. I was pleasantly surprised to see the fresh high color the cold wind had given to his face.

"So late, Béla." Ditta walked over to him. "Did you have a hard day?"

"Oh no. On the contrary. A very good day, and a fat one too." He handed his bulging briefcase to her. "See how heavy it is? I deserve my dinner today."

But later, when dinner was ready, Bartók hardly touched the food on his plate.

"Can't you find anything on the table you like enough even to taste?" Ditta asked him.

"Oh, everything is fine. This is just not my evening for a lot of food," he told her.

Somehow he seemed nearer this evening than at any time during that whole winter.

"Why Ditta," he said, looking at her as if he hadn't seen her for a long while, "how thin you look, and what happened to your chin?"

"My chin," she answered, not knowing what to make of his remark. "What about my chin?"

"It has become so small," Bartók said with surprise. "So pointed, and sharp. You must have lost a lot of weight. Just look at that small chin." He turned to me, but as I was looking at it a broad smile spread over Ditta's face and all at once the taut sharp lines relaxed and her features became soft and round.

"It must have been a shadow," she said lightly, and moved her chair closer to the table and the bright circle of the electric light.

"Oh," Bartók said, relieved. "You scared me for a moment."

"Did I?" she said, almost happily, glad that Bartók was noticing things once more.

"Any news of Péter?" Ditta asked, encouraged, after a while.

"I heard nothing today, but I'm sure that everything is going well. Don't worry so much. It's only a question of a little time."

"How much time?"

"A few months perhaps," Bartók said. "It depends on so many things. And it will happen much sooner too, if you don't weigh every passing moment in your hands."

"But I can't really believe it," Ditta answered. "I try, but I can't make it real to myself at all."

"The reality will come naturally. When you spread his bed for him on top of the radios, he will be standing right there watching you. Or maybe it will begin by buying a bed for him."

"Oh yes, a bed," Ditta said slowly. "And soon I'll begin to fix up his room too."

We sat at the table for a long time, and when Ditta brought in the coffee the cats came too, prancing right up to Bartók's chair, shiny and almost full-grown. Bartók's hand touched them, as if pouring into them his reassurance and his love, and they purred loudly.

Outside the wind was rattling the dry branches of the rose-bushes, knocking them rhythmically against the windowpanes. Bartók was listening now to the scraping sound right next to the house, and not to the deathly bombs falling somewhere an ocean away.

"These roses are not without their proverbial thorns," he said. "I am afraid that if the wind keeps on wreaking its havoc on those tangled branches there won't be anything left of them by the time spring comes."

Later in the evening we settled in the living room to look at the fresh manuscript Bartók had just brought home from Columbia. First he spread out the pages on the table before us, then spent a long time manipulating the ailing victrola, winding it up with care before he placed a record on it. The machine finally began to sing in its fragile and distant voice.

It was hard for me to follow his small notations, which covered like ants every inch of the manuscript. So, closing my eyes, I just listened to the faint sounds of the victrola that was whispering songs for some reason touchingly familiar to me.

"Are you asleep?" Bartók asked me suddenly. "If you are not following the script, how can you compare the sound with my notes? Why, that's what my whole work is about! Can you tell me where we are right now? Then why don't you show it to me, please?"

Ditta, who sensed that I had not been following for some time, slid her hand lightly across the page to the right place.

"Don't show it to her, Ditta," Bartók stopped her. "It is no use." He got up, walked across the room, but stopped when he realized that the record was coming to an end.

"To compare the records with the manuscript is the only way to tell what I have really done," he told me firmly. "And besides, you ought to remember that this is the only time you will have a chance to look at my manuscript. For this six months of time is running out again and, judging from the slowness of my progress, you must realize I will never be able to bring to completion any amount of it that would be worth while to publish."

But by the time he had placed both the manuscript and the records back in his briefcase, he was calm again. Ditta and I remembered and talked about this evening for a long time. Ditta called it his evening of homecoming.

"Isn't it just like Béla," she pointed out, "to go all the way to Canada and back with his eyes and ears closed to what was was going on around him, then to walk from one room into another, and for no apparent reason be alive and alert again."

Perhaps alive and alert, but frailer than ever before. How frail he really was I only noticed when I happened to see him one early evening descending the staircase of the 231st Street subway station only a few steps ahead of me. We must have arrived on the same train. My first instinct was to call out to him, but I could not so suddenly overcome my diffidence. And by the time we were on the street I felt it was too late, and I was even glad to be unseen. So I walked slowly behind him, gradually increasing the distance between us, watching his disheartened slow advance up the busy sidewalk. He was weaving in and out among the late shoppers, the baby carriages parked in front of stores, and the people hurrying home from work. I was amazed as always by his power to separate himself from all outside impressions, and to walk with what seemed like the sixth sense of the blind man, and in that blind-man's rhythm — unaware of the people around him and yet avoiding them at the same time. His head was bowed low, he cast no glances around, as if what there was to see held no joy at all for him. And yet this was the same street that had given him such an elated sense of discovery when we walked toward the subway station after finding the house. Now I felt that it must have been a dream — the sunlit blueness of that day in early spring, the soft silence and Sunday emptiness of the wide street.

After he passed the long block of clustered stores, the crowd had thinned out, and now there was only a long stretch of empty sidewalk ahead of him, slippery with thick transparent ice underfoot, and, to his right, the bare winter trees. Bartók stopped to rest, standing still and looking, as if he could suddenly see with his eyes again, into the slowing moving faded arms of the trees, and with upturned face examined the murky, low-hanging sky. He waited for some time before crossing the wide highway that separated him from the hill. Arriving at the park, he hesitated, but did not choose this time the path that wound inside it. Instead he turned into the parallel side street that rose steeply upward. A sudden gust of strong wind held him still for a minute, but he began to walk slowly up, past the quiet houses with their lighted windows shedding pale rays of yellow into their dead gardens.

Only now did I realize what a long walk it was from the subway station to his house, how completely winter had taken over the winding street, caking the sidewalks with layers of ice, and how penetrating the damp coldness was here under the open sky.

"But I love that walk," I had often heard Bartók answer when Ditta expressed her concern over the distance from the subway station to their house, a distance that grew longer as the winter wind grew icy cold.

"Please take a taxi, Béla, please," Ditta would plead with him from time to time. "It's only fifty cents."

"Sixty with the tip," Bartók would answer her, smiling. "However, that's not the reason, or the only reason. I like that walk. I find it a good way to clear my head and do some reflecting of my own."

I was wondering how good he found it now when he had to stop every few steps to rest before continuing on his way. Was he warm enough in the faded old winter coat that seemed to have no life left in it any more, all its warmth used up by too many years of wear — nine, ten or twelve, how many years? He himself could not quite remember. When Ditta had taken it out of mothballs in the fall, and, looking at it despairingly, suggested that it was surely time for a new one, Bartók had stared at her as though he had not heard right.

"A new one? Why, this coat still looks beautiful to me." He had spread it out carefully on the rug, and looked at it fondly.

"It's only the sleeves that need a little attention from time to time."

"But those sleeves are too short already," Ditta had protested. "If you have them fixed again, they will be up to your elbows."

"This coat," was Bartók's grave reply, "is permeated through with the essences of places I knew. It breathes their flavor warmly right into my body and I wouldn't part with it for anything in the world."

Climbing ahead of me in the coat with the short sleeves and narrow shoulders, Bartók looked as frail as a boy in the darkness that had suddenly settled over us. His steps were slow and difficult as he walked on one of those streets he "did not really know, but merely recognized." And I carefully kept my distance behind him, while the biting raw wind flapped around him, pushing itself through the fibers of the ancient coat, forcing its own new flavor into them, to mingle there with the faint, cherished essences of the old.

Bartók reached his own house at last, and I saw him lean heavily against one of the two tall trees in front of the doorway, waiting there perhaps to catch his breath before going in.

I turned around quickly and hurried down the hill, feeling an unaccountable sense of guilt, and did not dare to stop until I was almost at the subway station again. I was happy to find the poorly lit Greek restaurant open. Then, much later, after a terrible dinner, I walked up the hill once more and shamefacedly rang the Bartóks' bell.

"But I thought you were coming for dinner," Ditta said as she led me straight into the kitchen. "I have kept the coffee hot for you — and that was all," she told me soberly, "that Béla wanted for dinner tonight.

"I wish you had come before," she continued. "You might have saved me from doing something silly. Oh, it was nothing serious!" she smiled. She was rummaging in her pocket. "Just one of those letters. It was addressed to me but actually meant for Béla. The writer of it is an acquaintance of ours, someone who is really concerned about us, and maybe that was the reason I didn't hide it from Béla. But now I wish I had. Most of the time he doesn't pay the slightest attention to this sort of thing, but tonight, for some reason . . ."

She handed me a letter. "Read it aloud. I'd like to hear how it sounds. But not too loud; Béla is resting."

She pointed out the place where she wanted me to begin.

" 'As a practical policy of the moment,' " I read, " 'the pieces of Bartók which are played in public should be chosen with discretion. This is no time to perform pieces which the public has no chance of understanding or liking because they are so different from what the public is used to. There are plenty of characteristic Bartók pieces which won't sound like all wrong notes to the public and the reviewers.' "

"It's even worse the second time," Ditta interrupted.

I went on reading. " 'Finally, I don't think that Bartók, if he concertizes, should give all-Bartók programs, because it's more than an audience can take with pleasure.' "

"That's all," Ditta stopped me. "The rest of it is all right." She folded the letter quickly and put it back into its envelope, eager to have it out of sight.

"What ever made me show it to him? He has plenty to worry about as it is."

When Bartók came out of his room later, he did not seem annoyed, but rather as if the letter had given him a painful satisfaction and proved something he had known for a long time.

"Now what would you suggest?" he asked us. "What manner of disguise should I assume the next time, if I am given a chance once more to concertize? Under what beguiling mask shall I hide my own identity as I steal out onto the stage to assail the public with those excessively irritating Bartók compositions? Would seven thick veils do the trick, or do I need something much more substantial to transform my pieces into something they are not?"

Then he turned to me, still smiling. "I am glad you didn't tell me, with your usual soft-pedal technique, how unimportant a letter of this kind is. For I would like the opportunity of pointing out to you how *important* it is, how revealingly it speaks not only for that one person who wrote it but also without any doubt for the majority of all those here who have ever heard me or my compositions, warning me sharply of my precarious position in this country. The question for me, of how to exist here at all — I did not say 'succeed' — has one very simple answer: not to be myself. For I, as I am, can only irritate those finicky ears and cause them more suffering than they can bear. How to give them pleasure or joy — that doesn't even enter into it — but, instead, how to be less painfully offending, how to hide my own identity under a well-padded bushel basket that would turn me into something acceptable."

His cheeks were burning, his eyes gleamed at us, and his mouth had a bright, challenging smile.

"Luckily we don't have to put our heads together in conspiratory fashion," he went on. "For there is no answer to this dilemma, never was and never will be. The idea of treading cautiously has never appealed to me. And besides, this is not my problem alone, but the eternal problem of all those creative artists who are trying to follow their own chosen paths. It shouldn't be hard to understand that to me none of my pieces sound like so many false notes, and that to separate the less offending from the more offending ones is beyond my power. For since I am the source, my work is what I am. From the smallest in scope to the largest of my compositions, they have all seeped to the surface and are flowing along from the same spring, the rivers feeding the ocean in one work or the entire ocean feeding the tiniest rivulet in another. In the end, they are so closely related and inseparably mingled that they must be accepted or rejected in their entirety the way they are. And only time will tell which it will be."

He walked around the still room. "Time, and most likely a long time. For our present does not promote healthy growth. To cure our present," he said, already at the door, "is the only thing that matters."

18

ALTHOUGH THERE WAS no visible sign that Bartók was feeling any worse these days, there was something alarming about him. It was a change that was invisible, that happened deep down in him, so deep that the effect of it had not yet worked itself to the surface, but it was more frightening than anything one could see with one's eyes. And it was at this time that he fell into the habit of reading every available newspaper. He buried himself in the pages, and gave to each item he read an interpretation of the starkest despair, although in his untiring search he seemed to retain one last straw of hope that he would find somewhere a hidden promise of encouragement in the increasingly dark news from all fronts of the war.

By now Péter had succeeded in leaving Hungary with a visitor's visa to the United States, but there had been no word from him since. How had he fared, crossing all those countries at war, what dangers, what horrors had he met? The fear was clearly written on Ditta's face. When finally in February a short letter came from him to say that he had safely reached Lisbon, and was waiting there for a boat to bring him to the United States, it was a relief that hardly had a chance to penetrate, for there were months to come again without any news from him.

Ditta was subdued, very calm, and unusually silent now. Whenever she talked at all, it was about remote places and people whose lives were in no way connected with her own. One evening, finding her busy in the kitchen, I sat watching her as she strained all kinds of vegetables into a bowl.

"Supposed to be potato soup for Béla," she said. "The things he wants to eat these days — only starches and nothing else. Just now, when none of the doctors can think of any cure for him except a good diet, all he wants for his dinner is potato soup. And I'm sure, too, that nothing would please him better than a big earthen bowl of it in the middle of the table, with a spoon in it for each of us. The best I can do is to mix all these vegetables into it, hoping he will not detect them — but what a waste of time it is, for I'm certain he will not touch it."

She sat down at the table and talked to me now the same way she used to, though now her face and eyes were hidden away from me, always turned at such an angle as not to be seen.

"I want you to know," she said, "that Béla's 'dismissal' from Columbia is final this time. There is no chance for that six months' reprieve to happen ever again."

"I'm sorry," I said.

"Oh yes," she answered, with her face turned away. "Everybody is sorry."

She got up and gave her full attention to the potato soup again. The little I could see of her face was as tightly drawn as a clenched fist, and not much bigger.

It did seem certain now that Bartók's appointment at Columbia would come to an end this spring. This time it was a more serious threat to their existence than before, because the pension from the Academy of Music in Budapest had ceased when Hungary entered the war, and there was also no hope of receiving his royalties tied up in other European countries.

"No need to be sorry about Béla's dismissal from Columbia," Ditta said to me one afternoon, continuing our conversation of the week before exactly where we had left off. Ditta had a way of remembering certain remarks she resented, although she seldom showed her hurt at the time they were made. Her reference to them, months later even, as if she were freshly wounded, amazed me again and again.

"For there is another place waiting for him where he can go any time, if he needs to." There was a hollow depth to her whisper.

"Where?" I asked.

"Far enough away so no one will be inconvenienced by us any more."

As I did not answer, she went on in a voice more like her own.

"It will be the end of everything to go to a place so far away from the center of things and begin over in another strange world again. However, I'm gaining a thorough education these days in getting used to most anything, and I'll show you what I mean," she said, walking straight to the sunroom and pointing, without a word, to the empty space where her own piano used to stand. "Called back on short notice by the company whose pianos Béla always uses on the concert stage here. It seems there's a piano shortage too, now, and perhaps we should consider ourselves lucky that they left Béla's here, but who knows for how long that will be?"

Winter was ebbing away. The days turned brighter and longer and in the noons one could feel the real warmth of the sunshine.

"Still, our house is colder inside than any time during the winter," Ditta told me. "I don't think the old man should have shut the heat off so soon, but Béla won't even let me breathe a word about it. He is so sorry for him, struggling to make ends meet, since we are the only tenants in the house."

Bartók walked around the rooms bundled up in his old flannel bathrobe and with a thick scarf around his neck. His bed was pushed away from the window against an inner wall, where it was more sheltered from the wind, and this change made his room look even smaller — although it had already shrunk so much by now that with the addition of small tables and piled-up papers he could hardly get in and out the door without turning sideways.

His fever began to take a more consistent course again after the long weeks during the winter when he had been completely free of it. It returned to remain, fluctuating evenly back and forth on its small course. At first it did not seem to make Bartók feel any worse, and he accepted it in a matter-of-fact way. What really irritated him was that none of the doctors found any good reason for it.

"It could be this, or it could be that," Bartók said once. "Your choice is as good as mine. So far I have a basketful of suggestions and can pull out whatever I like. Perhaps a slight renewal of my TB that was healed more than twenty-five years ago; or it could be some kind of allergy, even related to the asthma I had in my youth, which I had almost entirely forgotten. It could be my head, or my feet, or any part at all of the complicated machinery."

The fever wasn't really high, just a few degrees in the evening, steadily rising and falling, and there was no pain with it to speak of. It only made him feel a little more weary every day, and a little paler too, in spite of the spring that finally arrived with its sunshine, coming right into every corner of their house to replace the gray winter air with the new light, and to unfold on the climbing roses outside the windows the light green leaves and the sharp, pink, tiny buds.

While Péter was never mentioned at all, there was always a silent awareness that there had been no news from him. It came as a surprise to me one day when Ditta suddenly asked me to go with her to buy Péter's bed. We started out in blazing noon to look into the small secondhand store near the subway station, hoping that we could find one there. But instead of walking down the hill, Ditta turned in the opposite direction, into the path of the sunshine.

"Although I never walked on these streets before, they don't seem strange at all," Ditta said. "When even the unknown streets seem familiar, then one begins to have a real feeling of belonging. Somehow I am full of hope today, and it's such a fine day to get the bed for Péter. I'm glad you could come with me."

However, we did not go toward the secondhand store, but walked from street to street, aimlessly wandering, following the magnet of the strong sunshine. We stopped from time to time to look around us as we found ourselves on wider and more lifeless streets, flanked by larger grounds and more imposing houses, set far back from the sidewalk, almost hidden in the faint green foliage of the newly sprouting trees. We came upon a rambling garden fenced in by walls, and stopped in front of its closed gate to look at the big forlorn-looking house at the end of the neglected path. The rows of windows were closed in by faded shutters, and the wide entrance boarded over. Without thinking, we pushed the gate and found it open. And though we soon became uncomfortable about trespassing and found ourselves stealing along cautiously, almost on tiptoe, we could not seem to tear ourselves away from this scene of deserted loveliness. We walked in a long way among tall, overgrown bushes and long-armed trees, and over the soft neglected ground that was covered by a thick matted growth resembling the winter-yellow grasses of a beach. Then as the shade grew almost into darkness, Ditta suddenly stopped.

"But why did we come here? I thought we were going to get that bed for Péter." She gripped my hand, suddenly afraid.

"We were, in a way," I said. "But I was following you when we left the house."

"I thought I was following you," she retorted. "You are the one who is always so sure of where to go."

"So we were following each other, it seems." I tried to make her laugh.

But she remained serious, hardly listening, watching the tangled growth on the ground below her as if aware of some secret motion of slowly creeping things hidden in its depth. She let go of my hand with a jerk and began to run. All at once I could see her ahead of me on the brushy path that curved down in an undulating long line beyond us. She was running lightly and smoothly at first, as one might run out of a sudden sense of freedom, but her tempo quickly increased and became urgent and wild. For a second I lost sight of her, although I was following as fast as I could, then, there! I saw a flash of her again, leaping among bushes and trees, a hunted animal fleeing from danger.

When I reached her at last she was quietly stretched out, face down, on a patch of matted grass. We had come to the very end of the grounds, for there was a fence, made of criss-cross black wire, very strong and very high, and beyond it I suddenly saw, bright and unexpected in the sunlight, the slowly flowing Hudson River.

I called to Ditta softly, as to a sleeper, "Are you all right?"

She did not answer and did not move. I was panting from

the wild run, but she did not even seem to be breathing, lying still and completely motionless, sunken into the ground, clinging to it hard, hiding and burying herself right into the depth of it. I stood at the wire fence staring at the river. Any word I could think of was too light to say out loud to her. Just softly, "Ditta, Ditta, Ditta" — but even that only in my mind. I didn't dare speak. I was afraid. When I heard her shriek I slowly turned. I had been anticipating that very sound with my whole body. It rang and careened among the trees with long painful echoes before it finally died away.

She raised herself onto her knees. I was on my knees too, next to her, but she moved away. She let herself down on the ground and sat leaning against a tree, looking around her with lost eyes, as if searching for a point where she could find rest for them. But finding none, she fastened them on me.

"So this is where the grand conspiracy was leading us. Everything is clear to me now." Her voice was neither soft nor loud, but for some reason it was unbearable. "The complete collapse. The end. Everybody knowing all along where it was leading except poor unsuspecting Ditta. Me. The one who was so easily fooled and so easy to lead anywhere at all. Oh no, but it wasn't so," she said with a tortured sound that was meant to be laughter. "I was the one who was fooling you all along, nodding my head believingly to all your lies. Oh sure, Péter will come. Soon now, very soon. Let's buy a bed. You knew very well for what reason you didn't take me to buy that bed today, knew it all the time that Péter needed no bed any more, or any other thing. Nothing. That is all over. There is no more Péter."

She spoke rapidly now, as if everything she was saying was printed on her mind in clear, large letters.

"And everything is just like that with Béla too, going on day after day. Being dismissed like a bad servant and then letting him stay on a little bit longer, not knowing how much he suffers behind his closed door, alone. Another job a thousand miles away and then perhaps another one again. And you all expect me to believe that, too!"

Her laughter came out like a sharp arrow, and was gone just as quickly.

"But I know better, and he does too. He has no need for your jobs any more. He has already turned away from all of you and, like Péter, needs nothing. He's on his own way already. And now I am the only one left, and that should be easy enough."

Her voice went up and ended in a quaver.

"Yet I can see through all of you. Just like mirrors." She spoke more slowly and on a lower tone. "There is the Ditta none of you know, and could never imagine what she is like."

She stopped, and leaned back against the tree with her face lifted high. On it there was an expression of enduring pride that her final helplessness could only emphasize.

I turned toward the river, and only sensed her letting herself down lower and lower until she was lying on the ground once more. When I looked at her again, she was spread out, unsupported, limp, her thin neck bent all the way back and her unconscious hands flat, as if painted on the grass. I could only think of a bird fallen out of its nest. I had to turn away and press my face against the cool wire of the fence until I felt the pain it gave me. Then she called me and I sat down beside her and helped her to sit up and supported her for a while. I don't know how long it was. It seemed like a very long time.

"Isn't it time to go home now?" Ditta asked me as casually as though we had just been having a cup of tea together.

"If you are ready. There is no hurry."

"I think we had better," she said mildly, and getting up, began to brush the twigs and dried leaves from her dress.

We walked slowly, cautiously, side by side, picking our way carefully out of the grounds until we were back on the street again, right outside the gate.

"Which way now?" Ditta asked, almost cheerfully. "I hope you know the way."

"No, I don't," I answered, and we walked at random on the now sunless street.

We turned from street to street in the sharp cool air of the spring twilight, until we found ourselves under the dark structure of the elevated's last station. Still a long way from home, but at least knowing which way to go, we hurried on, and although dead tired, it did not occur to either of us that we could take either a taxi or the subway. Slowly we recognized landmarks: there was the pet shop, and there, with all its lively display on the sidewalk, the secondhand furniture store. Surprised, we both stopped and looked excitedly in at the cluttered room.

"Would you like to come in and see if we can find what we want?" Ditta asked hesitantly. "Or shall we let it go for another day?"

We decided to go in right then, and it didn't take us long to find and buy the bed.

19

Not more than two or three days after this excursion I answered my telephone one early evening and an unfamiliar voice said "Good evening, Agota" in the bright and fresh tones of a young man speaking a clear, unspoiled Hungarian which somehow did not seem entirely strange to me. Although nothing in the whole world should have been more unexpected than to hear him say, "I am Bartók Péter and I arrived here less than an hour ago," still I took it quite naturally even in the first minute. My surprised exclamations, "But when did you come? How did it happen?" were not intended to be questions, let alone answered. But they were, promptly, and in great detail.

"I came by train, of course, from Philadelphia, where my boat landed, and arrived at the Grand Central Station. I asked the first man I saw in uniform which was the quickest way to get to 231st Street, by subway or by taxi. His answer was 'By subway, of course,' so naturally that's the way I came. But just listen to this," he said, and now he did not sound like a young man any more, but like the boy I had imagined him to be. "I hardly walked a few feet down the street after I got off the subway, when who did I see walking a little way ahead of me but my father! Not only did I recognize him, but I recognized his briefcase too. So I ran right up to him, and took his arm and said, 'Here I am, Apu,' and we walked home together."

"You mean you walked home just like that, and rang the bell, and Ditta opened the door for you?"

"Yes, we rang the bell, although Apu had a key. But we rang just the same because we didn't want to surprise her too much."

"But what did she say?" I asked, and even as I spoke I realized how impossible it would be for him to understand all that it meant to Ditta to see before her a sturdy and alive Péter without having even a few minutes to prepare herself for this reality.

"She just kissed me and cried a little, but she was surprised, of course."

Then he went on to tell me how much he loved the cats, and how they seemed to take to him right away.

"But of course," he said, "Apu is the one they like the best, and he has demonstrated to me already how he can walk around the room on all fours with a cat sitting on each shoulder, completely unsupported, but secure and happy."

After a while, it was Ditta's voice on the telephone.

"So Péter is here." She spoke almost in a whisper, as if afraid that a mirage she was seeing would disappear.

"But how was it when they just walked in together?" I had to ask her again and again.

"As natural as in my dreams. My good dreams," her still voice answered me.

She called again late that same evening.

"Péter has come home," she said, as if I hadn't heard the news before. And we touched upon the miracle of it, a little surer now, but still in whispers, still with great care. For

Péter, although he was not a reality yet, was no longer a phantom, either, but like someone leaving a dangerous illness behind him, finally brought to safety, and sheltered now in a deep and healing sleep.

When I saw Péter the next day, I found him most decidedly real. And Ditta gave forth a radiant aliveness, as if washed all over by happiness. Her steps were light and her eyes had a rainbow smile in them.

Bartók was calm, immensely relieved and soothed. The deep shadows and twisted lines had vanished from his face. The entire house seemed to be filled with a harmonious and restful joy. And it was a pleasure to see how much Péter looked like both of them. In spite of his friendliness, he had a quality of remoteness so like Bartók's; but whenever he broke into laughter, Ditta's gaiety was there.

Péter grew even more substantial to me the next day — a day that reminded me of that first one Ditta and I spent together traveling in and out of downtown bargain basements. Only it was Péter now who needed just about everything. We went to Gimbel's this time, and here Péter demonstrated his independence by selecting with confidence and decision a suit and an overcoat, paying no attention to Ditta's suggestions, or mine. The difficulty came when Ditta tried to persuade Péter, against his will, to buy a hat. And she enlisted me on her side, whispering in my ear and tugging at my arm.

"You must make him get a hat. Tell him that everyone wears a hat here."

"But they really don't," I whispered back to her.

"No matter. I would love to see him in a hat." She was speaking rapidly, for Péter was only a few steps away. "He is really a young man now, and his last hat I remember was the little sailor he wore when he was about ten years old."

Péter finally gave in and chose a soft rainhat that he folded up and sank into his pocket even before the salesman had a chance to put it in a bag.

Later, at the end of an evening, Péter offered to take me to the subway station, suggesting that we walk there the long way in a circle, all around the hill. Alone with him for the first time, I was trying to establish our own personal way of communicating, but I could think of only the most trivial questions to ask him.

"Do you think you will soon get used to this part of the world?"

Péter kept still for a long time. "My problem is not how to get used to this part of the world, but how to forget that other," he said finally, refusing to consider my question in the same manner he refused the hat.

While Péter was no longer the little boy Ditta believed him to be, still he was like a child playing with his toys when he discovered the radios. He took those radios apart and put them together again so many times that their intricate inner workings were as well known to everyone in the house as the clumsy designs of the cabinets that held them. And Ditta, watching him, would look as happy as Péter himself.

"I wonder if you know how good it is to see him doing things with such pleasure like this," she said, and I noticed tears in her eyes that I had never seen there before.

"If only it could be kept from him, how uncertain the ground is beneath our feet. If he could only have a happy time for a while, now that we are together again, after he has been alone for such a long time."

But in spite of Ditta's fears, nothing came in to disturb the joy of the weeks that followed Péter's arrival, with Bartók looking and feeling much better. Péter was a fresh breeze, a living link with home, the source of history, and a witness to so many happenings that he made the past two years seem almost like a lifetime. There was no end to Bartók's questions, and I was always struck by the surprise written on his face while he listened to Péter's long and detailed accounts. For out of these continued talks there emerged a whole intact countryside, and both Buda and Pest too, standing just as they were at the time when Bartók came away, with people still moving on the streets alive and unhurt. Bartók's premonition of the destruction of his land had run far ahead of actual events, and it was planted so firmly in his mind that it was difficult for him to rearrange his image to fit the present reality. He had to erase the vision of dusty stone piles and see again the streets with their upstanding, life-filled houses, and that well-known small stretch of the Danube not yet stripped of its proud bridges. And it was a shallow source of relief for him to realize with his conscious mind that his picture of destruction had been only imaginary, although as far as he was concerned it was so certain to come that it might as well have taken place already. It was as though Péter were showing him a book of pictures that he recognized with a pleasure that was mixed with deep yearning pain. And out of it all he seemed to gain a wistful calmness — many times I saw him with his eyes closed, leaning back in his chair, listening to Péter's lively voice and laughter only an arm's length away.

Ditta had a hard time, too, catching up with time. It wasn't easy for her to comprehend that the two years which separated her from Péter had turned the boy she had left behind into a grown-up young man almost old enough to fight in a war. And a frightening thought followed that one: if he had stayed in Europe only a year more, he might have perished fighting on the side of the enemy.

"What a world of difference," Bartók remarked more than once, "to know that as long as he has to be in it, as he undoubtedly will be in a year or two, he will be on the right side, not with the enemy, but against them."

A moment of time to breathe in, to rest from anxiety! It

wasn't long, however, before it became obvious that Bartók did not really feel better but was in fact worse again. The approach of summer failed to do its healing. The wild blooming of flowers, the dusty streets, the heavy breezeless afternoons already gave a foretaste of what the midsummer city would be like. As always after a period of lightheartedness, Bartók sank suddenly into an even more hopeless mood than before. Unexpectedly there was another six months' extension of his work at Columbia, but there was not a single concert engagement for the coming season.

"Just as well," Bartók said. "For even if there were a line of concerts waiting for me, it's highly improbable that I could fulfill a single one of them." And he added, with a smile, "You see, as a pianist I could not exist, and as a composer I have become nonexistent." He shrugged his shoulders, as if to say it did not matter to him at all.

In the middle of June when I left for Vermont, the Bartóks still could not make any plans for the summer. It was not until the latter part of July that any decision was made and Ditta could write to me about it and the various problems yet remaining to be solved before they would be able to leave the city.

It was hard to say anything definite about the state of Béla's health, she told me, but the doctors seemed to think his illness chronic. It was better not to try to do anything about it and to accept the idea it would be a long time before he could be cured. At the moment he was planning to go to the seashore in August, a place only a few hours by train from New York, to remain there a few weeks perhaps. That would be the time for her to come to Riverton, and how long she could stay would depend on circumstances. Meanwhile, New York was not really unpleasant, and when it rained the fragrance hanging in the air afterwards reminded her of Vermont and brought tears of delight to her eyes, and made her wonder how the rosebushes were, the Sleeping Beauty and the poor little Cemetery Pine.

The Sleeping Beauty and the Cemetery Pine were two small hemlock trees we had carried home the summer before after a long walk in the woods with the idea of planting them in a pot for Ditta to take back to Bartók. But they were so wilted that we put them quickly into the earth right near the house, and gave them their melancholy names because of their sad, drooping branches. It did not look as if they would survive, and Ditta worried about them constantly throughout the winter.

There were many changes and postponements of these plans, but finally only one problem remained: What to do with the cats? I suggested sending them to me, but Bartók could not bear the thought of exposing them to the long trip alone. At the end they decided to leave them in a nearby animal home. I heard from Ditta that the place was nice and clean, seemed to be well run, and that they would not be there too long anyway.

So, at long last, Ditta was in Riverton again. She arrived late in the evening. Happy and excited, she not only hugged and kissed Martha, but the surprised Matthew as well. Even before taking off her coat, she ran outside with a strong flashlight to see her hemlock trees.

"Just look at them, how they grew. Look at them, Martha! Look, Mr. Matthew! What do you think of it? Did they develop the way they should have?"

I held my breath, afraid of what "Mr. Matthew's" answer would be, but I needn't have worried at all.

"They did pretty good and grew the best they could," he hemmed and hawed as politely as I had ever heard him before.

"Soon we'll have to move the house if they keep growing like this."

"But can they really be the same wilted things I planted myself? These beautiful, alive trees?"

"They are. They are," all three of us reassured her.

"Oh yes, they must be the same," she decided for herself after a little while. "I cannot help but recognize them."

She insisted that we have dinner in the kitchen, as if she wanted to re-establish the happy mood of the year before — of those last carefree days at the end of the summer.

But it wasn't like that at all. It was instead like the shadow of something once bright and real. An invisible, colorless ghost seemed to be crowding our minds with memories too sharply aching to remember. Just by following Ditta's eyes I could guess what she was seeing, and a word or two was enough to assure me that I was not mistaken. How often she would give a quick glance to the closed door of the room that had once been Bartók's own.

"You will never know his aloneness in there," she said gravely, not looking at me, but through me. "His fight to make order out of his conflicting desires that were pulling him with equal strength in different directions — to return to Hungary or stay here for ever. You may understand one day, perhaps."

And as we went on our old walks again, it seemed to me at times as if we were following Bartók's light footsteps among the confusing shadows in the dark woods.

"He is so thin," Ditta once said. "You can't even hear his steps on the ground any more."

Whenever she talked about Bartók, her words had an unfriendly, almost accusing edge, but at the same time she trusted me fully, or she wouldn't have spoken her worried thoughts out loud, just as they entered her mind, without trying to arrange them coherently. She knew that I would be able to supply the unuttered links that gave meaning to what she said. But once when I answered her, for it was awkward for me to remain silent all the time, saying "I know, Ditta. I know," her tone quickly changed, as if she were refusing to be soothed in any way.

"Béla can be understood only through his work. For he is himself only when he is doing his own creating, and all other times whatever is visible is no more than the surface dust that falls away from him as soon as he gives himself fully to his work.

"And if you could really know, besides everything else, how much more he is shaken and moved by the suffering of others than by his own, as now, during the war, the big universal sufferings. He has no easy quick feelings for the small everyday complaints, and almost no vocabulary of small words to make himself appealing!"

How different our talks were from the long and excited conversations of the year before. We walked on the same ground, sat under the same trees, tasted the same fruits and rested in the same sunshine — but there was no peace, no relaxing into the summer's warm bounty. Although Ditta leaned against the trees, she held herself rigidly, her face often twitching as if in pain. But even that was better than the hopeless sadness that spread over it when in repose.

During the first week we wandered for miles and miles, but after that Ditta mostly slept. She slept almost the entire day, throwing herself into slumber as into a deep river, to be carried on and on by the lulling current, and emerging only with difficulty. Looking dazed and tired and puzzled, she would sit in her bed trying to remember where she was and where she had been. I brought her breakfast in bed and had some with her, too, although most of the time it was already after lunch for me. I drank my coffee silently while fragments of Ditta's dreams or confused night thoughts were finding their way to the surface. Sometimes she shuddered, remembering.

"Oh, Seattle. Even the name is painful to me. Please don't tell me it isn't true, for I'm sure the name Seattle means the end of the sea. And the place is not covered with darkness as America was for me before I came here, for don't forget I have been to Seattle while on a concert tour and I know that I don't want to live there ever. And neither does Béla, I am sure."

After these days spent with Ditta, who was like someone living half in the present, half in the past, it seemed completely unreal when a cheerful letter arrived from Bartók from Nonquit. He said that Péter was well, and he himself neither better nor worse than he was when he left New York. Except the weather — so stickily damp that from his socks to his manuscript paper everything was dripping wet, including himself. Péter wrote too, promising to visit us in Riverton, but not for a while yet.

And another day there was a letter from the place where the cats were boarding, only a few lines to let Mrs. Bartók know that both of the cats were very sick, and she should come to see them at her convenience, for there was not much hope for their recovery.

"What is this supposed to be?" Ditta asked in a sharp, curt tone. "Is this a conspiracy to steal them? You know in what perfect condition those cats are! They are sparkling with health."

"But they might have caught some disease," I said anxiously. Ditta's only answer to this was an angry glance and no more.

Another letter came the day afterward. I handed it to Ditta, trembling, afraid of the news it might contain. But in a completely matter-of-fact manner, with no comment, Ditta put the letter, unopened, into her pocket. And it was not until we got home after a long and tiring walk that she took it out of her pocket as if accidentally finding it there. She opened it then and read it aloud. The cats were dead and Mrs. Bartók could call for them within twenty-four hours. I was afraid that the distress I felt would show on my face, and I was afraid to see her own, so I turned away and waited for her outburst. But to my surprise, her voice was cold and angry.

"What a diabolical lie! They admired those cats so much when I took them there that I'm not surprised at all they found a way to steal them."

"But the letter says they are dead and they could be called for," I reminded her. She refused to listen, and put the letter back in her pocket, indicating firmly that she wanted to hear no more about it.

Yet, for some reason, I went on insisting that she should face the fact squarely: the cats were dead, not stolen. Why did I try so hard to make her realize the truth? I am sure I was glad the pain of it had not touched her. But I could not let it go, and almost against my will kept on making new attempts to convince her, and only gave up when I saw her resolve not to accept the facts was stronger than my desire to force her to do so. My failure filled me with a worry and an apprehension that stayed with me from then on.

The rest of Ditta's visit was uneventful, and one day blended into another. Péter was expected, but his trip was postponed again and again. Finally Bartók wrote that he had decided to go home earlier than he had planned, and so Ditta went back to New York too.

After she left, Péter came at last. It was a great comfort to spend a few days with him. Péter had Ditta's capacity to experience the countryside with inexhaustible delight, but he also had some of the slow, searching curiosity of his father. And it was consoling that he shared my sorrow over the death of the cats, although his sadness was soon dispelled by his healthy vigor and enthusiasm.

Furthermore, Lulu had a new brood of kittens, looking so much like the poor dead ones that it seemed very natural for Péter to suggest taking at least one of them home with him to fill the gap the others had left.

This idea, which seemed so natural at the time, did not turn out quite as we expected, however, because Bartók showed no interest in the newcomer. In fact he actively withdrew the affection he usually gave to animals. He treated the kitten with gentle respect whenever their paths crossed, but his personal feelings obviously remained faithful to the ones who had died. And for Ditta, the presence of the new pet seemed to be cause for increasing apprehension.

"But what will ever become of him? We don't even know what will become of us."

He was never even properly named and was called merely "Puss-Puss" or "Péter's Cat."

"It hurts me how good he is," Ditta used to say. "How hard he has to work for a little love. He feels so uncertain and always a bit afraid. Oh no, not scared of us, but of something unknown."

This nameless cat did seem to have, from the very beginning, a dubious air, looking questioningly at everyone, with a vague fear lurking in his large, slightly crossed green eyes. And I myself found those eyes becoming a symbol of the tension in the Bartóks' atmosphere in that early fall of 1942.

When I first saw Bartók after the summer, I could only stare unbelievingly into his face. The beautiful order of his features was so ravaged that at first glance he seemed almost unknown to me. But after a while I became accustomed to his new appearance, his paler and thinner face, his more cautious movements about the house, and the stretches of time he spent alone in his own room.

"Do his doctors have any new suggestions to offer?" I asked Ditta carefully one day.

"Nothing," she answered, "but the same old thing. Nothing new. Only food and rest — and this, you see, amounts to less than nothing, for he barely eats and cannot really rest at all. And the foods he wants I've never even heard of before — potato dumplings, corn mush, and all kinds of other things we never used to have in our house. He must have discovered them in those days when he was wandering in search of folk songs. Perhaps he desires them because they remind him of the time when he was active and forever tireless — the happiest days, as he has often said himself, of his whole lifetime."

Ditta's perception was borne out nearly always by the stories that unexpectedly welled up in Bartók's descriptions of peasant houses he had stayed in many years ago. One time when Ditta offered him an apple, he took it from her and held it as if weighing it in his hand, and smiled as he began to speak.

"Oh, this reminds me of another apple — one that fell on my head from the top of a cupboard. It was in one of those pungent-smelling peasant houses, where I slept in the best room on a bed piled high with goosefeather bedding. The apples were kept in a row on top of the cupboard. They were very rare by then, for it was wintertime. All night I was inhaling the pure ripe smell, until all at once one fell practically into my hand. But what a dilemma came with that apple! To eat it or eat it not? It wasn't exactly the forbidden fruit, only it wasn't mine. I sat up in my bed and held it in my hand just like this, and I never tasted any apple as intensely or one with as many concentrated flavors as that apple I never ate. I climbed up on the headboard of my bed and placed it very carefully back with the rest, and that was the end of it."

He put the apple he held in his hand back on the plate, and that was the end of that too.

There were so many times that Bartók did not come to the dinner table at all that Ditta and I more and more often ended up eating a bite in the kitchen. And again, as we used to, we fell back on talking about Péter. But how much easier it was, now that Péter was merely a subway ride away, at night school instead of at the other end of the world.

"I am so glad Péter is doing well with his studies," I would say, and Ditta's reaction would be instantaneous.

"And with many other things, too!" And by that she meant mostly the radios he had already fixed, and the sick gramophone that he not only cured but electrified as well.

Ditta had even more reason to be proud of Péter's great skill when she unexpectedly received an invitation to play an all-Bartók program over WQXR. It gave her enormous satisfaction to know that Bartók could listen to his own compositions on a radio that Péter had put in shape. Ditta and Bartók worked out the program together with great care, pouring tremendous thought and energy into the choice of the pieces, as they always did, whether it was to be a performance in a public school or in the biggest concert hall in the world. And a concert was an even greater occasion these days, for it happened so very rarely.

I went with Ditta to the radio station and sat next to her while she played. As I saw her so immersed and concentrated, I discovered yet another side of Ditta's I had not known before. An unsuspected power tightened the softness of her face into firm lines, growing steadily tenser and stronger as she guided her performance, with great restraint, preserving carefully the purity of the sound she was creating.

"You played beautifully," I told her when we were down in the busy street. She merely smiled at me, with raised eyebrows, and suggested having a cup of coffee immediately. We turned into the first cafeteria we found on our way. Quite at home in the noisy crowded place, she sat warming her cold hands on the heavy mug of hot coffee, happy and relieved.

"I was remembering throughout the whole thing," she said, "that Béla was listening to me, and on one of Péter's radios! But it was with my sixth sense that I remembered it, for one needs all the other five for the work itself." She was relaxed, without a cloud on her face.

We went home by the long subway trip, but Ditta didn't seem to mind it this time. Her music was open on her lap and her head bent down over it. She was following the notes and it seemed as if she were hearing the music all over again in her mind.

"I wonder if Béla liked it."

We walked rapidly after leaving the subway, and on the last stretch ran up the hill toward the house in the crisp clear air. The inside of the house was in semidarkness, and all was still.

Ditta knocked on Bartók's door and we went in. He was lying in bed, covered up to his chin.

"It was fine, it was very fine," he greeted Ditta as soon as we entered. "Just as it was intended."

"And the radio?" she asked. "How was the radio?"

"Oh, quite a clear transmission," Bartók answered casually, "with the exception of a few minor disturbances, of course."

Ditta was overjoyed, and moved around the apartment as if lifted from the floor, gliding back and forth from the kitchen preparing something to eat.

It never failed to surprise me how completely they forgot about themselves, about the uncertainties of their existence, about everything else whenever it came to a performance. This was the truly important thing.

In no time at all the coffee was ready, and Ditta brought it in, though she could find no place to put it in this room that seemed to have become more crowded every time I saw it again. Ditta quickly brought in a folding table and put it near Bartók's bed, pushing away the table that was there, cluttered with glasses and bottles, a thermometer and pencils, pads of paper, a box of rubber bands, and a book or two. One of the books was a French edition of Proust's *Swann's Way*. Next she brought in a snow-white tablecloth and then a plate of the wonderful-smelling nut cake that was Bartók's favorite. Bartók sat up in bed. There was a red spot on each side of his face, burning warm and alive on his sunken cheeks. He took a piece of the cake and held it in his hand, inhaling deeply the sweet aroma.

"A secret formula of my family," he said, "kept alive like the folk melodies from mouth to mouth throughout the generations." He smiled, and to make sure we understood his point to the full, he raised the cake to his mouth. But without tasting it, he put it back on his plate.

"By tradition it is a Christmas cake, but it keeps so well that it lasts a long time after Christmas. Almost through the entire winter. The flavor of it gets more and more concentrated with time, and as the supply of it keeps on dwindling away, it becomes an ever rarer treat. Something very precious. You get at first thin little square pieces and later on only morsels. Slowly it develops great strength of its own, like old wine, and has magic powers like a tonic, a medicine, a potion."

Ditta poured him a cup of coffee, and he reached out for it.

"You did play excellently," he said to her earnestly. "Your performance always comes the nearest of all to my intention. The simplest, the most articulate, the purest."

Ditta was sitting on the edge of her chair, barely breathing.

"And still I am not saying that you are absolutely the best pianist." They were looking at each other. "Just that you perform my works in the truest style. And always remember, you are the one who will have to preserve this style, keep it alive, keep it going."

Ditta was gathering up cups and plates. Her face, just as when she was playing earlier that evening, was drawn into tight, strong lines. She was straining to listen to every word Bartók was saying. She reached for his cup.

"If only your hands could be twice as big as they are!" he said, and a smile broke out on Ditta's face.

Bartók held out his hand and Ditta put hers into it.

"But already they are twice as strong as one could believe possible, judging from their size. And what pure strength they possess for those *parlandos* and *pesantos*."

Suddenly tired, he lay back in his bed. His eyes were closed now, but he began to speak again, a little lower, and somewhat more slowly.

"Yes, you should help to keep it alive, to continue, if there is to be a continuation. I like to believe that there will be. But sometimes I am afraid."

20

ALL AT ONCE it was cold dark winter again. Somehow it seemed as if time had changed its steady pace, and were both standing still and running wildly ahead at the same time, only to be measured now by a new device unrelated to the old familiar calendar. The leisurely step-by-step progress toward the return of each season was replaced by erratic sudden jerks, accompanied by a rhythm of irritatingly shrieking bells. And then again, all would be hurled to a standstill.

Bartók continued going to Columbia twice a week, although it had become a real hardship, and not the exciting adventure it had been. And now that it would have given him such comfort to let one of those fifty-cent taxis carry him to and from the subway station, the long line of waiting cabs had disappeared, and not one was to be found. So he had to walk those long blocks down to the subway, and climb them again in the evening, through the gloomy fall rain or against the cold winter wind.

As soon as he arrived home, he went straight to his room and fell onto his bed, sometimes without removing his overcoat. When Ditta would urge him to make himself more comfortable, or to come to dinner, or take some nourishment in his room, he would only signal no with his hands to all her suggestions. He wanted nothing except rest, his blanket pulled up to his chin, stretched out on his bed, without turning on the light, in the stillness and solitude of his own cluttered little room.

I can still see that room. In the middle of the floor stood one of Péter's ingenious devices to keep Bartók warm, a small electric plate transformed into an old-fashioned stove by a long black pipe placed over its hot coils to spread the heat around it in a large circle. The one window near the bed was draped with a heavy gray blanket, creating a half-dark stillness, made even deeper by the thick new snow visible from the other window, lying heavily in windswept mounds rising all around so that the room was like a cave, closed away from the outside world.

Sitting in the warmth of the long pipe, Bartók, huddled in his old flannel robe, reminded me of a chestnut vendor bending over his tiny stove. He would be working on his Romanian collection, spread all around the room, and he needed only a glance at these single pages to place each one on the pile where it belonged. Every featherlike sheet added still one more link to the complicated system of classification, where every small variation of rhythmical pattern played a part in revealing relationships between peoples and places.

Perhaps for Bartók these notes, like pressed flowers in an album, still retained traces of their original fragrance, potent enough to draw him back to the land where he first found them and releasing him from the shadows of the room where he sat.

Gradually I sensed that this hushed and oppressive atmosphere was lifted and charged with a renewed vitality and anticipation.

"Yes, some good news is on the way," Ditta told me when I asked her about this, "but I can't tell you any more just now, not until we are sure it is going to happen," she said with finality. "You know how superstitious I am, and besides, Béla asked me to keep it a secret."

Whatever it was, this untold news already seemed to have its good effect on Bartók. He emerged from his room looking stronger again, fully dressed and moving vigorously about the house, and even sitting under the brightest light he bore a closer resemblance to his old self, as if his face had been poured back into its original mold once more.

The longer I waited for the mysterious news to come out into the open, the greater my hopes grew. And naturally they circled around those things that would basically change their life, perhaps a new source of income, but, above all else, a turn for the better in the course of Bartók's illness.

So when Ditta finally told me that the New York Philharmonic-Symphony was going to give a first performance of Bartók's *Concerto for Two Pianos and Orchestra* in Carnegie Hall, with Fritz Reiner conducting and with Béla and Ditta Bartók at the pianos, I did not instantly recognize this information as the secret news I had been waiting to hear for so long. And although it took only a moment for me to make the connection, Ditta immediately sensed that this was something less than I had hoped for, and before I could summon up an enthusiastic response, she began to express her disappointment at my reaction.

"How could anyone fail to realize how important it is that Bartók will be heard, both as a composer and a pianist, just when it seemed so unlikely that such a thing would ever happen again! Or could it be," she probed more deeply, "that you think I am exaggerating the importance of this because it is not just for Béla alone, but for both of us, and I have my part in it too!"

But when I quickly reassured her that this idea had never

crossed my mind at all; she didn't quite like that either.

"At the same time, I'd like you to understand it is not un-important to me that I am included in this new performance. For of course it's important, but that is not the reason why I am able to see this event in its true significance."

I could sense, with apprehension, that she was deeply ruffled, but this time, however, her happy excitement kept her from developing her feelings to the point of a crisis, and she continued almost calmly, "After Béla was so completely neglected here and sentenced into silence for so long, this opportunity may give him the feeling of a fresh beginning, perhaps even new health, and who knows, even put him on the road of composing again."

These words of Ditta's kept ringing in my mind like a prophecy when the rehearsals began, and I was sitting in the almost empty darkness of Carnegie Hall listening to the performance taking shape under the wise hands of Fritz Reiner. With the most natural ease Bartók himself was blending with the members of the orchestra, and working with them toward the mutual goal of creating a performance that would fulfill all that this new idiom demanded and inspired. He no longer resembled that lonely and aloof man who had retreated so far into his isolated detachment.

Although only a few weeks before he had barely the strength to hold a pencil in his hand, Bartók was now bringing forth from the piano sounds of such fullness and controlled force that they flooded every corner of the big hall, each tone an echo of his long suppressed power released into creation again. I could not help wondering whether this energy would continue its flow, or spend itself, only to come to a standstill when these concerts were over. Would he sink back into the hopelessness he was caught in only a short while ago, would he say again with the same final despair in his voice, "For me, nothing seems more impossible than to imagine that I will ever compose again"?

Even if everyone taking part in these rehearsals had known that it was to be Bartók's last appearance, he could not have been given more devoted cooperation. Many times Reiner turned thoughtfully to Bartók, asking, "Is this what you meant, Béla?" and Bartók would nod his head, "Yes, yes, it is exactly what I had in mind!" And Ditta for her part worked smoothly and steadily, with an inexhaustible eagerness to assume her full weight of responsibility.

The excitement gave Bartók's face a glowing alertness, and with a single glance he could suggest almost superhuman strength. But when one time he removed his jacket in order to play with more freedom and sat down at the piano in his shirtsleeves, a shocked hush and a long sigh came from the members of the orchestra, for now they saw how ravaged he was by illness, weighing hardly more than ninety pounds, his wasted shoulders and thin arms giving him the look of a frail, undernourished boy.

At the last rehearsal the performance, now hewed into its final shape, kept the few of us who were in the hall in a fever of excitement. I remember Tibor Serly, score in hand, moving from one part of the hall to the other to hear how the balance of the instruments came through. After it was over, a few friends gathered around Bartók and Reiner, talking enthusiastically. I went up on the stage to join Ditta there.

"You were so wonderful," I said in answer to her questioning smile, "that I was hardly aware of your playing apart from Bartók's. It was inseparably one with his." She took hold of my hand in response so tightly that it hurt.

"But do you know," I said in a lighter tone, "your piano is not quite at the right angle, and you cannot be seen well enough from all sides." Pleased and amused, she burst into laughter. An attendant was passing by just then and I asked him if he would help me move the piano a few inches forward, but he only looked at me and continued on his way. So I gave it a push myself, and Ditta sat down at the piano again, while I went back into the hall to take another look.

"It's fine now," I told her when I came back.

"I'm glad," she said. "But you should have heard yourself talking to that man. No wonder he went away in such a hurry. You overcame your shyness so completely for my sake that you turned into a lioness protecting her cub."

Later on that day, when I was helping Ditta lay out the clothes she was to wear at the concert, she seemed very tense and very quiet.

"Any performance of a work of Béla's fills me with concentrated anticipation. It was always that way, even when it happened every week — in London, Paris, Rome. But here in New York, now of all times, it means even more than it ever did before."

So, in New York City, on the evening of January 21, 1943, in Carnegie Hall, the performance of the *Concerto for Two Pianos and Orchestra* was for many reasons of the utmost significance to the Bartóks. Perhaps they could not have told all the reasons why, for they were not consciously aware of them, but their nerves, stretched to capacity, seemed to sense with some foreboding the great importance of this moment.

And it was a moving occasion, too, for that handful of Bartók admirers who finally had a chance to hear him again. Many others in the large audience must certainly have been interested and inspired as well, although there was the inevitable antagonism from still another group in the hall. A few old ladies left their seats and demonstratively made their way toward the exit. And for the rest, it was probably only another number on the program.

I can remember sitting in the crowded hall entirely lost in the music that was a runaway river upsurging and rushing in a wild flood over the land, then, calm, falling back within its banks again, to move with brooding slowness through its own channel toward the ocean.

But presently I became aware of a sensation that the music, so familiar to me by now, was no longer anything I remembered. I looked at Bartók, who had made himself completely at one with the piano and with that particular abandonment of his had entered a world his alone. He was playing something entirely unknown to me, something that had an immediate and bright existence of its own but still seemed an integral part, inseparable from the rest.

One glance at Ditta and I knew I was not dreaming. For while playing as steadily as before, she was obviously under great pressure. There seemed to be two separate spheres, each moving in its own orbit: Bartók belonging to one, alone, while the conductor, Ditta and the entire orchestra were crowded into the other.

But it all passed so quickly, it seemed as if scarcely any time had gone by before the two worlds blended into one again. I couldn't even be sure at all, when finally the wild dancelike gaiety reached its climax, that a momentary illusion of my own had not made me hear the music so differently from the way I remembered it.

When I went backstage I saw only a few people, talking in hushed tones at one end of the artists' room. I did not see Ditta, but far from the small gathering, almost hidden in a corner, Bartók was leaning back in a chair, with closed eyes; he was looking very tired now, and seemed to be almost asleep.

After a while Reiner came in, looking grim and disturbed. He did not speak at first, but finally walked over to Bartók.

"What on earth came over you, Béla?" he said in a voice that was cold, but somehow compassionate too. "How could you endanger everything, risking disaster for a momentary whim? Didn't you realize what an impossible task it was, trying to follow you through your wanderings? For all of us, not to mention Ditta!"

Bartók looked up at Reiner and did not say anything, and seemed to remain detached and undisturbed.

He held his brooding silence in the taxi on the way to Riverdale, and we were already going up the hill when he sat up straight and turned to Ditta.

"The tympanist," he said, "the tympanist is the one who started everything. He played a wrong note, suddenly giving me an idea that I had to try out, and follow through all the way, right then. I could not help it — there was nothing else for me to do."

This explanation appeared to be so natural and logical to him that it was impossible not to accept it as inevitable. But later, at home, while lingering at the round table over a cup of coffee, he brought up the subject again, this time turning to Ditta with a smile.

"I am sorry, I must have made it terribly hard for you. But not for very long, at any rate."

"It wasn't exactly easy," Ditta said, with some reserve. "Not that it was any harder for me than for all the others. But I, for one, at least understood."

I wondered if Bartók offered the same explanation to Reiner, or whether he ever gave any for what had happened at the first performance of the *Concerto for Two Pianos and Orchestra*. But one thing is sure: at the second performance on the following afternoon, he kept his eyes faithfully on Reiner, and played his music with the greatest fidelity to the printed score.

The performances were over, but the high spirit they left in their wake lingered for a while. Nothing significant or important resulted from these concerts, but the full sense of accomplishment felt by both Bartók and Ditta was not marred by any sudden letdown. And now it became clearer than ever to me that the tremendous excitement which had mounted so high before the concert did not spring from any hope of worldly gain, but had risen purely and entirely for the purpose of bringing the music itself into life, and was by the same token purely and entirely consumed by the act of the performance.

The unsatisfactory reviews did not appear to affect Bartók very much. He looked at them thoughtfully, and even singled out the one from the *New York Times* and gave it to me to read a few days after the concert.

"Although I have read this over many times, without making head or tail of it, maybe you would give me an idea what it means, or translate it into any language for me, from Sanskrit to Mohammedan, and make even the remotest sense out of it?" With that, he took the clipping out of my hand, and placed it in front of me upside down.

Actually, Bartók was more interested in the letters he received than in the reviews in the press. Some of these communications were filled with infinite admiration, while others just as eloquently expressed vehement distaste. Bartók found their direct, clear-cut style much more satisfying than the roundabout and pretentious innuendoes of the reviewers. And he brought this up again, even much later on, pointing out how helpful it would prove to be for both the public and the performer if the reviewers would adopt a more simple and coherent style, though by now his interest in the subject was more impersonal and abstract as the Carnegie Hall performance was already fading into the past.

None of the presentations of Bartók's major works, however, faded away entirely for Ditta and Bartók. They could recall any one of them at will, and with an astounding amount of detail. They remembered not only the performances and how they were received, but all the people who took part in them, too, together with the special mood of each occasion.

And now as if this latest concert became in its turn a part of the long chain of performances, Ditta began one day to speak of it.

"I only found out a short time ago that Béla was not entirely happy about the way the concert in Carnegie Hall came about. Because it was arranged by Reiner, who is an old friend of ours, Béla could not escape the feeling that it was more like a 'family affair' and did not originate from impersonal interest. No one knows better than Béla that Reiner's integrity cannot be affected by such considerations, but the neglect Béla has experienced here these last years has made him sensitive about these things."

Ditta thought for a while, then continued. "Somehow the way he was lured into changing his music right on the stage while it was being performed must have been connected with the disturbed, uneasy feeling inside him. What happened then is ever so much more than an anecdote, although it has the perfect making of one. But realizing that this is not the first time it happened might give one a deeper insight into the whole affair.

"The first time I went through this experience," Ditta explained, "was in London, when the terrible fear was growing in Béla that the war was certain to come and was making him feel entirely lost. It wasn't even his own composition that time. I was playing a long solo part when all at once I felt as if a strange hand were touching my shoulder, and then, like a hallucination, a few very soft and heartbreaking chords were floating toward me. Even when the sounds grew stronger, turning into wild, human voices, I still didn't know where they were coming from. But after the plaintive piercing last tones, so much more like a flute or a violin, had subsided, I realized they were coming from Béla's piano. However, after a while, everything fell into order again and remained so to the end.

"It was weeks later that I mentioned it to him. 'Really, did you notice it?' he said, suddenly interested. But when I asked him what made him do it he shrugged his shoulders. 'I don't know,' he said. 'I had a vision, for a second, that that very moment was my last, the last standstill, before everything should get lost in chaos and panic, and I felt I had to hold on to it.'

"He did it another time," Ditta said, "at a recording session of one of his own works that was held in London just about the time when he realized there was no power on earth to keep the war from coming. He told me about it as soon as he came home, very excited and pleased with what he had accomplished in that moment of inspiration."

So again, in New York, there came to him that irrepressible flood of creative energy, and once more he was unable to hold back the tide. Was it that he sensed in a moment of unearthly insight that this might be the last time he would ever be heard in a concert hall? Or perhaps he was so filled to the brim after the long years of silence that his desire for release could not be contained another moment. This desire was fulfilled, and the moment passed: but the need for expression subsided after the performance, and ended without carrying him any farther along the way to compose again.

The strength he had summoned up during the preparation for this concert at Carnegie Hall had lasted exactly as long as it was needed, and no longer. Soon afterward he became sick, perhaps even sicker than ever before, while at just about this time his work at Columbia was halted again as another six months had come to an end.

21

LIKE TWO PARALLEL THEMES deepening each other with their dark shadows, Bartók's illness and the uncertainty of his position at Columbia ran side by side from the beginning of his stay in America to the end. And out of these two, a third one slowly emerged: Bartók's silent conflict over the offer from Seattle.

The communications between Professor Carl Paige Wood of the University of Washington and Bartók began just about when he started his work at Columbia in the spring of 1941, and were in progress without ever reaching any conclusion almost to the time of his death. He found it reassuring at first to think about this position that he had tentatively accepted, but whenever the move to Seattle loomed nearer, and seemed inevitable, he was struck anew by an inability to make a final decision.

Then later, when it was evident his health was getting worse and not better, he began to realize he had just enough strength to remain where he was, within this small area that had been slowly and painfully accepted by him as part of his life. And whenever the threat of losing it came closer, he became aware all over again how much he wished to be left where he was and remain at Columbia in the basic security of three thousand dollars a year, just to go there twice a week, probing farther and farther into that remarkable Yugoslav folk song collection of Parry's, and accomplish as much as he possibly could.

But if it had to be, as he had known from the beginning, that his work at Columbia would sooner or later come to an end, even this disruption would not be an insufferable loss if there were only some way of finding a similar occupation in this part of the country instead of facing a move so far away from the center of musical activities he still hoped to become part of and to a place so altogether remote, besides. Then they would not have to forsake the Riverdale apartment where they were so thoroughly settled, that small secure island of their own, the nearest thing to a home they could ever have hoped to find here.

The mere thought of such an uprooting brought back some of the anguish of their departure from Europe, that shock which had never been dissolved. Perhaps during the upheaval of leaving Hungary the pain was actually a source of strength to Bartók, reassuring him that he was paying in full for his self-chosen exile from his country. But this pain must have become an unbearable burden as it continued to lie heavy within him, quietly and steadily growing. For the passing of time seemed to increase rather than heal the wounded spot in him.

Bartók never restrained himself from occasional impatient remarks when problems seemed impossible to solve — as, for instance, the obstacles encountered at every step of bringing Péter to America, when he would exclaim fairly often, "Perhaps it would be best if we ourselves went back, instead!" But all this expressed no more than a momentary annoyance. He never in any way revealed in words the feelings that were gnawing at him in the deepest level and remained, as far as he knew, hidden from everyone. Despite this it was transparently clear that underneath all his disappointments here — including even his frustration as a creative artist, and his illness, together with his fears — there was spread a heavy velvet layer of homesickness, absorbing into itself all the current problems and in return nourishing them into vast proportions.

That he was driven so far as to seek a way out by devising an actual plan to go back to Hungary immediately, and while the war was still in progress, had never entered my mind. So it came as a complete surprise to me one evening after he had eaten his small supper when, sitting up in bed with the tray on his knees, he slowly began to talk about his plan of going home, a plan completely worked out in his mind. It was only with a great effort that I could hide my feelings as I listened to him, fearful besides of what Ditta's reaction to this unexpected revelation of Bartók's would be. I was amazed to see her sitting calmly on the edge of his bed showing no sign of disturbance whatever, even when Bartók went on to say that he had no intention of exposing her to all the difficulties certain to be encountered in wartime traveling, and that she by all means should remain safely in America until the end of the war.

"Péter, of course, will soon be joining the armed forces, and that is how it should be," he went on, with resignation in his voice.

Neither Ditta nor I had interrupted him with as much as a sigh. Yet he suddenly raised his quiet voice as if someone had challenged him with strong opposition.

"If either of you thinks that in going back to Hungary I am denying entirely the original meaning of my departure three years ago, it doesn't matter to me at all. Besides," he went on, leaning forward so that the intensely shining eyes in his tightly drawn face seemed all at once very near, "there comes a time probably in each man's life, when he is allowed to do the one thing he wants the most, whether it involves the utmost heroism for the fulfillment of a deed, or embraces only a very simple desire, as in my case, to lean back on a hillside somewhere, in Buda, and smell the breeze floating in from the Danube."

Although we were as silent as the inanimate objects around us, Bartók's voice swelled in volume again.

"I cannot be used wrongly by anyone any more, for I am in the hands of the strongest force of all, held in that final grip that keeps me separated. Whatever I do, or wherever I go, is my choice alone. And so I am freer and more elusive than all the birds."

He leaned back on his pillow, holding his eyes on us for a second with a strangely triumphant smile.

This plan of going back to Hungary, if it was a plan at all, did not find its way into words again after that one evening, but must have withdrawn into the deep silent pool, the only place where it could attain even a semblance of reality.

As always, the most significant feelings remained submerged, while accepting the blow of a sudden hardship drained all Bartók's endurance. It seemed almost out of proportion how much vitality was ground up by his emotional reaction when this time his own piano was taken away, recalled by the company whose pianos he used exclusively at all his public appearances here. For this, as he said with tense restraint, was the first time in his life that he was without a piano, and perhaps this emptiness served as a symbol for his entire present existence. Soon, however, a battered upright piano stood silently in the old piano's place; but this instrument, lent to him by a friend, was never anything else but a source of irritation to both of them.

About this time everything began to happen in a faster tempo. Bartók's health was still deteriorating visibly, and there remained no question any more that his illness was as serious as it was lasting.

The few people who were close to Bartók finally realized that some kind of steady assistance would be needed, for Bartók's health had not improved by the force of hope alone, and it was proved by now that left without any medical help he would only be even further exposed to unpredictable consequences. Considering all possibilities, it was decided to inquire if ASCAP was willing to take an interest in his welfare, even though Bartók was not one of their members.

And after approaching ASCAP, there was no need to seek any farther, for they instantly took up Bartók's case, assuming full responsibility. With all the efficiency of their powerful organization, they placed at his disposal doctors and hospitals, all of the very best. Immediately after ASCAP took over, a long and exhaustive series of examinations began. Even then none of the doctors seemed ready to offer a diagnosis of Bartók's illness. Perhaps they were not entirely sure, but perhaps they kept him in the dark because they knew only too well.

"Although these tests are very tiresome, to say the least, yet finally I am officially sick and not merely ailing," Bartók said one day. "I find it very encouraging, besides, that there is so much attention being spent on me; for I doubt that if my case were entirely hopeless these practical doctors would give so much of their time and effort to try to restore me to health, especially at this time when all doctors have such heavy demands on them. I feel I have become an investment by now, and so I'm sure of being well taken care of, and I hope it won't be long before I stop being a burden to myself and everyone else."

But at this time something else came along that seemed to

give Bartók a fresh breath of energy and, like the Carnegie Hall concert, made him for a short period feel almost healthy again. It was an invitation from Harvard University to give the Horatio Appleton Lamb lecture series for six months. This offer seemed to arrive at the best possible moment, just when his work at Columbia had come to an end once more and he was convinced, as each time before, that it was irrevocably and finally over.

"This Harvard engagement wasn't at all as unexpected as Béla's surprise would seem to indicate," Ditta remarked, "for the negotiations have been in progress for quite some time now, but he can never believe in anything until it is signed and sealed, especially when it is so deeply important to him. He really was not quite so hopeless as he seemed to be, since he has already almost worked out an outline for the entire series."

And on some evenings Bartók would try out on us part of the material he happened to be working on, searching our faces to see if we found it interesting, and if we understood fully the meaning of what he was attempting to say. Ditta and I, and occasionally Péter, made up his audience, but we were never a very inspiring group.

"You should not sit there in such passive silence," he complained repeatedly, "but act more alive, besiege me with questions until I exhaust all my resources, reaching down to the very bottom of my subject."

He made Péter draw complicated diagrams to help him illustrate certain points.

"Of course my subject will not only be supplemented by drawings," he would say, "but naturally by music too." And he would get up from time to time and go to the clumsy upright piano standing ignored against the wall, hardly ever touched by either of them. Now that this despised object had become useful to him he played on it without giving way to any scornful remarks, although he touched its keys with restraint, careful not to encourage its harsh and booming voice.

When Bartók left for Cambridge for the first time, he felt suddenly very well, and so full of anticipation that even the train ride looked like a great treat to him.

"It's no distance at all," he kept on saying, sounding very pleased, "and since I don't have to change anywhere, I don't see why I can't work and rest on the train, just as if I were at home in my own room."

He arrived home frighteningly pale, completely exhausted, and took to his bed again. Still his enthusiasm remained intact.

"I feel this is the most important thing that has happened to me since I came to this country, as if I'd gained a different view toward everything here. For the first time now, instead of being abandoned outside the flow of life I feel actually part of it. And just to remember the wide and lively interest of that student body at Harvard and the way we understood each other, and all the other people I came in contact with, makes me feel certain and reassured."

When the time drew near for his second lecture, he continued to be so weak that he could only move around the house with difficulty. Through his eagerness to go he almost hypnotized himself into feeling well again.

He came home with a high fever but still not admitting, at least outwardly, the threat that he might not be able to finish the course at Harvard. While at home, he spent every minute of his time resting to store up enough energy for the next trip — and to return in his thoughts to Cambridge and keep talking about it seemed to preserve for him the reality of the place he felt slowly to be slipping away from him.

"Walking around those quiet side streets, I could easily believe I was strolling in a well-kept, well-to-do village, and I found myself stopping often to look yearningly into the deep, quiet gardens, deserted to the silence of their very old trees. At moments I had the feeling that even the village had disappeared and there was nothing left but undisturbed nature. But then I'd turn around and take a few steps into another street — and find myself surrounded by a buzzing, live city, with libraries filled with the richest concentration of books you could find anywhere, and also with that steady flow of people of cultural curiosity who make good use of them all the time.

"That place is just tingling with life, and this vitality in the atmosphere suggests the presence of a great many productive thinkers and artists. I could not help feeling how easily one could find everything there one needs in order to exist peacefully, occupied with one's own work."

He had brought home an essential but incomplete picture of Cambridge, an image that kept producing a series of new forms for him to keep pace with.

"Ever since I came home from Cambridge this time," he said one evening, "a vision seems to appear to me, right out of history, and I am able to place it somewhere about the middle of the nineteenth century, at the time when there were so many European towns gathered around a court or a university, each existing independently and creating its own rich culture. These small complete towns did not have to turn for their nourishment, as they do today, to one large city that inevitably became polluted by overpopulation, and in addition by the constant invasion of people in search of a quick and superficial dose of light entertainment."

Bartók stopped, and the room was very still. Péter's cat, who by now had been accepted in this room, was lying on the bed, his steady round eyes never leaving Bartók's face. Bartók caressed his smooth fur gently and sorrowfully whenever he was within reach.

"Yes, I saw many cats, too, in Cambridge, mingling with the people as if they were with trusted friends, walking leisurely on the sidewalks, but still aware of their own secret purposes." Seeing us smile, he shook his head, and went on with greater emphasis.

"But that is an important sign of real civilization too, accepting and making room for those other children of the earth."

When the third trip came around, Bartók still managed to go, but well knew when he came back that it was the last time. And while he never put it into words, this was accepted in all its finality.

An essence of Cambridge lingered in his thoughts as he lay confined to his bed. "It would have been just the right place for us, and I wish we could have lived there."

"Maybe Seattle will be just as right," Ditta said, trying to reassure him in spite of her own feelings.

"No one place could be just as right as the other," Bartók answered firmly. "But we'll see, we'll see," he continued, as if already resigned. "After all, there again I will have my work to do."

Now Seattle loomed up once more as the only way out, when his health should improve enough for him to take another position. No one dared to think, let alone mention, the possibility that he might never be well enough to take any position at all again, for his sickness was still treated as something temporary, something that came and went. And that such a severe attack had to come just at the time when the Harvard lectures were scheduled was one of the things giving Bartók his deep sense of loss and disappointment.

If there was any doubt that his condition might remain unchanged for a long time, it was hidden in vague forebodings and in a certain heavyheartedness shown by both Ditta and Bartók as they began weaving the idea of Seattle into their conversation, and trying to turn it into a reality.

"A home could be made there too," Ditta would say, "just the way we have it here, if we really could take our furniture as you said we might."

"Oh yes, that seems to be all arranged," Bartók would reassure her, "and it is a good thing, too."

For by now the furniture was important to Bartók, and he was just as eager to hold on to it as he had once been reluctant to accept it for his own.

During this period of uncertainty it never occurred to me that the Bartóks might give up the Riverdale apartment, even if they didn't go to Seattle, until Ditta made some vague reference to it one day.

"Leaving this place," she said, "would be like finding myself in the middle of the ocean without a boat."

When I asked her, taken aback, if they were considering such a move, she did not answer me directly but suggested by the expression on her face that she did not know one way or the other. The idea began to haunt me more and more. To imagine the Bartóks living anywhere else was impossible for me then — they blended and merged with every part of that place so completely I couldn't separate them in my mind from those rooms, even long after the house actually was empty, standing like a hollow shell, with the strips of gardens around it overgrown with grass, as in deserted places, and with the strange stillness of the basement, where the radio had once boomed so loudly, and the small windows now blinded with faded green shades.

For the old Italian was to move shortly after the Bartóks left, giving up his battle to save the house, the pink stucco, the climbing roses. Although I did feel his heartbreak of leaving all this behind, yet I could easily imagine him in some other dark rooms, surrounded by the waves of "O Sole Mio," or bending over a little piece of land he must surely have found for himself again.

But the Bartóks were to be there, for me, always, long after the years piled into a decade and time had made those slow changes it inevitably makes, spreading its dark transparent cloth over the bright surfaces. In my imagination a semi-twilight deepened around them; the empty rooms closed in by blue-green shades and Bartók and Ditta were woven into the stillness as in the waving standstill of a tapestry, entangled in the rocking arms of the trees laden with low-hanging fruits, their grave eloquent eyes following me with changing expressions wherever I moved in the room, while in the deep background tame animals were scattered, their questioning eyes ever the same, softly tender, pleading and tragic.

Into this one persistent vision my imagination now has merged all the places where I ever saw the Bartóks, including the rooms they lived in after they left Riverdale. And their faces are part of it, too, changing as they changed when I knew them, in shape, and in intensity, and in their different hues of graveness they seem to be made of shifting materials, as they look out of shadowy corners, or are exposed to glaring lights, carved now from marble, then put together roughly from clay, from putty, from paper or mist, and suddenly again, in sober daylight, from suffering human flesh once more.

Among all these I remember perhaps most clearly Bartók's face as he lay stretched out on the sofa in cold winter light, covered by his old flannel robe, in the Riverdale apartment for almost the last time.

A taxi! A taxi was needed at once to take him to the hospital where his doctor was waiting for him. If we could only find a taxi! But there was none to be found, and Ditta and I were running around the house blindly, calling every possible number.

"An ambulance, perhaps." I must have spoken very loudly, for suddenly Bartók was sitting up straight, saying the most energetic No! I ever heard in my life. "I absolutely refuse. Leave those things to the people who are really in need of them. I am not, as yet."

It took a long time, but at last there was a taxi standing at the door, and Bartók was slowly helped into it. Ditta got in too, and covered him with a warm blanket.

"My briefcase," he called to me, just before the taxi started. "It's on the table near my bed. In case they make me stay there!" In a second I was back with the bulging briefcase, and Bartók reached out a hand for it.

Probably the fear that they might find themselves in an even more urgent crisis than this one brought on the still reluctant decision to leave the Riverdale apartment. Those almost always cold rooms, such an impossible distance from the city and medical help, now finally had to be abandoned.

I stayed with Ditta throughout the long days Bartók spent in the hospital. We were to pack everything to be sent to the warehouse, but if we did pack, it must have been done blindly, for I have no recollection of it. All I remember is sitting around the house, with the shades half pulled down, speaking in whispers, and moving aimlessly, feeling the empty sadness that was already closing in on the rooms, as if everything were coming to an end.

How difficult it became, to disturb those hair-fine roots that after three years were still running barely under the surface. To demolish this lightly planted setting with no certainty that another would take its place, or whether there would be any need for one, brought me without warning to the thought that Bartók was in grave danger, and his time was running out.

22

How easily all could have come to an end right then, so frayed was the thread that held their lives in balance. But the clock rewound itself instead, and there was another beginning.

It must have been desolate for Bartók, lying in his small hospital room with nothing to hinge his hopes on, sad over the uncompleted lectures at Harvard. But more than anything else, he must have come to the realization that his politely called "uncertain health" had all at once become a very certain illness. No doctor would yet attempt to give a name to it, in spite of another series of exhaustive examinations, made with the financial assistance of Harvard University. No diagnosis was made, and no medicine prescribed other than good food and further rest. *Further rest!* Could anything have sounded more hopeless to him? How far would it be to the end of this road of "further rest" which seemed to stretch ahead into infinity, taking as its toll every new breath of energy, promising no relief?

But this seemingly hopeless road, as it happened, opened out into an expanse of new exciting vistas. It came unex-

pectedly, and with the simplicity of a fairy tale, with Koussevitzky coming to visit Bartók in his hospital room one day,
offering him a commission of a thousand dollars from the
Koussevitzky Foundation for an orchestral work in memory
of the late Madame Koussevitzky.

The offer seemed almost unbelievable to Bartók, and he
was unable to relate it to reality. His first reaction was one of
warm gratitude. But he instantly made it clear he could not
possibly promise to fulfill such a commission when he had no
idea of how long his illness would keep him helplessly inactive,
and, even more than that, the feeling had grown strong within
him by this time that he could never under any circumstances
bring himself to compose again.

Koussevitzky, however, with one sweeping motion of his
hand waved all arguments aside and promised Bartók that this
offer would put no pressure on him, and he would be left completely free to undertake this work any time in the future,
whenever he saw his way clear to do so. While Bartók was still
protesting that he could give no assurance the composition
would ever be born at all, Koussevitzky left a check for half
the amount on his bedside table, and departed.

And perhaps it was instantly, in this first moment of excitement, that the restraint so heavily crusted within him began to
dissolve and melt away, for only a day later, when he was home
again and relating the story to us, an enormous change seemed
to have taken place in him already — a change that no one
could fail to see. It seemed as if the obstructed forces within
him were released at last, and the entire center of his being had
been restored and reawakened, even though he was still lying
limp on his bed, hardly any stronger than he was before he
went to the hospital.

He did not seem to notice that the apartment was almost
stripped and ready to be abandoned, or, if he did, it was not
important to mention now that suddenly such exciting de-

velopments were taking shape and bringing a significant change into his immediate view.

For by now an arrangement had been completed by ASCAP for Bartók to spend the summer months in a private sanitarium at Lake Saranac, with Ditta, and for Péter to stay with them too whenever he wished. It was a hardship for Bartók to wait for the moment to come when finally they could leave the city. The flood of impatience he had not released since his departure from Vermont came back now in full force, ready to sweep all obstacles out of its path. He even found strength enough to pack the great bulk of his papers himself.

Beyond the summer, the Bartóks seemed to have no plans and no idea where they were going to live when they returned from Saranac. But these details did not even occur to Bartók; he was living already in the work he was going to do, and the thought of leaving the Riverdale apartment had lost the significance for him that it carried before.

Both Ditta and I felt a deep sadness to see the apartment almost deserted. For the small happenings within the radius of the one big event that strikes the final blow never lose their power to give many sharp stings of pain until all things cease to matter. Only when the final frost puts its freezing finger on the limbs of the strongest tree, only then will the numbing cold reach to the thinnest blades of lowly grass.

I could hardly bear to see the victrola pushed aside among those objects which were to be left behind.

"Please, let's not leave it here," I implored Ditta. "I would love to send it to Vermont, if you'll let me."

"Why, of course," she laughed. "But Péter has ripped all the insides out, and it's no more than a shell now."

"But, even so . . ." I said, and Ditta seemed very pleased.

And it was depressing for both of us when I came to call for Péter's Cat the day before I left for Vermont, to take him with me for the summer.

"Remember, for the summer only," Ditta was saying, touching him with tense fingers. "And after that . . ." She stopped in the middle of her sentence, keeping her hand on him now. "We'll see what will happen after that."

Before we parted she promised she would come to Riverton as soon as she could find time during the summer.

Then, as soon as I arrived in Vermont, I was confronted by another painful task — to write a letter to Ditta telling her that Péter's Cat had run away. For the minute I opened his traveling basket, he tore out of it and ran right into the woods like a streak of fire and was not seen again, though I mobilized everyone to look for him.

At the end of my letter I mentioned that the victrola had arrived safely. Ditta answered me with a short note, pleased about the victrola, and sending her love to the "darling Puss-Puss," without paying any attention to the news of his disappearance. I wrote her about it again, explaining that the cat was still gone but we had not given up hope of finding him.

It was therefore with the strangest feeling that I read the opening words of her letter of July 2 from Lake Saranac: "How is the sweet and only Puss-Puss? He is well, isn't he?"

On the fifth of July I heard from her again, a detailed description of how Béla, now resting so much more clamly than ever before in America, was waiting for another hospital examination the very next day. So far he had been visited in their cottage only by a doctor who had been accurately informed of everything. About his food, of course, there had been some confusion, but the woman who ran the place had been kind enough to allow her to make use of the kitchen from time to time to prepare something special for him.

Every word of her letter reflected a great sense of relief and enthusiasm for the beauty of the place. However, Péter, who was looking very well, was eager to go to Riverton for a few days around the fifteenth, and could she herself come for a little visit about the twenty-fifth? Not that either one of them knew how to get there from Saranac! She concluded by asking me to write about everything, with a long separate chapter about sweet little Puss-Puss.

About a week later, when I was walking alone in the woods, I suddenly sensed a slight motion behind me, and when I turned around I had a quick vision of a gray shadow darting into the thick underbrush. Could it be that this was the lost cat? I wondered. Could he have kept alive in the wild woods, this cat who was so timid, gentle and so afraid of everything? And several times after that, this gray image kept reappearing during my walks, but always so fleetingly that I was never quite sure. One early morning, however, I saw him from my window, sitting motionless a few yards from the house. But not to be lured inside, this time nor at any time later, as the weeks passed into August.

It was near the end of August, the beginning of autumn in Vermont when Ditta came. Together with Martha and Matthew, I was eagerly waiting for her at the station — but even though she was the only one getting off the train, it took a moment for me to recognize her. She had become very thin and altogether much smaller, and was moving with a strange air of uncertainty, as if she were here at the Riverton station only by some mistake. But she was instantly restored by our outburst of happy greetings as we hugged her each in turn.

A heavy silence fell on her again in the car on our way home, and I did not dare turn to her and try to draw her out for fear of perhaps not asking just the right questions. After we arrived and she had begun to feel at home again, however, she could hardly wait to begin talking about how their days were spent at Saranac and to describe for me, to the last detail, their small house there and every turn of the land lying around it, until finally I felt I could walk all over that landscape with my eyes closed, without losing my way.

This seemed to be the one thing that gave Ditta some degree of assurance and a sense of reality — that she could cling in her thoughts to their existence at Lake Saranac, the place that had worked miracles for Bartók's health as nothing had before.

"From the moment we arrived there," she told me several times, "Béla began to get better, waving away his sickness by his own strong will as if it had never been. For in order to do his work of composing, he knows that the first step is to feel completely free, and guarded from all disturbances, and remain for a while calm and restored in his own world."

Ditta, although subdued most of the time, was calm, friendly and communicative these days, and never moved by those sudden sharp resentments I used to fear before. But she seemed to have lost, too, all her impulses of fresh joy that used to come bubbling up even during the times of greatest hardship. She came closest to it when she found the empty gramophone standing in a corner of the living room and lifted the top, opening both its side doors wide.

"Our Péter left nothing in it but a piece of wire curled up in there like the tail of a little pig!" Her laughter came out freely, and like a singer with a precious high note, she held it for a long time.

But her seriousness remained unrelieved during most of the time she spent in Riverton.

"You do know, I hope, that I wouldn't have left Béla, even for this short time, if he weren't receiving the best of care at Saranac," she repeatedly assured me, "by all the doctors and nurses, but most of all by the woman who is running the entire place. I wish you could see her with the patients, so you

could understand her great kindness mixed with that overwhelming authority. The very type of woman who would
bring out in Béla the eager small boy ready to please.

"Once I saw her giving him a spoonful of medicine and he
took it so willingly he almost swallowed it spoon and all." She
smiled at me uncertainly. "I like her too, but I am somehow
just a little bit afraid of her. Perhaps because it has such an
altogether different effect on me to be reminded of my mother.
For I was my father's little girl, you see, and remained so always, even if only in my dreams, after he died in the war. I was
so young then that I never really knew what he was like. But I
will always remember the terrible gap I felt after he was gone."
Her face was pulled by all kinds of taut lines. It was not very
often that Ditta talked about her childhood.

"Béla's mother, on the other hand," she went on, "continued to be a strong reality behind him for a lifetime, and the
close relationship that existed between them never lessened as
long as she was alive. And perhaps this was one of the reasons
why he remained all that time so completely unaware of his
own age."

Ditta smiled, as if to pass these thoughts off lightly. "And
neither did the great difference between his age and mine ever
occur to him at any time. For that matter, I never thought of
it, either, until recently, and only because I am asked the question every once in a while these days by a nurse or a doctor how
old my husband is, and when I am made to say out loud 'He
is just a little over sixty,' I can't believe it myself. And it makes
me feel strange to mark him like this with a definite limit of
time. For whenever he surrenders himself to his work of creation, as now, he seems to become free of all earthly ballast,
and even sickness can no longer hold its power over him."

And it was in the flow of thoughts like these that Ditta
found the means to restore her own inner forces.

From the first day of her arrival, I had been fearing the moment when she would inquire about the lost cat. But I had no reason at all to be apprehensive, for she did not mention him at all until the end of her visit, and then in such an even and calm way that she might have been referring to the most natural development in the world.

"So Puss-Puss took to wandering in those lovely woods. I only hope he is really happy there, for I am afraid he was in great need of a little happiness. But still I wish," she went on, "he could tear himself away for a short while, just to let me see him and put my hand on him for a second."

And the cat did appear one day when Ditta and I were walking in the woods. He came on us swiftly and lay down silently on the ground in front of Ditta. It all happened so fast that she jumped back at first, bewildered, and only realized a minute later that she had seen her own cat. And by then it was too late, for as she leaned down to touch him he was already gone.

"Cat!" she cried after him, pleading, but he did not come again.

We had almost reached home before Ditta remarked sadly, "It is just like everything else these days. All real things are eluding me, and I seem to be living in the haze of a dream."

Ditta had returned to Saranac before Péter arrived. He came with the definite purpose of rescuing his cat from the woods, and he went about it with his usual ingenuity and patience.

From the storm windows and doors he found in the barn he built several large comfortable cages, each with its own harmless trap, and placed them at strategic points all over the neighborhood. During his early morning inspection tours he found many different kinds of prisoners: a very young skunk in one cage, and an angry squirrel running wildly around in another, and once, even, an outraged raccoon.

Finally, the cat himself! There never was a happier face than Péter's when he knocked on my door practically at dawn with a very lean and disheveled cat resting in his arms. It was a triumphant moment for both of them, the cat clinging tightly to Péter, safe and calm, his eyes half closed, as wan and listless as a sleepy child.

Péter put the cat in his own bed, and for the rest of that morning the entire household was busy carrying offerings upstairs, until the whole floor of Péter's room was covered with an assortment of tempting food. And even after Péter left Riverton, the cat remained in his room, and lay on the bed all day long, disinterested and melancholy, with no desire to wander out of sight again.

In the end I had to give him up, because back in my New York apartment my cat Lulu, usually so very tame, fought him with wild fury, though he never tried to defend himself or to supplant her in any way. What a relief it was when I found some people who became attached to him and were eager to have him. But they were not to keep him, not even as long as a day, as he found a way of escaping from their apartment almost as soon as he was taken there, without even touching the first meal that was offered to him. And I could not stop asking myself if it wouldn't have been better if we had left him in the woods, where he was learning to live in his own way among the sheltering, rooted things.

How he fared in the deafening noise and clutter of the city, among the unprotecting stone houses no one ever knew, for all search for him was in vain, and he was never found again.

23

BARTOK AND DITTA came back from Lake Saranac in the late fall and moved into the Hotel Woodrow at 85th Street on the West Side.

When I went to see them there and was greeted by Bartók, I found him so completely changed, with so little resemblance to any of the pictures I had of him in my mind, that a strange feeling came over me. It was not only as if I were meeting Bartók for the first time, but also as if this meeting were taking place sometime in the past, long before he came to America. And as if all that had happened in the so-near past never happened at all.

For when I saw Bartók at the Baloghs', only a few days after his arrival from Europe, the fear was already beginning to grow in him that it would be impossible to continue his creative work here for a long time, if ever at all, since he could not see in the tangled maze of problems ahead of him a resting point, a continuum of time free from the pressure of establishing a new day-to-day existence in completely strange circumstances. And so whatever move he chose to make would be accompanied by the hopelessness that it was only to carry him farther from his goal.

But now, on his return from Saranac, a new aliveness was radiating from him, filling and vibrating the atmosphere of the drab hotel room, an energy that seemed almost too strong to be held in by the cramped walls of that place. His strong active steps around the room were an instantly visible sign of his improved health and renewed spirit, denying the oppressive smallness of his quarters and suggesting a freedom of sweeping fields stretching around him without limits in all directions.

It was only after a while that the apartment shrank into reality, and I became aware of a bed that reached through the doorless opening of the dark bedroom almost into the living room, and the piles of books and music that covered almost all the floor. The clutter inside, the noise from the corridor outside, and the rattle of the rushing cars below in the street went entirely unnoticed by either Bartók or Ditta, losing all importance now like so many other things that had mattered so much before.

Except for our greetings, I believe no words were spoken until Bartók turned to me with the question: "I wonder if you would be interested in taking a look at my score of the *Concerto for Orchestra?*" And he took my arm gently, leading me to a small table, where he lifted out of a drawer a thick sheaf of papers. He switched on a light and stood beside me as I slowly turned its pages.

"Even if you are too lazy to follow a score, and are interested only in books besides, at least you may see for yourself how many notes I wrote!" His tone was friendly, and only mildly teasing.

I was too moved even to attempt reading the score, and could see nothing except a blurred mass of notes before me as I stood there turning the pages, unable to speak. The first work he had done here! These words ran through my mind so strongly that I felt as if I had spoken them out loud. A handful of fruit, the first harvest of these long hard years. This thought alone made everything seem right and good, and not in vain. The vibrancy I had felt in the air ever since I entered the room was touching me now, as if through the contact of my fingers with the pages.

"But what nobody could possibly see in this score," Bartók was saying in a lively, confiding way as he took the pages from me and put them back in the drawer, "is that through working on this concerto, I have discovered the wonder drug I needed to bring about my own cure. And like so many other discoveries, it just happened accidentally, and was only a by-product of what was of true importance to me, and I was almost unaware, at the time, that it was happening."

As I was leaving, Ditta followed me out into the dark hall, and I was surprised to see that now, out of Bartók's presence, her brightness had faded away from her, as if it had been no more than a reflection of his own intense brightness, and she was left almost as uncertain and shadowlike as in Vermont. She held on to my hand tightly. "You see," she said, "why I believe in miracles."

Long after I left them, I was still overcome by the immense change that had taken place in Bartók, and felt the impact of his new lightheartedness and hope as strongly as I used to feel, so many times before, the different hues and intensities of his dark hopelessness. Now I realized that in spite of all his varied moods, I had never seen him happy before, with this strong and natural joy suffusing his entire being.

Although this freely flowing joy went quickly underground, yet a general hopefulness remained with them as Bartók's health kept on improving, and he felt assured that his first completed work in America was only a beginning, and he had finally entered into a new period of creativity. Compared with the years in the Riverdale apartment, when time seemed to stand frozen, those few weeks the Bartóks spent in the Hotel Woodrow were crowded with happenings.

"To be reborn and return to life gives me a joy that seems to bear no relationship to all the worn-out dogma I have heard on this theme," Bartók remarked one evening, his voice light yet not entirely free of that note of seriousness he could inject into any seemingly unimportant conversation.

"To be awakened one day, even from a few degrees this side of death, and not by the sound of trumpets but only by the slow trickle of alive minutes passing evenly like rain. To feel dissolving within you the crushing bulk of solidified time; to move, free of all ballast, with the flow of days again. To use the hours in that steady, well-remembered rhythm which has carried you for a lifetime, and put your trust in it once more. If that's what it means to be reborn, I understand now why this concept has taken such a strong hold on the imagination of people for so many centuries."

His feeling of elation grew as offers, arrangements and events were all occurring simultaneously, each one appearing as a new miracle, entirely unexpected and unhoped for at this late date.

This seemed to be the time for Bartók's wishes to turn into realities. During all these years he had been waiting to hear his Violin Concerto, whose first performance in Amsterdam he had been unable to attend. Then the solo part had been played by his friend, Zoltán Székely, to whom the Concerto was dedicated, and now at last it was to be performed in Carnegie Hall, this time by Tossy Spivakovsky, in October 1943.

"Strange," he remarked, still deeply moved, after the performance, "although all this time I imagined that I would hear this work someday played in this country by Jóska [Joseph Szigeti]; yet Spivakovsky brought it to life exactly according to my original image of it."

The sudden and unexpected reappointment for another six months at Columbia University, after he had been made to view the project as definitely and finally ended, meant yet another abandoned hope renewed. It was fortunate Bartók did not know and never suspected that the Alice M. Ditson Fund — the source of his salary — this time was supplemented by contributions collected, with Szigeti's, Reiner's and others' cooperation, from various organizations, like orchestras, music publishers, recording companies, and many individuals.

Bartók was ready to begin his work at Columbia at once, for his health seemed to be holding as the weeks went by, although he was wearing it with a little more wisdom and caution than he had at the time when he returned from Lake Saranac. So it was a sobering blow to him, a disturbing disappointment, when his doctors advised him to postpone this appointment for a while and not even think about it until the fall of 1944.

I wonder if Bartók would have accepted this suggestion with such mild opposition if two other opportunities had not presented themselves at just about the same time. One was a tentative arrangement made by ASCAP for Bartók to spend the winter months in Asheville, to guard his improved health further. The other was a commission offered to him by Menuhin for a violin composition.

As soon as Bartók realized that these two developments, coming at the same time, formed again the ideal situation, as the Koussevitsky commission and his first trip to Saranac had the previous summer, he instantly began to immerse himself in the contemplation of this new work, and a wide ring of detachment spread slowly around him, separating him from all present reality. And he would have liked nothing better than to transport himself into that promising situation he was anticipating so eagerly.

But in actuality it was not quite so easy to bypass everything else that lay in between the present life in New York and the winter to come in Asheville. In this month of November 1943, an event of great significance awaited him: Menuhin was to play Bartók's First Violin and Piano Sonato in Carnegie Hall. Even more than the importance of having this work performed, it meant a great deal to hear it played by Menuhin, for Bartók admired Menuhin as an outstanding artist, and counted him among those very few for whom he had a warm personal liking besides. And that meant indeed a very strong liking, for Bartók demonstrated in his day-to-day life either strong likes or strong indifferences, and nothing in between.

Of course, he had feelings of concentrated hatred, too, but these were reserved for and directed toward those almost symbolic figures he considered to be elements of evil; and it made no difference to the actual force of his emotion whether these individuals lived far back in history or whether they were forging their harmful and destructive deeds right now, in our present time.

When finally the day of the performance came, I called for them at the Hotel Woodrow as planned, with not much time to spare to get to Carnegie Hall before the concert was to begin. When I arrived there to my surprise I found that Ditta, usually so very prompt, had not even begun to get dressed as yet and was moving around the bedroom in such a slow and dazed way I could not imagine how she would ever be ready to leave in time. When I reminded her it was getting late and offered my help, she merely sat down on the bed, putting an end to her slow preparations altogether.

Bartók, already bundled up in his winter coat, was sitting in the living room on a small straight chair, unaware of what was going on in the other room and as if he were completely withdrawn into the immense pool of silence that lay around him.

"Perhaps you ought to go on alone," I said, crashing into his detachment almost against my will. "I have a cab waiting downstairs."

Bartók merely drew a long horizontal line in the air with a softly relaxed hand, not as an answer but only to make me silent.

It seemed forever before Ditta was ready to leave, but we arrived at the concert just as it began and took what seats we could find in the very last row, sitting down in the already darkened hall.

With the first sound of the violin, Bartók's detached mood disappeared, and he followed with active participation Menuhin's playing throughout the Bach Sonata, his intensity increasing when the performance of his own work began and growing steadily until the very last sound subsided. And he always remembered this interpretation of his First Violin Sonata by Menuhin as one of great beauty and integrity.

Ditta remembered that concert, too, long after Bartók had gone to Asheville and the apartment in the Hotel Woodrow had become a thing of the past.

"I don't know what came over me that day," she said, as if out of an uneasy conscience. "Perhaps because Béla's moods always extend in such large circles around him, there seemed to be no surface left untouched in that crowded place to allow me to move in my own rhythm. So there were times when I found myself almost hypnotized into inertia."

After Bartók's departure for Asheville, Ditta planned to stay with me until she could find a suitable place for herself. At first we looked around lightheartedly, but when Ditta realized how much harder it was to find a place now than at the time when they had taken the Riverdale apartment, she began to be restless and impatient.

There were days when she cut herself away in complete isolation, as if barricading herself into a corner of her own, and did not seem to care how much motion was going on around her as long as she was not approached directly and felt that she could remain unnoticed. But then, like a coin flipped over, she would return, eager for laughter and filling every minute of her days with activity.

Her freshly washed clothes were constantly hung dripping and drying in the bathroom, and whenever I mentioned to her that I never failed to receive a cold shower when I went in there, she answered me greatly amused.

"At last you've found out the secret of my tremendous wardrobe of 'always new' clothes, the infamous luxury and extravagance that is so widely talked about."

"I've never heard it," I told her, although of course I had heard it mentioned by mutual acquaintances — how much money she must spend to look so immaculately dressed all the time.

"Don't try to fool me," she said. "Most everybody I know talks about it." This did not disturb her at all, in fact she felt rather proud of it.

"I don't know how it came about, but I am just unable to wear anything a second time without refreshing it with soap and water. Washing, ironing, steaming out every wrinkle — I've become a real expert. Perhaps because Béla loves the pure smell of freshly dried clothes, while the slightest staleness makes him feel almost sick.

"Besides, it's hard to keep up with Béla when it comes to cleanliness. He is not at all interested in having his things washed all the time, but that is because he doesn't need to; he seems to be made of a substance dirt cannot cling to, and he could climb through a monumental garbage heap without the smallest speck remaining on him."

But whatever Ditta's mood, I no longer had to beware of those sudden sharp irritations that used to lead her into such fearful depths. They never happened any more. And now I found myself almost wishing for one of those momentary up-heavals. For no matter into what unreachable distance she had disappeared at those times, I could always follow at least part of the way and then wait for her return with much more hope than I felt now that her moods of gaiety were almost gone and I was watching her sink ever deeper into sadness and resignation. And even physically she seemed to be affected, getting smaller from day to day, huddled into herself, always occupying the least possible amount of surface, as if a sea of danger were lapping around her and she could find protection and safety only within herself.

As the days went by, she hardly ever retired to her bedroom at night, but would remain sitting in the corner of the sofa in the living room, looking at books and music, just as if it were daytime. Often she made coffee for herself in the small kitchen, and the penetrating aroma would draw me out of my room, and I would join her in the living room, drinking cup after cup of the dark strong drink she brewed in the middle of the night.

"I have the strangest dreams here in your house." It was hard for her to find words, yet she was eager to speak.

"It seems to me, now that Béla has disappeared into his work, with all his emotions and energies poured into that alone and drawing his own boundaries closer and closer around him, I am the one who has to take over his homesickness and keep it alive, and blame myself, besides, for having felt so completely free of it all this time. My mind seems to be occu-pied by our home in Buda, and I see images of our gardens, the shapes of the flower beds, and the way our house looked inside, as if I were lying in my own bed there, knowing that my bare feet could carry me from one end of the house to the other in the quiet darkness.

"Night after night I have the same dream, compelling me to go and search for our old home, and although it takes a long time, it always happens that I get there somehow, after tremendous hardship and often not without actual pain. In a moment of great joy I recognize 'Csalán ut,' and see our house in front of me, but at the same time I remember that we moved out of it before we left, and took all our possessions away. But, strangely, it seems that all those pieces of furniture found their way back to the house of their own accord, and arranged themselves again exactly the way they used to be, except that now they are standing with their faces turned toward the wall as if they were hiding, and I cannot turn them around, although I try and try and almost collapse trying. And all at once, I know they have to hide themselves this way, because my presence there means great danger to their safety, and I make a feeble attempt to run away or hide, but I'm unable to do either. As I stand there, helplessly, all of those inanimate objects are becoming as vulnerable and alive as people.

"Then to my greatest horror, I realize that a few pieces of our furniture from the Riverdale apartment have followed me to Buda and it dawns on me that merely on account of my being there all these innocent objects will suffer terribly and will die one by one a most agonizing death. And a pointing finger is raised toward me, as if saying I am the cause of all this destruction and many other things, and all that is happening to Béla too.

"These dreams keep on clinging to me for days — I cannot untangle myself from them. It's like being only half awake and closed in by a heavy fog, unable to see through a thickness that is heavier and stronger than any wall I could touch with my hands."

It began to be almost impossible to lure Ditta out of the house and away from the corner she had made into her own. And the harder I tried, the more resistance she developed against going out into the street at all.

However, when unexpectedly some of her friends found a small furnished apartment for her on 57th Street, she moved in there and settled down with all outward signs of contentment. She seemed to find a great sense of assurance that she was not completely alone in a strange new house, since the friends who had found the place lived only a few floors above her.

I continued to see her almost daily, for she still came to teach and practice at my place while in the process of renting a piano from Steinway. If I had not seen when she was living with me how difficult it was for her to pass the days and nights, it would never have occurred to me that she was not accepting all that was happening with complete adjustment and calm, but whenever she left I was always made to think how hard her struggle must be with the long and empty hours she had to face alone.

She had one pupil, a talented young girl who came to her twice a week. These lessons gave her some sense of purpose and momentary importance, dividing the mass of time into days, something positive to wait for. And what lessons they were! Lasting for hours, as if she were unable to end them.

"If I only felt," she once remarked, "that I could give back to this girl even the smallest part of what I've received from Béla. To be able to plant the seed exactly the right way, so that it could take hold and spread farther on its own. To be as useful, as vital, and infallible as Béla was."

She looked around, bewildered. "Did I say was? But he is, he is! Getting better and stronger every day, and working harder than ever before."

"Getting better and stronger every day" were Bartók's own words, repeated in almost every letter he wrote to Ditta from Asheville. He was getting better, while the new violin sonata was growing bigger and the winter months were moving toward spring.

A short while before Bartók was to return to the city, Ditta mentioned to me that he had been suffering from a bad cold that hung on so persistently his Asheville doctor had even feared he was perhaps developing pleurisy. Something about the offhand way Ditta communicated this news gave me an impression that all this had happened some time ago, and there was nothing left to worry about any more. And Bartók's illness had disappeared even farther into the background, because Ditta told me at the same time the other news: Bartók had completed the Sonata for Solo Violin and seemed to be very pleased with it.

The first time this "prolonged cold" of Bartók's appeared in a more serious light was after he returned to the city and had had several examinations by his New York doctors before they attempted to express their opinion: Bartók did not seem to show any symptoms of pleurisy but rather of a minor disturbance of the spleen. A few X-ray treatments were suggested as the best remedy for it.

The tiny apartment on 57th Street seemed even smaller now that Bartók had moved in, together with the huge bulk of papers that followed him wherever he went. To see him there reminded me of the last months in his old crowded room in Riverdale, where the slow days dragged along so painfully in the rhythm of the small degrees of his fever fluctuating insistently back and forth on their steady course.

Even the slips of paper were spread out the same way — all over his blanket. The only difference was that the silence so deeply guarded in his Riverdale room by the wide arms of the trees and the tall overgrown bushes was replaced here on 57th Street by the shrieking late afternoon traffic noises, which came crashing into the room and were caught there inescapably within the close, crammed walls.

That lighthearted meeting in the Hotel Woodrow after Bartók's return from Saranac no more than a few months ago, the fresh strongness of his face then, the sudden impression of renewed health had no meaning any more. All seemed to be taken back and canceled out entirely. For now it was clear — even during that period, when he appeared outwardly to be on the way to recovery — he was sinking deeper into an illness that had not taken any time out at all, but was steadily and slowly enveloping him even then.

What does it really mean, I asked myself, this "minor disturbance of the spleen," that could change his appearance so much again? Would a few X-ray treatments really take it away, or would it continue regardless, day after day, month after month? But wouldn't it add up to an earthquake then, to such a force that would carry him far beyond any help? Already the great order of his face seemed to be thrown into random lines, leaving only his eyes untouched and still familiar though sunken deep into his face, the brooding distant look in them shining like dark water from the bottom of a well.

But as soon as Bartók would begin to speak this extreme impression I had of him vanished, as if it were only a passing image created by an intricate play of light and shadow; for his voice was still his cured voice, suggesting a cured spirit, and his smile helped, too, to straighten somewhat the tangled planes of his face.

"I am well enough," he answered my usual question as to how he felt, "considering that soon there won't be any sickness left in the medical dictionary which I have not been diagnosed

as having, at one examination or another. I am a walking en-
cyclopedia of human frailties." The pencil in his hand was
moving fast as he put his small marks on the white leaves of
paper spread out before him.

"But perhaps I am not much help to the doctors, either, in
giving them the right clue, for most of the time I am uncertain myself of what my symptoms really are, and except for a
small degree of fever, which I already consider my normal
temperature, and my occasional complete lack of energy, I
have nothing to tell them.

"Actually it is not the worst thing that could happen, to be
convalescing like this and to be able to pour every minute of
the time into work — although perhaps it is hard on you," he
turned to Ditta, "to move around as silently as a mouse all
the time, and not be able to use the piano you went to so much
trouble getting. As for myself, looking at that big shiny instrument gives me only a pang of sadness. It makes me realize
finally that my piano-playing days are over for ever, although I
must admit that in spite of my aching arm it's still a luxury
to feel the keys underneath my fingers now and then. Yet
there is a feeling of remorse that in order to spare me, you
cannot plunge into practicing as freely as you would enjoy."

"But I have learned so well how to practice in my mind,"
she reassured him quickly, "the way you taught me, and the
way I used to do during our trips, in hotel rooms, and even on
trains. Please don't think for a minute that I am idle these
days. I wish you knew how many interesting things are happening during those long hours of work I do in silence."

"Why, of course," Bartók said, readily accepting Ditta's
remark. "One has so much more room to hear if left entirely
free and not confined to sounds."

"Well, at least it's a relief," Ditta said after we left the
room, "that Béla doesn't realize how starved one gets not

working on the piano most of the time. But he cannot find anything wrong with his life now that he is composing. It is only when he cannot solve his working problems that all things seem to be reflecting their dark side toward him. Then at those times the best of conditions becomes meaningless to him as he tries to clear himself of all obstacles, and feels tortured by the most innocent objects lying in his way. And this accusing and helpless anger makes him feel more thoroughly ill than when he is actually very sick. But when he is free to arrange his twenty-four hours in any way he desires, as now in his abandonment to the process of creating, everything from the smallest annoyance to the most tragic happening is swallowed up by the hungry churning waves of his work."

And that is exactly how it was. Although life was reduced to a confined space, and was unvaried from one day to the next, there was a steady sense of satisfaction in every hour of it; and if Bartók ever complained at all, it was only because of his desire for a still greater frugality and an all-over rigid austerity in these crucial and decisive days of the war.

"But I thought sugar was a rare commodity these days," he remarked in his old irritated way once when Ditta poured a heaping spoonful into his coffee.

"I got this with a special card given to you," Ditta explained, "to have while convalescing."

"But that's all wrong," he shook his head. "There ought to be many more important uses for it these days. Please remember, do not get it for me any more."

His great anguish over the war — his hopelessness over its slow progress, and the collapse of so many of the small but complete worlds he had known — was not spoken of any more. It was only expressed by his eagerness for personal sacrifice, and it seemed to reassure him that there were signs that the effects of the war had finally reached into our everyday life, and that everyone was being called on to contribute at least in some small measure.

"I saw a long line standing for bread," he said one day on arriving home, as if relating some exciting good news.

He could not possibly imagine that this long line might be standing for anything else but bread, for this had become the symbol of the most dire and basic needs of those other motionless long lines winding endlessly in the streets of Hungary which he no doubt remembered from the other war. He quite naturally wished to believe that the line he had seen in New York was also standing for bread, and most likely would have refused to believe it if anyone had suggested to him that these people were waiting for meat, or even perhaps for nylon stockings. And it could have been that the line he saw was not quite as long as it grew to be in his imagination.

The X-ray treatments began, and Bartók spent a large part of his time trying to rest away the tiring effect they seemed to leave behind. But he did not appear at all discouraged.

"Perhaps the fact that I am so deeply stirred by these treatments means that they are reaching down to the very source of my illness, and it is only a question of time for the cure to follow."

"Would you like to hear," he asked me one day, "the most recent example I have been able to add to my collection of names that have been given to my illness throughout the years?" And as I shook my head, he drew a deep breath before he pronounced it slowly: "Polycythemia."

"Since this diagnosis is already quite old, I can't promise you that it would still stand today. But no matter, for since my illness has been christened with such an impressive name it seems to make little difference to me any more.

"At the beginning of all this, I did feel a great need to know exactly what was wrong, and what was in store for me, in order to make my plan how to meet it. But by now I understand how little difference a name can make. I must have needed all this time to realize that I would have preferred to keep this disease of mine nameless. For now an understanding is growing clearer in me day after day, that none of these fatal illnesses are completely separated from one another, and each includes within itself almost all the inexhaustible symptoms and characteristics of the others, forming a large family circle, closely related by blood. For nature is working steadily ahead with immense purposeful care to make it unfailingly certain that the new layer of shoots, ever stirring on their way and pushing up through the old, will be provided with room and nourishment by them, in the final completion of the cycle.

"Why couldn't all these fatal illnesses be called by a general and calm-sounding name like 'Malady,' embracing them all together? A mere warning, standing for all that is to be, the fate we were given over to as soon as we came into being, a firm reminder of that monumental common home that is awaiting us all."

Bartók's voice sounded like a single instrument, as he spoke on with immense calmness, like someone who had long ago turned away from the disturbing chaos of the close view, and was reflecting only from an infinite distance the final meaning of complete order.

I heard Ditta's muffled moan, and after a while Bartók's quiet voice again.

"But what's wrong with what I said?" he asked, surprised. "I didn't say anything new — only repeated what you've heard from me a hundred times before in the woods. You didn't think that we humans were outside the law, did you? Wouldn't it be monstrous if we weren't counted in? Isn't it soothing to you to be part of that great design?"

Ditta's eyes, tightly closed, drew her features into deep lines, and one could almost see that her ears were just as forcefully shut, making her face as small and colorless as a withered apple in the grass.

"I wasn't saying, don't forget, that it will happen today or tomorrow," Bartók said to her strongly. "But I still remember that it could have been yesterday, and how thankful I am that it didn't come then. For I am in great need of a length of undisturbed time, and so I am counting hopefully on gaining a postponement."

He leaned back against his pillows, as if he had said all and more than he intended. But Ditta still did not move, her small face remaining clenched in its tight, frozen lines, and it seemed that she was refusing even to draw a breath.

Bartók turned directly to her, changing his serious tone into teasing.

"But right now everyone can see that I am just approaching my prime, and have even gained twelve pounds in the bargain, and so increased my food value as nourishment for the new shoots. And since man does not live by bread alone, I am at the same time intent upon increasing the spiritual legacy I hope to leave behind me. For there is nothing more deeply disturbing to me than the thought of carrying any of my work back with me unborn. I'd like to take my final leave as stripped and empty-handed as I came.

"What is it you find so wrong with all this?" he asked Ditta, for she was still as rigid as before.

"I just can't bear it," she said finally, with difficulty. "The way you made it so terribly real."

"On the contrary, I'm afraid I didn't make it real enough," Bartók answered her. "For if I had, you would naturally understand that I was only trying to draw the inevitable conclusion, and I merely added to that my own personal desire to postpone my final leavetaking until I have completely emptied the rucksack on my back."

But as Ditta remained inconsolable, Bartók spoke to her as if she were a child.

"Then there is only one other thing I can try to do for you — to put all this down on paper, so you can decipher it in your own way. So far you have never failed to grasp my meaning when it was turned into a score."

But Ditta hurried out of the room without giving the slightest indication that she heard him at all. It was not until much later that I learned how well she took in every single word that was spoken that afternoon.

24

EACH TIME WHEN Bartók emerged from one of his periodic relapses, as in this late spring, he seemed to be infused with such a forceful sense of general well-being that no less than a complete recovery seemed to be the eventual next step. An immense relief spread throughout the atmosphere with featherweight swiftness, lifting life far above the confining sickroom, and plans already abandoned many times naturally crowded back into focus to be pursued with much more insistent hope than before. These plans, however, always remained a step behind fulfillment, and kept on falling away as if by their own accord, for they were never allowed time enough to ripen into reality.

Now Bartók was no longer floating aimlessly, but was caught up and pulled by the mainstream and given the hope that he perhaps would have a chance to release his own energy into its current. The few performances of his works in Carnegie Hall were not single unconnected events any more, but the natural result of a slowly growing knowledge and acceptance of him on the part of the public, and he was elated by a sensation of gaining a foothold here, and of being discovered anew.

Now, for the first time he was being made to feel sought

after by great conductors, while performing artists were offering him commissions for specific works. And he felt reassured by the realization that he had the freedom to fulfill these commissions without any financial worries, and in peaceful surroundings. Furthermore, as the immediate steps ahead of him seemed unobstructed, he began to visualize his long vista of undisturbed time, and the accomplishment of all those works it was still imperative for him to create.

It was arranged by ASCAP again that Bartók's entire summer would be spent at Lake Saranac. And the name Saranac alone meant work accomplished, and the promise of a cure.

But it was the security of a probable annual income, from various sources, of around three thousand dollars for two or three years to come that gave Bartók the greatest satisfaction and confidence enough to plan on taking an apartment again, to move the furniture out of the Bronx warehouse and make an attempt to get settled as they had been at Riverdale. For there was no question in their minds but that Bartók would be able to take up the postponed work at Columbia by next fall.

With this assurance Ditta and I did set out one day to look for an apartment in the vicinity of Columbia University. At first we only walked around, turning from one side street to another, getting the feel of the place. Ditta seemed delighted with the small brownstone houses and began to visualize their life in one of them, dwelling on the thought of how very pleasant it would be for Bartók to be able to walk back and forth to Columbia and for Péter to be near the subway to use in going to school when he lived home again.

But in spite of the words Ditta spoke, I felt all along that she was only going through the motions of following a hope so weightless that it drifted in the air and never for a moment touched the reality of the ground. It was no more than a vague wish that their life, so painfully interrupted by Bartók's illness, could take on an undisturbed continuity again.

The apartment we found, however, was not in one of those homelike brownstone houses, but on the top floor of a tall building on 110th Street.

The first thing we saw as we opened the door was a bulky upright piano, left in the long hall.

"Oh," said Ditta, backing toward the door as if touched by a sudden fear. Almost instantly I became aware that, like those pieces of furniture in her dreams, this piano was standing turned toward the wall. Before I realized what I was doing, I found myself swinging the clumsy object around, and as soon as the piano was turned toward her Ditta cautiously came nearer, forcing herself to touch the keys, but she was again taken aback by the booming raw sound she had released.

Then, grateful for the comfort of being afraid of something that was not a nightmare, she gave way to relieved laughter. As if trying to tame a wild beast, she approached the keys very gently again, and bending over them began to play, and even sang a few words from one of my favorite Bartók songs, as if she remembered the joy I had always found in it ever since I had heard them play it together at their first concert in America.

"If it was really meant to be left here, maybe we could get it fixed up a bit, and own a piano again!" In the excitement of this thought, she actually started to run from room to room at random, without trying to keep track of them or to take them in at all.

"Look at this light and space!" she was saying. "Ample room for all of us. Room enough to give Béla the kind of privacy he needs, and for Péter and his machines! Really too much for me, almost like being out in the open air after all those cramped places we have been living in this last year."

I thought Ditta would never leave, she lingered so long in every room, standing at one window and then another, as if trying to plant herself there, looking at bathrooms and closets and kitchen equipment, but obviously not really seeing anything. She seemed to know that this was the only time she would ever live there, and she wanted to make this single occasion last a long time.

"I am almost sure we will take it," she said when we were out on the street again. Her mind was already working on how to present this apartment most favorably to Bartók.

"A hundred dollars a month," she said as if she were trying the sound of it. "I wish I could say instead that it was ninety-nine. It would seem like so much less when we have to describe it to the authorities." While Ditta often referred to these "authorities" whenever any final decision had to be made, she never really told me who these people were. But I presumed that probably they consisted of Bartók's doctors and various representatives of the ASCAP.

And although I met Ditta day after day, following our "successful" apartment hunting, and expected her to tell me what decision, if any, had been arrived at, she never made the slightest allusion to the apartment again, and never would have, perhaps, if I had not finally brought it up myself.

"Oh," she said, shrugging her shoulders indifferently, "the general opinion seems to be that it might be better not to take any apartment right now, but rather wait until we come back from Lake Saranac and, who can tell, we might even find that place still empty then." Her voice strayed off into complete evasiveness, "Or come upon another one just as good or perhaps even better."

So the plan of taking an apartment remained unchanged and became again postponed a little deeper into the future, until the time when Bartók's work at Columbia would begin and the need to settle down would become a more immediate necessity. Meanwhile, they felt fortunate to be able to hold on to their apartment on 57th Street, although even that seemed uncertain for a while. They had only a sublease there that had never been fully accepted by the landlord, and it was not likely to be renewed when it ran out toward the end of the year.

The early summer was already spreading a heavy breathless haze over the city, flooding the Bartóks' 57th Street apartment with motionless liquid heat. The thought alone that the transparently fresh atmosphere of Lake Saranac was only a few short weeks away was in itself an escape.

Bartók's papers were already spread out to be packed, separated from one another in neatly arranged piles with rubber bands and strings. He not only refused, horrified, the help Ditta and I offered him, but made us promise never to touch these papers at any time, for any reason, whether he was outside of the room for a moment or away from the house for days or weeks because of some unforeseen emergency. The papers slowly disappeared into their boxes, and by the time I came to make a last visit before leaving the city, they had vanished completely.

Coming to say goodbye this way and finding Ditta among the half-filled suitcases had already taken on a traditional feeling. Talking about Riverton and Ditta's promise to come to visit me there sometime during the summer had become part of the ritual.

But this was perhaps the first time since Bartók had left Vermont almost three years ago that he allowed himself to talk about Riverton. He was resting in his room, and his voice coming through the open door gave his words a stronger impact than he meant to give them.

"I could only permit myself to think about that place if I were fully reassured that Matthew's tottering barn, together with his long-suffering animals were mercifully swallowed up and well covered by the earth."

Although he was in the other room, I could still visualize, just as if we were face to face, the pained expression in his eyes.

"Surely you know that Béla didn't mean what he said about Riverton," Ditta offered soothingly, when she saw me to the door. "You must know that he doesn't feel like that at all. It is only that he cannot resist teasing you, and nothing more. Just wait and see how glad he will be to go there again some-day, one of these summers to come."

But while Ditta attempted to take away the sting of Bartók's words, she only succeeded in arousing a fear in me by so openly revealing the insistent hold she had on her hopes in spite of the meager nourishment they received.

I hardly knew what disturbed me more: the unreality of these hopes of Ditta's or the thought of Bartók arriving in Riverton again and occupying his room in my Vermont house when I knew with such finality that it could never happen.

And Ditta herself did not come again. In her occasional letters from Saranac during the summer, she never failed at first to talk about coming to Riverton just as soon as the improvement in Bartók's health should become more of a certainty. And no matter how short her visit would have to be, she still wanted to come, even if for no more than a day. However, later on all references to this proposed visit had completely disappeared from her more and more infrequent notes. She wrote only of birds and water, and how Bartók was teaching her about the stars from the clear map of the bright August sky. And then it was fall again, and we were all back in New York once more.

The summer months at Lake Saranac went by without producing the miraculous healing that had been anticipated with such complete faith. Bartók arrived home without feeling any better, but not much worse either, than when he left. That in itself was considered as progress this time.

The need for a new apartment did not exist any more, and just as if it had been their plan all along, the Bartóks went back to their place on 57th Street. Nor was Bartók's work at Columbia mentioned even as a possibility.

"Béla will most likely have a few private pupils," Ditta told me, as if this were the best news she ever had for me.

Bartók looked well enough as he sat fully dressed at his table near the window when I went to see them for the first time since their return. I could not tell whether his face, under its hue of healthy sunburn, actually looked better or worse than it did when he had left for his vacation.

By now I remembered Bartók's face in so many different ways, my memory of him had undergone so many changes that what once struck me as the most strange became the best known to me, and the constant changes themselves appeared so familiar that I seemed to lose my sensitivity to all the nuances. And even more so because these changes did not succeed each other in regular progression, but occurred in irrelevant leaps back and forth from one extreme to the other, often bypassing the in-between stages, until finally I could not tell any more his new and unknown face from the old and known.

I felt very conscious this time of how impossible it was to avoid disturbing him, either in his work or his rest, within the close walls of this place, where there was no corner to retreat to and leave him in privacy. Maybe I felt it so strongly now because Ditta was out when I called, for she never failed to improvise some sort of shelter for him, no matter how inadequate their quarters were.

"Tell me," he asked, hardly leaving time for a greeting, and disregarding my customary self-conscious questions about how he was feeling and what kind of summer he had spent, "Tell me, what ever happened to that poor cat of Péter's?"

His question surprised me, coming so unexpectedly after all this time, for he had never given the slightest indication that he noticed the absence of the cat at all.

"I keep on wishing," he went on, "that he has found a life as good as he deserved. At any rate, a better one than we were able to give him. It was at the wrong time he came to us," he shook his head sadly, "and how I wish he had never come. It was only adding one more straw to the load on my conscience, heavy enough with the thought of all the suffering animals keep on enduring from our hands. I often feel that something went wrong at the very beginning of time that left a hopeless void between us and the other living creatures who were here even before us, for I believe originally we were meant to share the earth with each other as brethren, and perhaps we would be less lonely if we had."

"But Péter's cat at least," I said in a hurry, "is happy now, very much loved, and has a wonderful home. In the country," I added after a while, looking at his narrow, sad face, and into his deeply sunken eyes.

"This is good news," he said, "indeed a great relief. It was very disturbing to me whenever I happened to think of him."

But no more was said about the cat, for Ditta had just come in, and Bartók turned the conversation to the papers in front of him.

"Perhaps these pages look the same as all those others I used to work on," he began. "However, this is the Walachian collection I am eager to put in order. Don't ask me the reason why I am so determined to do this, for most likely this work will follow the fate of my Romanian collection that took a lifetime to prepare, only to be buried alive in a Columbia University library." He stopped for a minute, but went on again with even more force.

"But perhaps someone has to provide the material to be sunk into oblivion and fill up those dusty archives, although I think that the tremendous bulk of my Romanian collection should be considered a fair enough contribution from me."

In spite of Bartók's ruefulness over the fate of his Romanian collection, he kept on working relentlessly on the Walachian, giving it every moment he could posibly spare.

"Don't you think that Béla must be feeling much stronger than he looks these days?" Ditta asked me once. "For he has never had such endurance before. In the past he always used to put aside his song collection whenever he was composing. But now he just goes from one to the other. For playing with those songs, he says, provides him with just the kind of relaxation he needs the most. But I can't help wondering how he will ever be able to keep this up, since he has more work planned ahead than at any time I can remember."

Just about this time Bartók was offered yet another commission, for a duo-piano composition, by the well-known piano team of Bartlett and Robertson. He accepted it only tentatively, including it among all those other works he was hoping to fulfill in the near future.

"He did have a good reason for this, of course," Ditta told me in such a pointed way that I instantly questioned her about it. But her answer was reluctant and evasive.

"Oh, some other composition he was thinking about for a long time now, the one he promised to write for me," she finally confessed, then turned away quickly to hide her embarrassment.

Once she had gone this far, however, she seemed almost glad to go on talking about it.

"Strange, how I never believed that Béla was really serious when he said he would put into music for me those ideas that were whirling so insistently around in his mind that terrible afternoon when he was unable to resist heaping up those frightful images of life and death until they became branded right into me, so thoroughly that perhaps they will never entirely come to a stop in my mind as long as I live. They are here with me right now," she said, putting her hands over her ears and keeping them glued there even as she continued to speak.

"It was perhaps the first time I really understood the story Béla had unfolded to me over and over again ever since I can remember. The innocent story of the fresh green shoots creeping over and covering the rotting tree trunks did not seem innocent any more, and I could not explain to myself how I could have remained blind for so long to its final meaning. And in that sudden flash of insight I was carried even farther, and all at once I was made to recognize in his music, too, that same life and death theme.

"Not that I have ever failed to hear in any of his compositions those heaving turning motions, sensing their presence long before they were fully unfolded, no matter how many different disguises they assumed in each case, as they were slowly approaching, in unearthly rhythms inevitably flowing into a distant stillness and calm. Yes, I know well the lulling smoothness of that slow-moving river, the pain of it, so tender, so far removed from anguish. But ever since that afternoon the abstract beauty has changed into something heartbreaking. Something that I am unable to bear. That ever-flowing river is sweeping him away now into eternity. Everything is linked to him now, and I wonder if I can ever listen to any of his work again."

She closed her head within her hands and rocked it up and

down as if she were crying, but when she looked up again her eyes were dry and searching, and her words became so intense that she could only whisper them.

"But if the passing of living things is to be taken as calmly as he would like me to believe, how can you explain then the torture he felt when once he accidentally stepped on a little green frog that was crouching unseen in the grass, and picked it up as if it was the most sacred thing on earth, trying to will life back into it with the warmth of his own hands. And just think of that time in Vermont, how desperate he felt when that tiny kitten was crushed under the ironing board, and never forgave you for it, remember."

Her eyes flashed at me with a bright green glare, insisting on my answer.

"Perhaps," I said, making the lowest possible sound that still could be heard, "because those things did not have to be."

"I know. I understand," she said, her voice turning against me. "What you are trying to tell me is that with him it must be."

She left me abruptly and walked to the window, pressing her forehead against the pane. When she came back her voice was abstract and calm, completely free from the wildness it had been touched by a minute ago.

"The thought that he might not be, that he would not exist any more the way he is now, comes to me sometimes, the way the soft outline of his white hair touches the air around him and keeps him separated as he walks in that old flannel robe, noiselessly, his worn felt slippers barely touching the floor, while his own stillness moves along with him. If all that were to come to an end, how would everything be then? I only know that I would have to go and look for him in all those places where he has ever been, in all the fields he once moved through, counting every blade of grass, and on city streets under tall houses, and go on searching in all those strange places where I have never been, where he wandered alone or with others, taking in everything on his way, whatever came into his view, and beyond that. And from all those things that had remained of him I would have to bring him into being, from all he has left behind to make him be again.

"But no, no, that couldn't be!" she answered herself in a whisper so tense that only her lack of strength kept it from sounding like an outburst.

"I don't want him to write that work for me, if he is going to link all those terrible thoughts to his own fate." She left the room and I did not dare follow her.

But nevertheless the Third Piano Concerto was completed. Bartók worked on it almost to the very last, and in a way even beyond that, for he left the last seventeen measures unfinished, merely indicating with a line where the notes should be, and putting the word "End" in Hungarian at the bottom of the page.

And Ditta was not able to bear it — she did fade away when Bartók died. I do not know if she ever looked at the concerto when she became herself again, and if she did, what it told her after such a long time.

25

EXCITEMENT AND ACTIVITY seemed to make the strong grip of Bartók's illness relax again, as the first performance of the Sonata for Solo Violin was scheduled to be played in Carnegie Hall at the end of November 1944. This was the work Bartók had composed for Menuhin, and it was to be performed by him.

"Reading through this work with Menuhin," Bartók said with enthusiasm a few days before the concert, "made me realize again how naturally he is able to fathom the utmost meaning of a work without the need of a single word of explanation."

On the evening of the concert Bartók did not seem to be touched by even a shadow of illness as he leaned forward in his seat, closing out everything between his own self and the sound that came from Menuhin's violin, watching it grow with such intensity, as if a tree were spreading before him of its own accord. Or perhaps his trancelike listening merely emphasized the image that possessed me every time I listened to a performance of his work. The spell that lay around him lasted undisturbed until the tremendous applause, which took him unaware, made him realize where he was.

A spontaneous demonstration arose from the audience, and calls were sounding everywhere for him to appear. Some time passed before he understood and left his seat. By the time he reached the podium, the applause had almost subsided. However, it gained new momentum when he appeared, making a stiff bow, and then he just stood there for a moment, pale and small, visibly moved and happy.

Of this performance, Bartók said afterwards, "There was nothing left to be desired. It was far beyond all expectancy."

But the day after the concert he battled with the newspapers again, choosing as the most typical example, as he always did, the *New York Times*.

"Regardless of my own song, this reviewer is so intent upon singing that same old tune of his he cannot possibly hear the changes time has brought to my singing," he said to us. "And I almost feel now," he went on, "contrary to my past belief, that there is a way to become known, over the heads of the music critics, bypassing the obstacle of their closed minds, if one is lucky enough to come in contact with the open-minded public."

But when the most important event of all was approaching, the presentation of the first work Bartók had composed in America after his long years of silence, his doctors firmly advised him not to entertain any plan to be present at this performance, pointing out repeatedly that health must be his first consideration, and that it would not be unreasonable to assume that the excitement of a first performance and the trip to Boston could prove too much for him. For the *Concerto for Orchestra* was to be performed by the Boston Symphony on the eighth and ninth of December, 1944, and to be conducted by Koussevitzky himself. Sergei Koussevitzky was, as Bartók once said, if not actually the father then at least the godfather to this work, and so became in a way instrumental not merely to the creation of this work alone but to all those others that followed afterwards. Bartók was determined to be present at the performance, and to pay no attention to his doctors' advice.

"But how can anyone believe that it would preserve my strength to remain at home, when I am being pulled with such a strong force to go? How much more energy would be wasted by trying to keep myself away than to follow my desire to be there!"

I wondered if it was this argument that convinced his doctors to let him go in the end.

"We would never know what might have been lost, if we had not been able to be present at these concerts, and to take part in the rehearsals," Ditta told me after they came back.

"What fulfillment it was for Béla that this time he did not have to wait long years between the birth of a work and its actual presentation. And how magnificent a presentation it was! And the festivity of it all! If I could only make you see how it was, how much reverence was shown to Béla there, and the simple and sincere kindness of Koussevitzky himself. I don't think Béla ever responded so readily and with so much freedom before, and how thoroughly happy he was!"

This happiness seemed to have followed Bartók home, and it emanated from him whenever he talked about the performance in Boston. He completely lost his restrained style, expressing his admiration for the thorough and accurate understanding, and for the unusually beautiful sound of the Boston Symphony Orchestra. And he praised Koussevitzky as "a great creative maestro."

"It would be no use for me to be excessively modest about my part in this concert," he said, "for some of the inspiration Koussevitzky poured into the performance must have been supplied by my own music. He assured me of this himself, and what's more, his appreciation seemed to grow by leaps and bounds as the days went by, for though at the rehearsal he announced that this work of mine was the very best of the last twenty-five years, after the actual performance he doubled his praise by another twenty-five years, assuring me this time that it was indeed the best work of the last fifty years."

His smile broadened as he went on.

"I wondered if I shouldn't have let it go at that, and simply thanked him for his high praise, but I couldn't resist reminding him that he had said the very same thing about a work of Shostakovich he conducted not too long ago. Yet as I keep on thinking about it, although this remark of Koussevitzky's might appear like a contradiction, it wasn't actually so, for he said that about Shostakovich's composition before he heard mine, and not afterwards.

"And so from that moment on, my concerto was to be considered the best work of the last fifty years, and this will hold true until another best work emerges again, perhaps no more than a few months from now."

The amusement over this incident left him, and he became serious again. "But one thing will stand much longer than that," he said with emphasis. "No composer could have hoped for a greater performance."

A greater *last* performance — Bartók most likely would have added, if he had known then that this was the last time he would ever hear any of his work performed.

The midwinter days had no breadth or length; they seemed to turn into night as soon as they began. The cold semidarkness stood outside the Bartóks' windows threateningly, changing the place inside into a warm and safe shelter.

I was increasingly hesitant about going to see them, for it was more and more difficult for Bartók to find privacy any longer. Since it had become the rhythm of his days to feel now a little better and now a little worse, he kept on transferring his work place accordingly, from his bed in his own room to the table near the living room window, and then back to his bed again.

Ditta, however, urged me to come, and pointed out many times that it did not seem to make any difference to him any more what was going on around him. Now that it had become impossible to maintain the absolute privacy once so necessary for him when composing, he had gone to the other extreme, and accepted his present working conditions to such an extent that he didn't even glance up when the grocery boy walked in and made all the various noises of unloading his packages and stamping out again.

"In the past, it was the first law of our household to guard the silence around Béla. Even Péter knew, before he learned anything else, that he must not make a sound in the garden under his father's window, and my presence, too, in the room where he was working, would have been unthinkable trespassing, while now he hardly notices that I am there."

But feeling she had not entirely dispelled my uneasiness, Ditta continued more definitely, "But you surely can come in the late afternoon, for Béla always relaxes with a cup of coffee at that time."

Whether Bartók did relax when I came, or merely took an occasional swallow from his cup of coffee and continued to jot down his small notes in rapid tempo, at any rate he did not register annoyance at my being there.

I became aware that the borderline of his own private world now stretched from one end of the apartment to the other, and Ditta and I had become two quietly moving figures within and not outside that separating line he always drew with such precision around himself. To be within this circle and almost feel the motions of his revolving mind was hard to bear, even if I tried consciously to make myself as unseen and unheard as a shadow and although my fear of being in the way was not borne out by Bartók's behavior.

Many times after his papers were pushed aside, he would begin to talk, allowing his thoughts to spill over so abundantly that his words almost touched us with a physical impact. Sometimes it seemed as if this conversation were merely a continuation of the work he had just concluded, or as if he were talking in his sleep, or even more as if he were thinking out loud his semiconscious thoughts in the intimate, close and dark silence of his own room. Whichever it was, the actual reality of the outside world never entered into what he was saying.

It appeared as if all the happenings of the recent years had undergone an organic change and had been distilled by the utmost degrees of pain into a fluid that could only flow in and out of his mind, but could not be turned into solid words any more.

Nor did the happenings of the immediate present have any part in these late afternoon talks, although the war was moving rapidly toward victory, with more certainty than he had ever hoped. The Nazism he hated with all his strength was suffering defeat upon defeat, and the ultimate blow was sure to fall in a short time. Why was it that during the darkest period of this struggle he had insisted upon expressing in words all the horrifying scenes he could envision, while now he gave the impression that he was not even aware the long conflict was resolving itself at last? Was the reason for it, I wondered, that he did not dare to touch upon it, and was holding his breath in fear that the tide would suddenly turn back and run in the other direction again? Or did he feel that the price being paid for this victory had to be too high and heartbreakingly real?

And so, weary from working, or just weary, resting in his

darkening room lit only by a sudden wayward beam from the noisy street, he would turn, as if in self-defense, toward some thoughts that would not fail to bring him relief.

"Perhaps I realize the darkness of this winter so keenly," Bartók once said, "because I escaped these depressing days last year. That winter in Asheville was filled with birds and light. I have never seen such a concentration of bird population anywhere before, and they all seemed to congregate on a big tree right underneath my window. I was constantly amazed by the busy life they were leading there, rushing in and out of the branches on their secret missions, chattering wildly like monkeys, and sustaining for an incredibly long time this highest peak of excitement. Until finally one of those birds decided it was time to take a well-deserved rest on a leafy branch, and do a little singing on his own. And then instantly hundreds of others seemed to be moved by the same impulse, as if that tree was the Tree of Life itself, lined with hidden nests under every bough. In the early dawn there came from every single branch a faint piping sound of awakening birds, slowly swelling into such full volume as every green leaf became part of a chorus more invigorating and lively than I could ever have imagined before. And this fluid sound did not penetrate the ears alone, but seeped into the body with the strength of a powerful healing potion.

"How well I understand that those people whose lives are lived in close proximity with nature, and far away from so-called civilization, from the questionable blessing of doctors and hospitals, are still entrusting their fate to those rituals of healing song. And I am not thinking of those tribes in the depths of Africa, either, but people not any farther east than the out-of-the-way provinces of Romania, for example. I recorded many of their songs myself. They are sung most of the time by women, in persuasive, mysterious and monotone voices, penetrating with a power strong enough to carry you along. I wouldn't mind trying the magic of those songs right now. I can't wish for any better cure to yield myself up to more happily," he said, smiling.

"There are songs against sickness, and against drought, and these of course always prove to be helpful sooner or later. And there are those songs to be sung over the dead, the hardest of all to make the people perform. For what could be more frightening and against any logic than to sing those songs that were made to be sung over the dead when there is no dead one to sing for? And wouldn't it bring bad luck besides? But just the same, I did persuade some of the women to sing those songs into my machine, and I can still remember one of them staring away at the distance and not daring to rest her frightened eyes on anyone even for a second.

"There was no shortage of dead ones in the time that followed, but there were still a few peaceful years ahead of us when I first wandered into Romania — it must have been thirty-five years ago, during the summer of 1908.

"It was only curiosity that made me investigate the Romanian folklore at the beginning, and not even conscious curiosity just then. Perhaps because it was so simple and natural to take that single step across the border, and after it had begun, I could not turn back any more. At first I was lured deeper into that country by the incomparable beauty of the songs. It was like picking flowers on a wild field, so pure and abundant was the song harvest there!"

Ever since the first evening when I met Bartók at the Baloghs', he had from time to time talked about his song collecting. I began to know, almost as well as a corner of my own childhood street in Buda, those distant villages of Hungary where I had never been, the small houses with the clean smell of their earthen floors, and the people who worked those endlessly stretching fields, through the long days, unable to call as much of that earth their own as would fill the palms of their hands.

And I came to feel, too, as his stories expanded, the steady rays of the burning sun in Egypt, and could see the red and lilac sunsets in Africa, and Bartók there in the midst of a group of dark and crouching figures, preparing an evening meal in the black smoke of an open fire.

But it was to Romania that Bartók's thoughts returned, and his brooding over the unpublished Romanian collection did not subside, but kept on with growing intensity during the long winter that was to be his last. Perhaps because he spent more time collecting there than anywhere else, fifteen summers at least, gaining complete knowledge of the language and establishing many friendships that endured throughout his life. There were names like Busita János, who adopted Bartók's cause for his own, and stood by him through every phase of the collecting. And there, too, was the nameless host of people, who gave trustfully to him their kindness and warmth. But for whatever reason, that country emerged as the most vivid and personal part of his past, and the one that he always remembered with yearning.

"Just think of those ancient forests in the depth of winter, with no human footsteps marring the immaculate snow for hundreds of miles around. To wake in the mornings to the thrumming sound of silence inside a small hut, where the breath of man and animal is mingled in the proximity of dependence, keeping each other warm and alive. While outside, the trees are standing guard in their gigantic bulging capes of snow that holds them so firmly that their immobility cannot be disturbed by the wildest outburst of the wind."

"I never knew, Béla, that you were there in the wintertime," Ditta remarked when Bartók stopped for a moment.

"But of course I never was," he said, "there were no open roads to those out-of-the-way places in the middle of the winter. But I like to carry many landscapes in my mind, and I always like to dress them up in different attire to match the changing seasons. Just as I always try to dress the songs in the color of the landscapes where they were kept alive."

And even if Bartók had to stop for an occasional rest, he never failed to pick up the thread and follow to the end his line of thought.

"And the very remoteness that separates these places from civilization made my collecting so much easier there than any place else. The open responsiveness of the people and their cooperation so warmly offered eased every step on the way, giving to the work a lighthearted quick tempo.

"Perhaps I pointed out these advantages too openly and too many times, for these words must have contributed to the hostility against me that was slowly building up at home.

"But of course during the excitement and joy of collecting I could barely afford to spend myself by giving too much attention to the rumblings that resounded in growing volume around me. After a while I began to take it for granted that I was being attacked from both sides of the border, and as long as there was much more work to be done than time to do it, I decided that the best remedy was to close my ears to the disturbing noises. So around the year 1912 I simply withdrew from every form of public appearance. It was not until the war was over that the waves of animosity met right above my head and I had to stop and stand still to listen to the full force of the outcry. The first thing I noticed was how cruelly I was assaulted in my own country, where in a momentary outburst of anger some extremists actually went so far as to call me a traitor, while in Romania they merely accused me of falsifying some of my findings and even challenged my full understanding of the language. But as long as I felt that no question could be raised over my understanding of the Romanian folklore, nor could any shadow be cast on my deep feeling for my own country, I was not at all hurt, but awakened by surprise.

"For I could not accept it as reasonable that my aim to forward the international science of folklore collecting provoked all that strange and hysterical sensitivity. And only when I began to interpret the political implications that brought on this earthquake of emotion did I realize that the map of folk song I drew with such care, relating us through mutual heritage, did not appeal to our noble countrymen or their lackeys in those neighboring Eastern countries.

"Oh, for a single drop of Western blood! If only I could have unearthed for their benefit the slightest proof of even a most distant relationship to the Western world, what a gracious offering that would have been to smooth over ruffled feelings. But the songs led me directly toward the East. Indeed, even in Turkey one evening I listened to an old man singing a song that could have been heard somewhere in Hungary. But all along I was unaware how dangerous it could be to point out any kind of relationship in that direction at that time, when the borders had been reshuffled and Hungary was enclosed within a much tighter line than before, and our neighboring countries appeared bulging with those mouthfuls they had bitten away from it.

"Yet neither new borderlines nor old, changed back and forth on the map, could ever raise any barricade to the wind that went on carrying the pollen and the seeds effortlessly over those expanses of land, green in the summer and white in the winter, wafting the songs, too, for centuries."

If Bartók stopped the story then, to lean back on his pillow and rest, there was sure to be another dark winter afternoon when he would return to the same theme and take up the narrative where he left off.

"These relationships must have begun long before we settled within our borderlines, for surely we have passed each other time and time again, and met in the waveless and waterless dry earthbed. And as our ways joined and crossed, we must have rested in our wanderings under the same bare sky, and perhaps many times we even mingled our blood."

After a while, as he pursued the story, he no longer made clear the distinctions of time, and he did not even suggest whether he was talking about the First World War, which had shattered for the time being all possibility of collecting and made his life a nightmare of fear lest people and songs would no longer exist by the time the war had passed over them, or whether his mind was filled with the war being fought right at the moment. Perhaps in his thoughts these wars had already blended into one, along with all those wars that were ever fought in history. Neither was he concerned with borderlines any more, for all the countries he remembered so well turned into an endless sweep of land suffering the terror of annihilation, with no more seeds and pollen left for the wind to carry — nothing but dark clouds of smoke and sharp tongues of fire lapping up all that was ever there before.

The thick darkness of the winter became thinner now. In the Bartóks' two rooms it was like being within the tent of a spider web, the faint light seeping through the dark map of zigzagged black lines.

It was only on rare occasions these days that Ditta and I had time for much conversation alone. The farthest retreat to be found in the apartment was the tiny kitchenette and even from there the most muffled whisper could travel right into Bartók's room.

It was in this kitchenette that Ditta told me in a tense, hushed tone one day, "It seems now that it's not entirely impossible Béla's illness has been arrested, for that's what one of his doctors told me." And as my answer was delayed, she added, "I hope you understand how good that would be."

"Why, of course I know!" I whispered back to her in the same muffled tone, careful not to awake Bartók, who was sleeping in his room. "I am very happy about this. You know that I am."

I wanted so much to but did not dare ask her what it really meant that his illness was arrested. Arrested for how long? It was so much safer to leave my question unspoken and unanswered, for then I could hope that it meant for a long, long time.

"Why don't you talk in your normal voices?" Bartók called to us from his room. "I greatly prefer it to whispering. Besides I wasn't sleeping at all."

As we came into his room, we found him sitting upright in his bed.

"I was just thinking about the time I was taken to a funeral," he started to talk at once, as if continuing a conversation. "I couldn't have been more than five or six years old, and I had never seen anyone dead before. It was a little girl next door who died, and I can see her before me, the way she was laid out in her coffin, in shimmering white, her small hands closed frozenly around a bouquet of jasmine. There were some freshly blooming roses too, somewhere around her, and her light blond hair was brushed very smoothly off her forehead, above a face as clean as wax. I remember glancing toward her with great fear, but a moment didn't pass before I saw her the way I used to from my window, running around with her hair flying after her. And at almost the same instant I saw her again sitting on the doorstep of her house, very slowly eating an apple. Her hair this time had fallen over and was almost covering her face.

"And then the many pictures that must have been heaped up in the back of my mind were passing quickly before me, each of them complete to the last thin line, even though I had no conscious recollection of ever having noticed her before. In one she was running home crying, rubbing her eyes; in another she was bouncing a ball on the sidewalk, her head bent down, and her face completely hidden under the heavy sheet of hair.

"And when I dared to look again at the girl in the coffin, I was unable to link that small statue lying there, her pale hair painted on the paper-smooth pillow, while the living images were still moving before my eyes."

Bartók stopped talking as unexpectedly as he had begun, and no one spoke for a while.

"The way you two are sitting there," he said, in a voice without a trace of resemblance to the one he had used a minute before, "like two scared old maids afraid of their own shadows! And how clearly it's marked all over your faces that you are thinking how I have given myself away now, revealing to you in spite of myself, a deep preoccupation with my own funeral."

He continued with the same trace of mockery in his voice.

"And to think how certain I was that you realized by now that nothing could concern me less than the fate that may befall my hulk beyond my life. In whichever manner or whatever style it is sent on its way. Except of course that one thing: that it really is no more than a hulk, freed from all that material I am striving to leave behind me. And that will take, as I see it, at least ten good years before it is ready to sink into that bottomless storeroom we all share. Thrown in a sheet to the waves, or scattered in the air as a handful of dust.

"And still," he said after a while, "although it matters so little, I think I would like it best if just directly and very simply it was given to the soil.

"But remember, this was not my line of thought to begin with; it was merely suggested by your scared faces. My thoughts, for no special reason, touched upon a memory from my childhood of a dead girl in her coffin and led me to wonder about the relation between motionlessness and motion, trying to find the reason why that one frozen picture broke into so many live ones, and why that small corpse did not want to stay dead in her coffin."

Like Bartók's illness, time seemed to be arrested too, standing still, keeping him apart from the rhythm of events around him. What mattered to him and what passed unnoticed was almost unpredictable. The same things that emerged to the surface with sharp pain one time would remain covered up with a sheet of ice in the next.

The war came to an end in Hungary, and while this must have been of greater importance than anything else to Bartók, he never alluded to it in his conversation at the time when it happened. Nor did he speak of it later when they received from an indirect source the news that Bartók's sister and her family, his son Béla by his first marriage, and also Kodály, were all alive and safe, and Bartók's own belongings left behind in Hungary, including a great part of his unpublished Hungarian folk song collection, had miraculously remained intact. It was Ditta who told me all about this. Bartók never referred to it with a single word until later, and then only indirectly.

And it was Ditta alone now who carried on the theme of going back to Hungary, weaving into her talk many fine details having to do with their return and the continuation of their life there. And occasionally as she talked it seemed that the reality was that they were already back in Hungary, and

America had become the faraway dream, the home she was now thinking of with yearning.

"I will never forget any of the places that belonged to us here," she once told me, "not even the apartment in Forest Hills, with the smell and the noise and those fragile gourds that Béla hated so much. And I am not sure that the years we have spent here were not somehow the most important of our entire life."

But going back to Hungary no longer seemed to be included among Bartók's plans, and he maintained his silence regarding the ending of the war there until one day when I came to see them and found him looking at a single sheet of newspaper that had been printed in Budapest. He put the paper down on the table and asked me to take a quick look at the long columns of advertisements, consisting mostly of notices from members of families looking for each other, and the oddest collection of objects for sale. Bartók put his finger on one of them and held it there tensely while I ran my eyes over it. For a reasonable price it offered a feather bed in fair condition.

"A good warm feather bed," Bartók said, not moving his finger from the paper. "To put back the warmth into someone who suffered the shelterless cold of that terrible winter without quite freezing to death. But how can that be done?" he said with an outburst of violence. "How can those people feel any warmth again, while they can still remember stealing along the dark frozen labyrinths that were once known as streets, covered with motionless heaps of dead horses lying in the places where they had fallen, with big hunks of flesh torn or carved out of them to keep thousands of people from dying of hunger. Won't the memory of those frozen limbs they fed on keep them cold beyond repair? For how could their blood be warmed again, feather bed or no feather bed, or even by the strongest sun?

"And look at this," he said, pointing to another advertisement offering hundreds of yards of khaki cloth for sale.

"You see, in that poor misery-ridden country, even *kaki* is for sale." He used the word that Hungarian children use to refer to excrement, but he remained so deadly serious that he did not even realize he had transposed the meaning of the word in his grief over the anguish these people had suffered as well as their immediate misery and gaping needs.

Perhaps because I found the strained expression on Bartók's face hard to bear I began to talk about the lucky escape of his own family from any fatal tragedy, and how fortunate it was that all his personal possessions remained unharmed.

He looked at me with narrow, questioning eyes, as if he had not understood the meaning of my words. Then he turned away from me abruptly and walked around the room.

"And what if they do happen to be among those whose lives were not claimed?" he said, as he came back with a strange restraint in his voice. "To be alive in that country today is no more than accidental, and what reality has it, if any, for those who were witnesses of all the dying, surrounded by those corpses still speaking to them of the agony that was theirs. It will be a long time before those who were left alive become whole again.

"All I like to think of now is softly falling lukewarm rain to cool the fever out of the naked bones of the dead and let them find their hollows in the earth, helping them to sink deeply into it, so the new sunshine of spring can grow a soft clean covering of green over them."

When I looked up, I saw Ditta standing in the doorway of the kitchenette. But I did not move.

"Did you say," Bartók went on, "that it is a great and unforeseen good fortune that my possessions are intact and not scattered ashes instead? And just think of the tremendous pleasure I could receive out of arranging them neatly in a line of display, along the edges of dark and sky-high garbage heaps composed of burned-out houses and those who died in them, the sweepings, the remains of the demolished life of an entire city.

"The only thing that seems fitting to me and that offers even a faint sense of relief is the thought, if I ever get there myself, it will be no more than my bones, to join up with those other bones that were pierced with pain, and mingle there with them, until we all crumble together into useful and pain-less dust."

26

I was so used to seeing Bartók blending in with the subdued gray during the long winter that when the sudden brightness of spring lifted away the murky shadows and left Bartók exposed to the brilliant glare his face revealed nakedly how every single hour of that winter had written its own dark mark upon it.

This change might have been only painted there, for actually he felt the same, and he kept on working as constantly as before. His days followed each other in their well-established smooth rhythm, and he moved within their flow with contentment, adapting himself to the smallness of the space around him almost with pleasure. His cluttered corner in the living room and the bed in his own room were like islands by now, closed in all around with towering stacks of papers, and he had within his reach all his notes, the pencils, erasers, and favorite kind of paper clips that he needed in order to work on without any interruption. It looked as if he were ready to expand into the sphere above and the region below if the surface itself was too full to hold any more.

Strangely, this further change in Bartók's appearance, so overwhelming to me, seemed to remain invisible to Ditta, or, if she noticed it at all, she must have closed her eyes against it. For she was determined to ignore any sign indicating that Bartók's illness could possibly change for the worse instead of taking a final turn for the better.

Nothing could have been more frightening than this deeply rooted hope growing like a tree, unhampered, in a sunless, airless room, freely expanding upward, unaware that its stretching arms had almost reached the limit and were about to touch the ceiling. However, this had come to be the only safeguard protecting her as she floated through her days in subdued negativeness.

With just this kind of muted calmness Ditta told me one day about Bartók's decision to go to a hospital at his doctor's suggestion, and that he would probably remain there for a while.

"Béla has never escaped a mild touch of illness of some kind or other in the spring, ever since I can remember. And that he should suffer from it somewhat more acutely now," she explained further, "is no more than natural."

Only with reluctance, later on, she finally told me the actual reason why Bartók went to the hospital — a mild case of pneumonia. She probably could not have talked about it at all if she had not been able to say at the same time he had been very quickly and so completely cured there with the help of the new drugs that he was feeling better and stronger now than at any time during the winter.

"And if you remember," she said, in a burst of recollection, "how it was before, how desperately he used to deny the mere thought of a hospital, how safe he felt every time he came back from even a short examination, you could never believe how mildly he has accepted it all this time. Now he does not struggle against everything as he did before, against the entire hospital routine. He lies just so calmly in his bed there, as if he were at home, his head buried in his pillow, his face without any resistance, soft and relaxed. Then there is only his work again. Everything beyond that is happening to someone else, as he said himself."

I remembered well enough. No one could help remembering the wild agony he suffered each time pressure was put upon him to tear himself away from the aloneness of his room. Exposure to the constant vigilance of strangers was absolutely contrary to his nature.

And yet, listening to Ditta's description, I was not so sure this complete lack of rebellion, this crumbling of his strong wall of defense, was really a hopeful sign, in spite of the comfort Ditta seemed to derive from the transformation. Besides, Ditta's mind was safely involved in immediate problems, the most troublesome of all — Bartók was hardly eating.

"Although the food is just as good as all the rest of the care Béla is getting in that beautiful Doctors Hospital, still it's the same difficulty as always when he is confronted with food unfamiliar to him."

One day when I was to go to see Bartók with Ditta, we were preparing to smuggle in some potato soup to him. It was not meant to be a surprise, for he did not like such surprises. He knew about it well in advance, and was expecting it on that very day.

"I did not tamper at all with this dish. It is truly traditional potato soup this time, thick enough for the spoon to stand up in it of its own accord," Ditta said as she was wrapping the small saucepan in a sweater to keep it warm until we got there.

When we finally reached Bartók's room, we found that he had many visitors already, Tibor Serly among them. As we sat down to wait, Bartók flashed at us a conspiratorial wink, either because he noticed that I was hiding the pot of soup under my coat, or else he smelled the strong aroma of it, and an approving smile remained on his face as he talked to the other guests. He looked altogether fresher and brighter than he had for a long time.

After the visitors left, Bartók turned to us instantly.

"And now for that potato soup," he said with exuberance. "For I hope it's not your favorite book you are hiding there so unsuccessfully," he told me.

With the soup in front of him, and sipping every spoonful of it slowly as if to make it last longer, he was trying to find the words that for him would mean the highest praise.

"If it had been cooked in a caldron over an open fire in a field, it could not taste better. How did you ever accomplish this feat on a mere gas stove?" he said to Ditta.

It did truly seem that he was accepting the hospital with an unprecedented amount of patience and, even more surprising, he was able to talk about it with a comparatively mild humor.

"This is not such a bad place for working as you might expect, if you are able to forget that your closed door is really open to the entire nurse population of the hospital, and to doctors of every possible rank, and your body is the common prey of all of them. And, looking at the river gives me the illusion that I might be anywhere, far away from here, although, to be sure, there is no way of escaping the incessant shrieking and wailing of the boats.

"I wouldn't mind even that so much, perhaps, if I were only separated from it by a greater distance. Yes, I could almost enjoy that sound, if it reached me in more subdued tones, accompanied by muted soft echoes. But as it is, most of the time it seems to be coming from right under my bed, and I almost feel the rocking motion of its insistent vibration."

Listening to him and seeing his manuscripts all around, covered with the flowing lines of his small, freshly written notes, one could easily imagine that he came to the hospital for the sole reason of finding out if he could do his work as well or better here than in his own room at home.

Driven now by the unrelenting urgency of his work, and by that alone, it did not seem to make any difference that the spaces were steadily shrinking around him, and were reduced by now to not much more than a surface large enough to hold him and the pages he was working on. He did not seem to need or want any more.

Bartók was home again, spending more time in bed than ever before. The door of his small room, almost always left open until now, was closed more often than not these days.

I came for a short time nearly every day, and Ditta and I sat in the kitchen again as we used to in the Riverdale apartment. But instead of the past, Ditta's mind was now always involved in the future, visualizing a long vista of untroubled time ahead, with most of the hardships left behind them.

"I wonder if you sense it as I do," she asked, but went on without any hesitation, "that now at last all the things we have been hoping for have actually begun to happen. Béla is feeling so much better that sometimes I think he is almost entirely well. And now just as if it were planned by providence, Menuhin has invited us to spend the entire summer with him in California and, to my great surprise, without any of his usual reluctance Béla accepted the invitation. Now he is planning with joy a whole summer under the huge sunny sky of California, the kind of climate Béla responds to most readily and that always works wonders with him. I really think the only reason he is willing to spend so much time in bed now is his hope of storing up enough energy to take full advantage of the summer ahead of us.

"It's almost certain besides," she went on, "that Péter will be coming home to stay sometime during the summer, for finally all those allergies that he has been suffering for a long while now developed into asthma, and as no medicine seems to help him it is assumed the cause must be the climate of Panama. I have the impression from his letters that he'd rather stay at his post until the end of the war, but I can't help feeling happy about his coming home, for you know what it would mean to us at this time of all times."

Whenever I went there I always saw Bartók, even if only for a few minutes. He was always ready to talk, although most of the time he did not lift his eyes from the manuscript he was working on.

"I hope you don't mind not seeing Béla today," Ditta told me once when I came. "Not because he is not feeling as well as usual, but his doctor thinks it is best for him not to talk more than is really necessary, to keep his rest undisturbed and complete."

In spite of the closed door, Bartók overheard us, and called from his room, asking me to come in to see him.

"Just for a short time," he said to Ditta, who was busy preparing dinner, "and I will let her do all the talking."

I entered the room, where I noticed that the window shade was pulled almost all the way down and the lamp, usually lit at his bedside, was not burning now. At first, in the dim shadowy light, only the white papers stacked high on a table in a corner were clearly visible. Then I saw a chair that had been left near his bed and silently I sat down.

Bartók was lying back, his head sunk in his pillow, completely lost in rest, his bed for once entirely free of even a single page of manuscript. On his face I discerned a look of unknown tenderness that made him seem nearer than ever before — or could it be that this warm and fragile smile was always there, but had remained hidden beneath the firm layer of his reserve? And as I looked at his face that seemed so close to me now, all that had been so unreachable before, like a secret writing, slowly began to disclose its meaning. Now that the marble strength of his features had collapsed, another kind of force moved into its place, revealing a strong and purposeful hope blended with a vague touch of very distant fear.

"Well, here is your chance to talk about anything you like," Bartók said, "so why don't you go ahead and begin."

But I continued to sit there quietly and he was the one who spoke again.

"Then I'd better ask you a few questions myself, so you can prove the worth of your claim to that exclusive interest in books, by telling me something I'd like to learn." His voice was serious and flavored only by a very faint touch of irony.

"I did read some Proust," he went on, "but I only had a chance to look into one book or another of his, and altogether did not accomplish much more than to feel the impact of his sensitive style. So could you, by any chance, enlighten me, please, since I am not qualified to draw my own conclusions, as to just what his position is in that long line of French writers beginning with Balzac, through Zola and Maupassant and all the others?"

Since I was considering very carefully what I wanted to say and did not offer any answer for a while, he became annoyed by my silence and did not restrain his impatience.

"Can't you see what I'm driving at? We all have to begin somewhere before finding our own place, choosing to follow the footsteps of someone perhaps far back in the past, or another no more than an arm's length away from us in the present. And only after trying out both can we make our final choice, at least that was the course I myself followed, getting my first real push from the Richard Strauss tone poem, *Also sprach Zarathustra*, but not satisfied there I turned in the opposite direction, hurling myself all the way back to the beginning. Through searching for my own path to follow, I came to believe one thing: that only from the entirely old can the entirely new be born. For all those complications that have been occurring in between the two were only obstructions standing in the way at the many forks of the crisscross road. And after those first confusing steps, I finally found my way through, bypassing all those shapes and forms of growth that wedged themselves in between the past and the present, cutting away everything between myself and that original strong, arrow-straight root, disregarding all the branches that sprouted from it at one time or another."

Entranced by his words and the way he spoke them, as if to make his idea unmistakably clear, I had completely forgotten about Proust. He promptly reminded me of it again, but I was unable to say a single word that would disturb the sound of his voice still echoing in my ears.

"But don't you see," he insisted, as always, when he put his mind on no matter how small a thing, "all I would like to know is whether Proust continued in the footsteps of Balzac, or did he go farther back than that, or stop somewhere midway, finding his own course, and did he give as important a view of his own period, as fully and in so many layers, as Balzac did of his own, or did he reveal it at least in fragments, or not at all?"

"I don't know," I answered, afraid to make any statements, but realizing that I could not escape any longer. "I think he reflected his own time, in a very abstract way. At least I myself have a picture of that layer of aristocracy, his main theme, and the different levels of people on which it balances its weight. And although he attains it indirectly, still, through the accumulation it becomes so positive and strong that as you keep on reading and are able to penetrate the slow flowing tempo, you find it impossible to remain an outsider and not to become involved in its midst — the people and landscapes, and the sense of the climate, the feeble warmth of the very early spring, and the faint color of a flower as the snow melts away from it, a flower that later takes into its petals the strong sunshine of summer — and all the hours that have passed in between are held together for you, until every minute of it becomes your own."

"Well, all that you say appeals to me deeply," Bartók remarked, "but it is still not the answer to my question. I want to know if, in the long run, the social structure of the society in that period he set out to reconstruct emerges as vividly as the landscape you describe with such affection."

Still hoping to evade the explicit answer he was insisting upon, it occurred to me to tell him about the Duchesse de Guermantes and her red shoes. He seemed to become interested as soon as I began to tell him about the time when Swann, already deathly ill, came to the Hôtel des Guermantes, bringing with him a present for the Duchesse: the immensely enlarged proofs of the engravings to be in Swann's book on the coinage of the Order of Malta, in which the Duchesse professed to be greatly interested.

Since Bartók did not stop me right at the beginning, I gained courage and went on more rapidly.

"But poor Swann could not have chosen a more inopportune moment for his call, as the Duchesse and the Duc de Guermantes were already late in dressing for an important dinner party and a ball afterwards. So Swann was left standing for a long time in the hall waiting for the Duchesse, until finally the Duc appeared, who could hardly restrain his impatience at finding Swann standing there. Fearing further delay, he was trying to get him out of there quickly before the Duchesse should come down. But before he could manage to accomplish this, the Duchesse appeared and greeted Swann in her own exquisitely polite style, expressing her gratitude for Swann's gift, although she had not had a chance to look at it as yet. But when she gave orders to the servants to bring in the engravings, the Duc was unable to hold back his growing annoyance any longer. 'But those pictures are of such an enormous size, they might not even pass through the door. Besides, there is no more time left, for the carriage is waiting outside, and as it is, we are already late.'

"Swann, preparing to take his departure, in the last minute mentioned to the Duchesse that this might easily be the last time they would meet, for he was ill and could very well die at any minute. The Duchesse, torn between her two duties — of not arriving late at a dinner party or of comforting her lifelong friend and admirer — found the shortest way out of her dilemma by simply sweeping away Swann's remark with a broad gesture, indicating that she found Swann's statement about his illness greatly exaggerated and not serious at all. 'Oh, but it is,' Swann said, 'and I assure you I have little time left. But I mustn't keep you any longer,' he quickly added, 'you are dining out, remember!'

" 'Oh, that dinner party is hardly important,' answered the Duchesse, already on her way to the carriage. 'Farewell, Swann, we will talk about this another time. And I do want to look at those pictures, together with you.'

"But as she lifted up her red skirt to step into the carriage, the Duc suddenly cried out, 'But you kept your black shoes on! Please go upstairs and change into a pair of red ones.'

" 'But you said we were late already!' the Duchesse protested.

" 'Nonsense! we have plenty of time,' the Duc reassured her.

"So the Duchesse went back upstairs, and the Duc remained alone with Swann again. 'I think you'd better go, Swann, before my wife comes down. She is so fond of you that she might start another conversation if she finds you here. And don't worry about your health. You may live for a long time. Doctors are donkeys, you know.' "

I had hardly finished my story before Bartók said promptly, "Oh, but I think doctors are apt to exaggerate in the other direction, making their patients feel that there is a long time left, when perhaps there is hardly any at all." Then he stopped speaking.

"Hmm, doctors are donkeys," he said suddenly alert and smiling, "I wonder if it is an alliteration in the original too.

"But about Swann," he went on, in a more serious tone. "Why would a dying man waste his time just standing around? I think he should have found a lot to do if he was worth his salt at all.

"And as for the Duchesse, there it is, you see — shoes again. Always too many pairs of shoes, and altogether too many other possessions."

With that he concluded all he had to say, and I sat silent for a moment. But as I got up, intending to leave the room, he spoke to me again.

"Now I would like to tell you about a book I just read, a book about Columbus Christophe, and I must say that this book caused me more irritation at times than any other I can think of. Whether Columbus Christophe was a good navigator or not is not the subject I am most interested in. And that he had no idea of how to handle his sailors certainly becomes more than clear every inch of the way through the account. He was not meant to be a leader." He shook his head.

As I listened to him, it seemed that he was not at all talking about a book he had read, but it was as if he were relating a recent happening which had aroused in him a strong disapproval.

"Neither do I admire the limited interest he displayed in the extent of his discovery, not showing the slightest inclination just then to navigate any farther, to investigate more fully how far the land he found himself on extended, and seemed satisfied to circle around the islands that were within easy reach.

"But he certainly had unlimited interest in the gold to be found nearby, and he showed no restraint in advertising this fact when he returned to Spain, arousing the greed of adventurers, gold-hungry exploiters, and pirates who naturally lost no time coming to this land to ruin its peaceful beauty for ever.

"The destruction began, however, with that first shipload of Columbus', for they did not hesitate to use their weapons, beginning then the chronicle of bloodshed that in the long run turned the inhabitants into hunted beasts, driven to the very last corner that was to be found.

"But there is that one crime which left the deepest sting in me and hurts with the same pain whenever I think of it, as if it were the first time. That first Indian who was caught alive and dragged onto the ship, to be taken back to Spain to be shown like an exotic animal, a sample to convince the Queen to begin with, and after that the Court, and then to be put on display for the curious mob to stare at what was left of him."

Bartók's face could not have held more anguish if he had been that captive himself, and I wanted to offer something to soothe that throbbing pain in him if only I could.

"But what made that so much worse than to be pursued and slaughtered?" I began vaguely but could not go any farther, as I was stopped right there by Bartók.

"How could anyone blunder upon a remark that shows such an insensitivity to human suffering? Even to try to compare two such utterly different fates is beyond me. Could it be that you really cannot see the difference?" he asked, somewhat less vehemently.

"Not that it isn't tragic to be an innocent victim and to be downed by a bullet, but the death it brings is quick, and ends it all right there on that piece of well-known soil. But to be pulled up from the ground, together with the rhubarb root, the corn, and tobacco, and carried away as a curiosity to throw in with the gold, to be dragged alive across half the world, bound helpless against strange winds, and forced to taste their unknown tang, and unknown food, and unknown water.

"And borne off into an unmeasurable hopeless distance from the place where you want with all your strength to be, knowing all along that you will never be there again."

I stood for a moment, following the tired motion of his head as he leaned back on the pillow.

"Is this so very hard to understand?" he asked me, his voice weak and his smile compassionate.

"No, it isn't," I said. And I never saw him again.

27

THERE WAS STILL another summer. But it was not under the huge sunny California sky. So distant a trip was at the last minute decided against by Bartók's doctors.

How hard it must have been for him to give up the idea of this visit could only be measured by his eagerness from the beginning to make this plan come true and by the way his tense seriousness mingled into the joy of his preparations for the approaching summer.

Still he accepted the decision silently. So Ditta said when she called me in Riverton late one night. And if not California, she added hopefully, there was always Lake Saranac.

But Bartók became so disheartened that he no longer had a desire to go anywhere. After a while, when they were able to rent a small makeshift place, his disappointment deeply buried, he went to Saranac just the same.

Half the summer was gone before I heard from Ditta again. She told me first of all that Bartók was feeling so well it was almost beyond belief. Just as in Riverton, he wandered long hours in the woods and never showed any weariness when he returned home. All the rest of his time was devoted to his work. to those two compositions he was so anxious to finish before the summer came to an end. The Viola Concerto for Primrose was already sketched out in its final form, and as for the orchestration, "all that was missing were the notes." For Bartók, that meant no more than finding time to put them down on paper. And the Piano Concerto she could not bear to think about was practically finished, except for a few of the concluding measures. At the end of her letter, in handwriting suddenly grown small and pale, she told me that as for herself she kept to her darkened room all day long and cried and cried.

It was a very long time before I knew anything about the rest of that summer. For a while the silence was soothing, and when I met Péter now and then I never asked any questions, for we both seemed to feel that they must remain unasked and unanswered. Yet, as the years passed by, the questions began to emerge almost of their own accord. Even then Péter's words would come only haltingly, and always faded into silence before the shadow of that final summer. At last he promised to write a long letter about it. And this is the letter he wrote, after many years.

Soon after I was discharged from the Navy, on or about August 15, I arrived at Lake Saranac very early in the morning and walked to the little hut my parents rented for the summer in the backyard of Mr. Max Haar. It was a tiny house with two rooms and a kitchen with ceilings barely higher than the top of our heads, a wooden outer shell with cardboard inside walls. Since it was very early I did not know if anyone was up, and I walked about to look in through the windows and found my mother sufficiently light-sleeping to wake up as I looked in.

Of course we were very happy at being together, also at the end of the war news. But what was most important to me was that I found my father in such excellent health; at least, it appeared to be so. We took many walks together, almost like the time when we spent summers in the Alps. Once we even climbed quite far up on a nearby hill, taking lunch with us. Father seemed to be able to do it very well, and it appeared that in another few months he should have regained all his former strength.

In spite of such an apparent improvement, just at the time when there seemed to be the least reason for it, my mother was sad almost at all times. Looking back later one is compelled to think as if she already knew what was to happen one month later.

During this time at Saranac Lake Father was very busy with some musical work, composing; there were two compositions in progress simultaneously. One of them was the Viola Concerto written for Primrose, and the other was something Mother should not know about. I am not sure why, but as if I remembered him telling me that it was a surprise for her (the *Third Piano Concerto*).

At the end of August or the beginning of September, Father again had occasional higher temperature in the evenings and so we decided to come back to New York a little earlier than planned. Our trip was a nightmare — it seemed to be about Labor Day and that year everyone seemed to pick the same time to arrive in Grand Central, and at one point after searching for porters in vain Father carried a piece of luggage for quite a distance before I was able to prevent him from doing so.

In New York he did not get much better. I had to learn to give him penicillin injections. Father protested against having a nurse for this purpose — the penicillin had to be given every four hours at that time — for nurses always talk silly things, like "How are you this morning?"

and things like that, even though the answer to that question does not in any way affect the patient's treatment, nor is a memorandum of it kept for the doctor; in other words, it would be unnecessary talk, and Father did not like that.

On top of everything, our apartment lease was to expire that month and our landlord showed no willingness to let us stay any longer. Could not have happened at a worse time.

One evening Father asked me to his bed and told me of the whereabouts of various manuscripts and about the will. I was horrified and assured him that this would be quite unnecessary, because he was getting better. His temperature suddenly did go down, and that was worst of all. Dr. Rappaport decided that Father should go to the hospital immediately. There was an argument. Father did not like hospitals. What could they do to help? Besides he had some important work to finish. (An extra day would have given him a chance to orchestrate the last seventeen or so bars of the *Third Piano Concerto*, which was practically completed at that time. As the extra day was not allowed, he marked on the score the number of bars still to follow.)

I can still see Father beg the doctor to let him stay home another day, and now, knowing what had to happen, I realize it would not have made any difference. Dr. Rappaport was adamant; the ambulance came and went. At this time already Father was very sick. We were there almost all the time, going home only to sleep. One morning early — about two or three A.M. — the hospital called. We went over. Father was getting a blood transfusion and was begging the nurse to take it away. Asked us to have the nurse with her needle taken away. He knew it could not help. "In my last moment they cannot leave me in peace."

Dr. Lax was in the hospital and paid Father a visit. We were not in the room at that time. It was later reported: Father mentioned to him "I am only sad that I have to leave with a full trunk."

(What was in the trunk was indicated by the works written in the last few years, like *Concerto for Orchestra*, *Violin Concerto*, *Viola Concerto*, and the *Third Piano Concerto*; which indicated the beginning of a new period in his writing, his crystallized period, as I like to refer to it.)

We were in the room when he died, when his eyes lost their conscious look and they slowly became like ice. I could not then realize what it was that happened, and still cannot fully accept it.

When I arrived in New York from Riverton on the morning of September 28, 1945, I did not know yet that Bartók had died. Not until I tried to call Ditta and an unknown voice answered her telephone and informed me that Mr. Bartók had passed away on the twenty-sixth in the West Side Hospital and his funeral would be held at the University Chapel at Lexington Avenue and 52nd Street that very afternoon.

I found the place and in it the long room. It was softly lit, and almost empty. Someone assured me it was the right place but still very early.

I sat down on a chair in the last row and waited. The West Side Hospital was not too far away, and I was wondering if I should go there to take a look at the place where he had died. How I wished it could have been at Saranac, or in his dark small room in Riverdale, or anywhere else than in the hospital.

"I cannot think of another thing more painful to me," I could hear his voice saying again, "than being helplessly exposed to the scrutiny of strangers. For my own instinct is so much more closely related to those animals of the wild whose only desire when wounded is to find a place far out of the way in the depth of a tangled wild thicket, and wait there in the far-reaching silence amidst the reassurance of the familiar bower for the end to come."

One side of the room looked like a stage, and I saw a mass of white flowers there, very large and frozen blooms, and I thought they must have grown behind tightly closed windows. They surely had never swayed freely against the wind, if they were real at all.

"All you have to know about Béla is that he loves everything that's real."

But when Ditta gave me this key, at the time when she first came to Vermont, I didn't tell her that there was one other thing besides, for you also have to know what is real.

Were these flowers real? This accommodating room slowly filling up with people? The music I heard? Or that closed black-covered narrow coffin?

Or were his tremendous anguish-filled eyes real, looking at me exactly the way they did in Vermont when we had stood in front of Matthew's collapsing barn and he had said, "Take one look at those poor beasts, those winter-wounded bodies. The summer sunshine is never long enough to smooth and heal their ravaged hides before the merciless cold is on them again. And now I will be forced to think of them every day this coming winter, every day I will feel through my own body the horror and torment of their existence, never knowing the hour when their icy hovel will finally collapse on them some bitter windy day."

"But Matthew moved his horses long ago into the beautiful barn of a neighbor," I heard myself saying now without hesitation or fear that he might detect I was not speaking the truth.

And what if he should ask me where was that clean and hay-laden barn he never saw anywhere there in all his wanderings? "It's hidden on the side of a hill well covered by trees." And I did not care if my voice carried above the very cloquent funeral speech. I wanted to say other things too, but there was no time left. Everyone was leaving and the coffin was not there any more on the empty stage.

I walked through the entry hall toward the street and then stopped, for in the midst of a small group I saw Ditta, and Péter holding on to her arm. I did not go to them, but without a word passed them by.

For with one look at Ditta's face, through her black veil, the distant glare and the lost blue of her round-open eyes, I knew she wasn't there in that crowded room, but was running down the city streets, through small villages and endless fields of green grass, gathering all he had left behind, and trying to make him be again.

Catalogue of Bartók's Works

CATALOGUE OF BARTÓK'S WORKS

FOR THE THEATRE

Bluebeard's Castle, opera in one act (libretto by Balázs), Op. 11 (1911).

The Wooden Prince, ballet in one act (scenario by Balázs), Op. 13 (1917).

The Miraculous Mandarin, pantomime in one act (scenario by Lengyel), Op. 19 (1919).

FOR ORCHESTRA

Scherzo, ms. (1902).

Kossuth Symphony, ms. (except for *Marcia funebre*, pub. in piano transcription) (1903).

Burlesque, Op. 2, ms. (1904).

Suite No. 1, Op. 3 (1905).

Suite No. 2, Op. 4 (1907); revised (1943).

Two Portraits, Op. 5 (1907–8).

Two Pictures, Op. 10 (1910).

Four Pieces: Preludio, Scherzo, Intermezzo, Marcia funebre, Op. 12 (1912).

Dance Suite (1923).

Transylvanian Dances (1931).

Hungarian Sketches (1931); transcriptions of piano pieces.

Hungarian Peasant Songs (1933); transcriptions of piano pieces.

Divertimento, for string orchestra (1939).
Concerto for Orchestra (1943).

FOR SMALL ORCHESTRA

Music for String Instruments, Percussion, and Celesta (1936).

CONCERTOS

Rhapsody, piano and orchestra, ms., Op. 1 (arr. of Rhapsody for piano solo) (1904).

Concerto for Violin and Orchestra, ms. (1908).

Concerto No. 1, for piano and orchestra (1926). First performed in Frankfurt, July 1, 1927, with the composer at the piano, Wilhelm Furtwängler conducting.

Rhapsody No. 1, for violin and orchestra (1928); versions for violin and piano, violoncello and piano.

Rhapsody No. 2, for violin and orchestra (1928); revised 1944; version for violin and piano.

Concerto No. 2, for piano and orchestra (1931).

Concerto for Violin and Orchestra (1938). First performed in Amsterdam, April 23, 1939, by Zoltán Székely, Willem Mengelberg conducting.

Concerto No. 3, for piano and orchestra (1945); unfinished; last 17 bars completed by Tibor Serly. First performed in Philadelphia, February 8, 1946, by György Sándor, Eugene Ormandy conducting.

Concerto for Viola and Orchestra (1945); unfinished; reconstructed and orchestrated by Tibor Serly. First performed in Minneapolis, December 2, 1949, by William Primrose, Antal Dórati conducting.

CHAMBER MUSIC

Quartet for piano and strings, ms. (1898).
String Quartet, ms. (1899).
Quintet, ms. (1899).
Sonata for violin and piano, ms. (1903).
Quintet for piano and strings, ms. (1904).
String Quartet No. 1, Op. 7 (1908).
String Quartet No. 2, Op. 17 (1917).

Sonata No. 1, for violin and piano (1921).

Sonata No. 2, for violin and piano (1922).

String Quartet No. 3 (1927).

String Quartet No. 4 (1928). Dedicated to the Pro Arte Quartet.

Forty-four Duos, for two violins (1931).

String Quartet No. 5 (1934). Dedicated to Mrs. Elizabeth Sprague Coolidge. First performed in Washington, April 8, 1935, by the Kolisch Quartet.

Contrasts, for violin, clarinet, and piano (1938). Dedicated to Benny Goodman and Joseph Szigeti; first performed in New York, January 9, 1939.

String Quartet No. 6 (1939). Dedicated to the Kolisch Quartet; first performed by them in New York, January 20, 1941.

Sonata for Solo Violin (1944). Dedicated to Yehudi Menuhin; first performed by him in New York, November 26, 1944.

FOR TWO PIANOS

Sonata for Two Pianos and Percussion (1937). First performed in Basle, January 16, 1938, by Béla and Ditta Bartók, Fritz Schiesser and Philipp Rühlig. Transcribed as Concerto for Two Pianos and Orchestra (1940); first performed in New York, January 21, 1943, by Béla and Ditta Bartók and the New York Philharmonic, Fritz Reiner conducting.

Mikrokosmos. Numbers 113, 69, 135, 123, 127, 145, 146 were transcribed by Bartók for two pianos.

FOR PIANO

The Danube River, ms. (1892).

Sonata, ms. (1897).

Four Pieces (1903).

Evening, ms. (1903).

Rhapsody, Op. 1, (1904).

Three Hungarian Folksongs (1907).

Fourteen Bagatelles, Op. 6 (1908).

Ten Easy Pieces (1908).

For Children, 85 pieces, 4 vols. (1908–9); revised 1945, 79 pieces, 2 vols.

Two Elegies, Op. 8b (1908–9).

Three Burlesques, Op. 8c (1908–11).

Three Rondos (1909).

Two Romanian Dances, Op. 8a (1909–10).

Seven Sketches, Op. 9 (1908–10); revised 1945.

Four Dirges (1910).

Allegro barbaro (1911).

The First Term at the Piano (1913).

Sonatina (1915).

Romanian Folk Dances from Hungary (1915).

Romanian Christmas Songs (1915).

Fifteen Hungarian Peasant Songs (1915–17).

Suite, Op. 14 (1916).

Three Studies, Op. 18 (1918).

Eight Improvisations on Hungarian Peasant Songs, Op. 20 (1920).

Sonata (1926).

Out of Doors (1926).

Nine Little Pieces (1926).

Mikrokosmos, 153 progressive pieces (1926–37).

Petite Suite (1936).

Three Hungarian Folk Tunes (published 1942; written 1914–17).

FOR VOICE

Three Songs, ms. (1898).

Love Songs, ms. (1900).

Four Songs (texts by Pósa) (1902).

Four Songs, ms. (1902–3? manuscript lost).

Twenty Hungarian Folksongs (1906); revised 1938.

Nine Romanian Songs, ms. (1915).

Five Songs, Op. 15 (texts by Balázs) (1916).

Five Songs, Op. 16 (texts by Ady) (1916).

Eight Hungarian Folksongs (1917)

Five Village Scenes (1924).

Twenty Hungarian Folksongs (1929).

The Husband's Grief (1945).

FOR CHORUS

Four Old Hungarian Folksongs, for a cappella male choir (1912).

Two Romanian Folksongs, for 4-part women's chorus, ms. (1915).

Five Slovak Folksongs, for 4-part male chorus (1917).

Four Slovak Folksongs, for mixed chorus and piano (1917).

Four Hungarian Folksongs, for a cappella mixed chorus (1930).

Cantata Profana: The Nine Enchanted Stags, for double mixed chorus, tenor and baritone soloists, and orchestra (1930). First performed in London, May 25, 1934, by BBC Symphony and Chorus, Aylmer Buesst conducting.

Székely Songs, for a cappella male chorus (1932).

Twenty-seven Choruses, for 2 and 3-part children's or women's chorus (1935). First performed in Budapest, May 7, 1937.

From Olden Times (with old Hungarian folksong and art-song texts), for a cappella male chorus (1935).

RECORDINGS

For a list of currently available recordings of Bartók's music, including some piano performances by Bartók himself, consult the *Schwann Long Playing Record Catalog*, issued monthly to record dealers throughout the country.

A CATALOGUE OF SELECTED DOVER BOOKS
IN ALL FIELDS OF INTEREST

A CATALOGUE OF SELECTED DOVER BOOKS
IN ALL FIELDS OF INTEREST

WHAT IS SCIENCE?, *N. Campbell*
The role of experiment and measurement, the function of mathematics, the nature of scientific laws, the difference between laws and theories, the limitations of science, and many similarly provocative topics are treated clearly and without technicalities by an eminent scientist. "Still an excellent introduction to scientific philosophy," H. Margenau in *Physics Today*. "A first-rate primer . . . deserves a wide audience," *Scientific American*. 192pp. 5⅜ x 8.
60043-2 Paperbound $1.25

THE NATURE OF LIGHT AND COLOUR IN THE OPEN AIR, *M. Minnaert*
Why are shadows sometimes blue, sometimes green, or other colors depending on the light and surroundings? What causes mirages? Why do multiple suns and moons appear in the sky? Professor Minnaert explains these unusual phenomena and hundreds of others in simple, easy-to-understand terms based on optical laws and the properties of light and color. No mathematics is required but artists, scientists, students, and everyone fascinated by these "tricks" of nature will find thousands of useful and amazing pieces of information. Hundreds of observational experiments are suggested which require no special equipment. 200 illustrations; 42 photos. xvi + 362pp. 5⅜ x 8.
20196-1 Paperbound $2.75

THE STRANGE STORY OF THE QUANTUM, AN ACCOUNT FOR THE GENERAL READER OF THE GROWTH OF IDEAS UNDERLYING OUR PRESENT ATOMIC KNOWLEDGE, *B. Hoffmann*
Presents lucidly and expertly, with barest amount of mathematics, the problems and theories which led to modern quantum physics. Dr. Hoffmann begins with the closing years of the 19th century, when certain trifling discrepancies were noticed, and with illuminating analogies and examples takes you through the brilliant concepts of Planck, Einstein, Pauli, Broglie, Bohr, Schroedinger, Heisenberg, Dirac, Sommerfeld, Feynman, etc. This edition includes a new, long postscript carrying the story through 1958. "Of the books attempting an account of the history and contents of our modern atomic physics which have come to my attention, this is the best," H. Margenau, Yale University, in *American Journal of Physics*. 32 tables and line illustrations. Index. 275pp. 5⅜ x 8.
20518-5 Paperbound $2.00

GREAT IDEAS OF MODERN MATHEMATICS: THEIR NATURE AND USE, *Jagjit Singh*
Reader with only high school math will understand main mathematical ideas of modern physics, astronomy, genetics, psychology, evolution, etc. better than many who use them as tools, but comprehend little of their basic structure. Author uses his wide knowledge of non-mathematical fields in brilliant exposition of differential equations, matrices, group theory, logic, statistics, problems of mathematical foundations, imaginary numbers, vectors, etc. Original publication. 2 appendixes. 2 indexes. 65 ills. 322pp. 5⅜ x 8.
20587-8 Paperbound $2.50

THE MUSIC OF THE SPHERES: THE MATERIAL UNIVERSE — FROM ATOM TO QUASAR, SIMPLY EXPLAINED, *Guy Murchie*

Vast compendium of fact, modern concept and theory, observed and calculated data, historical background guides intelligent layman through the material universe. Brilliant exposition of earth's construction, explanations for moon's craters, atmospheric components of Venus and Mars (with data from recent fly-by's), sun spots, sequences of star birth and death, neighboring galaxies, contributions of Galileo, Tycho Brahe, Kepler, etc.; and (Vol. 2) construction of the atom (describing newly discovered sigma and xi subatomic particles), theories of sound, color and light, space and time, including relativity theory, quantum theory, wave theory, probability theory, work of Newton, Maxwell, Faraday, Einstein, de Broglie, etc. "Best presentation yet offered to the intelligent general reader," *Saturday Review*. Revised (1967). Index. 319 illustrations by the author. Total of xx + 644pp. 5⅜ x 8½.

21809-0, 21810-4 Two volume set, paperbound $5.00

FOUR LECTURES ON RELATIVITY AND SPACE, *Charles Proteus Steinmetz*

Lecture series, given by great mathematician and electrical engineer, generally considered one of the best popular-level expositions of special and general relativity theories and related questions. Steinmetz translates complex mathematical reasoning into language accessible to laymen through analogy, example and comparison. Among topics covered are relativity of motion, location, time; of mass; acceleration; 4-dimensional time-space; geometry of the gravitational field; curvature and bending of space; non-Euclidean geometry. Index. 40 illustrations. x + 142pp. 5⅜ x 8½.

61771-8 Paperbound $1.50

HOW TO KNOW THE WILD FLOWERS, *Mrs. William Starr Dana*

Classic nature book that has introduced thousands to wonders of American wild flowers. Color-season principle of organization is easy to use, even by those with no botanical training, and the genial, refreshing discussions of history, folklore, uses of over 1,000 native and escape flowers, foliage plants are informative as well as fun to read. Over 170 full-page plates, collected from several editions, may be colored in to make permanent records of finds. Revised to conform with 1950 edition of Gray's Manual of Botany. xlii + 438pp. 5⅜ x 8½.

20332-8 Paperbound $2.50

MANUAL OF THE TREES OF NORTH AMERICA, *Charles Sprague Sargent*

Still unsurpassed as most comprehensive, reliable study of North American tree characteristics, precise locations and distribution. By dean of American dendrologists. Every tree native to U.S., Canada, Alaska; 185 genera, 717 species, described in detail—leaves, flowers, fruit, winterbuds, bark, wood, growth habits, etc. plus discussion of varieties and local variants, immaturity variations. Over 100 keys, including unusual 11-page analytical key to genera, aid in identification. 783 clear illustrations of flowers, fruit, leaves. An unmatched permanent reference work for all nature lovers. Second enlarged (1926) edition. Synopsis of families. Analytical key to genera. Glossary of technical terms. Index. 783 illustrations, 1 map. Total of 982pp. 5⅜ x 8.

20277-1, 20278-X Two volume set, paperbound $6.00

IT'S FUN TO MAKE THINGS FROM SCRAP MATERIALS,
Evelyn Glantz Hershoff
What use are empty spools, tin cans, bottle tops? What can be made from
rubber bands, clothes pins, paper clips, and buttons? This book provides
simply worded instructions and large diagrams showing you how to make
cookie cutters, toy trucks, paper turkeys, Halloween masks, telephone sets,
aprons, linoleum block- and spatter prints — in all 399 projects! Many are easy
enough for young children to figure out for themselves; some challenging
enough to entertain adults; all are remarkably ingenious ways to make things
from materials that cost pennies or less! Formerly "Scrap Fun for Everyone."
Index. 214 illustrations. 373pp. 5⅜ x 8½.   21251-3 Paperbound $2.00

SYMBOLIC LOGIC and THE GAME OF LOGIC, *Lewis Carroll*
"Symbolic Logic" is not concerned with modern symbolic logic, but is instead
a collection of over 380 problems posed with charm and imagination, using
the syllogism and a fascinating diagrammatic method of drawing conclusions.
In "The Game of Logic" Carroll's whimsical imagination devises a logical game
played with 2 diagrams and counters (included) to manipulate hundreds of
tricky syllogisms. The final section, "Hit or Miss" is a lagniappe of 101 additional puzzles in the delightful Carroll manner. Until this reprint edition,
both of these books were rarities costing up to $15 each. Symbolic Logic:
Index. xxxi + 199pp. The Game of Logic: 96pp. 2 vols. bound as one. 5⅜ x 8.
                                                            20492-8 Paperbound $2.50

MATHEMATICAL PUZZLES OF SAM LOYD, PART I
selected and edited by M. Gardner
Choice puzzles by the greatest American puzzle creator and innovator. Selected
from his famous collection, "Cyclopedia of Puzzles," they retain the unique
style and historical flavor of the originals. There are posers based on arithmetic,
algebra, probability, game theory, route tracing, topology, counter and sliding
block, operations research, geometrical dissection. Includes the famous "14-15"
puzzle which was a national craze, and his "Horse of a Different Color" which
sold millions of copies. 117 of his most ingenious puzzles in all. 120 line
drawings and diagrams. Solutions. Selected references. xx + 167pp. 5⅜ x 8.
                                                            20498-7 Paperbound $1.35

STRING FIGURES AND HOW TO MAKE THEM, *Caroline Furness Jayne*
107 string figures plus variations selected from the best primitive and modern
examples developed by Navajo, Apache, pygmies of Africa, Eskimo, in Europe,
Australia, China, etc. The most readily understandable, easy-to-follow book in
English on perennially popular recreation. Crystal-clear exposition; step-by-
step diagrams. Everyone from kindergarten children to adults looking for
unusual diversion will be endlessly amused. Index. Bibliography. Introduction
by A. C. Haddon. 17 full-page plates, 960 illustrations. xxiii + 401pp. 5⅜ x 8½.
                                                            20152-X Paperbound $2.50

PAPER FOLDING FOR BEGINNERS, *W. D. Murray and F. J. Rigney*
A delightful introduction to the varied and entertaining Japanese art of
origami (paper folding), with a full, crystal-clear text that anticipates every
difficulty; over 275 clearly labeled diagrams of all important stages in creation.
You get results at each stage, since complex figures are logically developed
from simpler ones. 43 different pieces are explained: sailboats, frogs, roosters,
etc. 6 photographic plates. 279 diagrams. 95pp. 5⅝ x 8⅜.
                                                            20713-7 Paperbound $1.00

PRINCIPLES OF ART HISTORY,
H. Wölfflin

Analyzing such terms as "baroque," "classic," "neoclassic," "primitive," "picturesque," and 164 different works by artists like Botticelli, van Cleve, Dürer, Hobbema, Holbein, Hals, Rembrandt, Titian, Brueghel, Vermeer, and many others, the author establishes the classifications of art history and style on a firm, concrete basis. This classic of art criticism shows what really occurred between the 14th-century primitives and the sophistication of the 18th century in terms of basic attitudes and philosophies. "A remarkable lesson in the art of seeing," *Sat. Rev. of Literature*. Translated from the 7th German edition. 150 illustrations. 254pp. 6⅛ x 9¼. 20276-3 Paperbound $2.50

PRIMITIVE ART,
Franz Boas

This authoritative and exhaustive work by a great American anthropologist covers the entire gamut of primitive art. Pottery, leatherwork, metal work, stone work, wood, basketry, are treated in detail. Theories of primitive art, historical depth in art history, technical virtuosity, unconscious levels of patterning, symbolism, styles, literature, music, dance, etc. A must book for the interested layman, the anthropologist, artist, handicrafter (hundreds of unusual motifs), and the historian. Over 900 illustrations (50 ceramic vessels, 12 totem poles, etc.). 376pp. 5⅜ x 8. 20025-6 Paperbound $2.50

THE GENTLEMAN AND CABINET MAKER'S DIRECTOR,
Thomas Chippendale

A reprint of the 1762 catalogue of furniture designs that went on to influence generations of English and Colonial and Early Republic American furniture makers. The 200 plates, most of them full-page sized, show Chippendale's designs for French (Louis XV), Gothic, and Chinese-manner chairs, sofas, canopy and dome beds, cornices, chamber organs, cabinets, shaving tables, commodes, picture frames, frets, candle stands, chimney pieces, decorations, etc. The drawings are all elegant and highly detailed; many include construction diagrams and elevations. A supplement of 24 photographs shows surviving pieces of original and Chippendale-style pieces of furniture. Brief biography of Chippendale by N. I. Bienenstock, editor of *Furniture World*. Reproduced from the 1762 edition. 200 plates, plus 19 photographic plates. vi + 249pp. 9⅛ x 12¼. 21601-2 Paperbound $4.00

AMERICAN ANTIQUE FURNITURE: A BOOK FOR AMATEURS,
Edgar G. Miller, Jr.

Standard introduction and practical guide to identification of valuable American antique furniture. 2115 illustrations, mostly photographs taken by the author in 148 private homes, are arranged in chronological order in extensive chapters on chairs, sofas, desks, beds, bedsteads, mirrors, tables, clocks, and other articles. Focus is on furniture accessible to the collector, including simpler pieces and a larger than usual coverage of Empire style. Introductory chapters identify structural elements, characteristics of various styles, how to avoid fakes, etc. "We are frequently asked to name some book on American furniture that will meet the requirements of the novice collector, the beginning dealer, and . . . the general public. . . . We believe Mr. Miller's two volumes more completely satisfy this specification than any other work," *Antiques*. Appendix. Index. Total of vi + 1106pp. 7⅞ x 10¾. 21599-7, 21600-4 Two volume set, paperbound $10.00

THE BAD CHILD'S BOOK OF BEASTS, MORE BEASTS FOR WORSE CHILDREN, and A MORAL ALPHABET, *H. Belloc*
Hardly and anthology of humorous verse has appeared in the last 50 years without at least a couple of these famous nonsense verses. But one must see the entire volumes — with all the delightful original illustrations by Sir Basil Blackwood — to appreciate fully Belloc's charming and witty verses that play so subacidly on the platitudes of life and morals that beset his day — and ours. A great humor classic. Three books in one. Total of 157pp. 5⅜ x 8.
20749-8 Paperbound $1.25

THE DEVIL'S DICTIONARY, *Ambrose Bierce*
Sardonic and irreverent barbs puncturing the pomposities and absurdities of American politics, business, religion, literature, and arts, by the country's greatest satirist in the classic tradition. Epigrammatic as Shaw, piercing as Swift, American as Mark Twain, Will Rogers, and Fred Allen, Bierce will always remain the favorite of a small coterie of enthusiasts, and of writers and speakers whom he supplies with "some of the most gorgeous witticisms of the English language" (H. L. Mencken). Over 1000 entries in alphabetical order. 144pp. 5⅜ x 8.
20487-1 Paperbound $1.25

THE COMPLETE NONSENSE OF EDWARD LEAR.
This is the only complete edition of this master of gentle madness available at a popular price. *A Book of Nonsense, Nonsense Songs, More Nonsense Songs and Stories* in their entirety with all the old favorites that have delighted children and adults for years. The Dong With A Luminous Nose, The Jumblies, The Owl and the Pussycat, and hundreds of other bits of wonderful nonsense. 214 limericks, 3 sets of Nonsense Botany, 5 Nonsense Alphabets, 546 drawings by Lear himself, and much more. 320pp. 5⅜ x 8. 20167-8 Paperbound $1.75

THE WIT AND HUMOR OF OSCAR WILDE, *ed. by Alvin Redman*
Wilde at his most brilliant, in 1000 epigrams exposing weaknesses and hypocrisies of "civilized" society. Divided into 49 categories—sin, wealth, women, America, etc.—to aid writers, speakers. Includes excerpts from his trials, books, plays, criticism. Formerly "The Epigrams of Oscar Wilde." Introduction by Vyvyan Holland, Wilde's only living son. Introductory essay by editor. 260pp. 5⅜ x 8.
20602-5 Paperbound $1.50

A CHILD'S PRIMER OF NATURAL HISTORY, *Oliver Herford*
Scarcely an anthology of whimsy and humor has appeared in the last 50 years without a contribution from Oliver Herford. Yet the works from which these examples are drawn have been almost impossible to obtain! Here at last are Herford's improbable definitions of a menagerie of familiar and weird animals, each verse illustrated by the author's own drawings. 24 drawings in 2 colors; 24 additional drawings. vii + 95pp. 6½ x 6. 21647-0 Paperbound $1.00

THE BROWNIES: THEIR BOOK, *Palmer Cox*
The book that made the Brownies a household word. Generations of readers have enjoyed the antics, predicaments and adventures of these jovial sprites, who emerge from the forest at night to play or to come to the aid of a deserving human. Delightful illustrations by the author decorate nearly every page. 24 short verse tales with 266 illustrations. 155pp. 6⅝ x 9¼.
21265-3 Paperbound $1.50

THE PRINCIPLES OF PSYCHOLOGY,
William James
The full long-course, unabridged, of one of the great classics of Western literature and science. Wonderfully lucid descriptions of human mental activity, the stream of thought, consciousness, time perception, memory, imagination, emotions, reason, abnormal phenomena, and similar topics. Original contributions are integrated with the work of such men as Berkeley, Binet, Mills, Darwin, Hume, Kant, Royce, Schopenhauer, Spinoza, Locke, Descartes, Galton, Wundt, Lotze, Herbart, Fechner, and scores of others. All contrasting interpretations of mental phenomena are examined in detail—introspective analysis, philosophical interpretation, and experimental research. "A classic," *Journal of Consulting Psychology.* "The main lines are as valid as ever," *Psychoanalytical Quarterly.* "Standard reading . . . a classic of interpretation," *Psychiatric Quarterly.* 94 illustrations. 1408pp. 5⅜ x 8.

20381-6, 20382-4 Two volume set, paperbound $6.00

VISUAL ILLUSIONS: THEIR CAUSES, CHARACTERISTICS AND APPLICATIONS,
M. Luckiesh
"Seeing is deceiving," asserts the author of this introduction to virtually every type of optical illusion known. The text both describes and explains the principles involved in color illusions, figure-ground, distance illusions, etc. 100 photographs, drawings and diagrams prove how easy it is to fool the sense: circles that aren't round, parallel lines that seem to bend, stationary figures that seem to move as you stare at them — illustration after illustration strains our credulity at what we see. Fascinating book from many points of view, from applications for artists, in camouflage, etc. to the psychology of vision. New introduction by William Ittleson, Dept. of Psychology, Queens College. Index. Bibliography. xxi + 252pp. 5⅜ x 8½. 21530-X Paperbound $1.75

FADS AND FALLACIES IN THE NAME OF SCIENCE,
Martin Gardner
This is the standard account of various cults, quack systems, and delusions which have masqueraded as science: hollow earth fanatics. Reich and orgone sex energy, dianetics, Atlantis, multiple moons, Forteanism, flying saucers, medical fallacies like iridiagnosis, zone therapy, etc. A new chapter has been added on Bridey Murphy, psionics, and other recent manifestations in this field. This is a fair, reasoned appraisal of eccentric theory which provides excellent inoculation against cleverly masked nonsense. "Should be read by everyone, scientist and non-scientist alike," R. T. Birge, Prof. Emeritus of Physics, Univ. of California; Former President, American Physical Society. Index. x + 365pp. 5⅜ x 8. 20394-8 Paperbound $2.00

ILLUSIONS AND DELUSIONS OF THE SUPERNATURAL AND THE OCCULT,
D. H. Rawcliffe
Holds up to rational examination hundreds of persistent delusions including crystal gazing, automatic writing, table turning, mediumistic trances, mental healing, stigmata, lycanthropy, live burial, the Indian Rope Trick, spiritualism, dowsing, telepathy, clairvoyance, ghosts, ESP, etc. The author explains and exposes the mental and physical deceptions involved, making this not only an exposé of supernatural phenomena, but a valuable exposition of characteristic types of abnormal psychology. Originally titled "The Psychology of the Occult." 14 illustrations. Index. 551pp. 5⅜ x 8. 20503-7 Paperbound $3.50

FAIRY TALE COLLECTIONS, *edited by Andrew Lang*
Andrew Lang's fairy tale collections make up the richest shelf-full of traditional children's stories anywhere available. Lang supervised the translation of stories from all over the world—familiar European tales collected by Grimm, animal stories from Negro Africa, myths of primitive Australia, stories from Russia, Hungary, Iceland, Japan, and many other countries. Lang's selection of translations are unusually high; many authorities consider that the most familiar tales find their best versions in these volumes. All collections are richly decorated and illustrated by H. J. Ford and other artists.

THE BLUE FAIRY BOOK. 37 stories. 138 illustrations. ix + 390pp. 5⅜ x 8½.
21437-0 Paperbound $1.95

THE GREEN FAIRY BOOK. 42 stories. 100 illustrations. xiii + 366pp. 5⅜ x 8½.
21439-7 Paperbound $2.00

THE BROWN FAIRY BOOK. 32 stories. 50 illustrations, 8 in color. xii + 350pp. 5⅜ x 8½.
21438-9 Paperbound $1.95

THE BEST TALES OF HOFFMANN, *edited by E. F. Bleiler*
10 stories by E. T. A. Hoffmann, one of the greatest of all writers of fantasy. The tales include "The Golden Flower Pot," "Automata," "A New Year's Eve Adventure," "Nutcracker and the King of Mice," "Sand-Man," and others. Vigorous characterizations of highly eccentric personalities, remarkably imaginative situations, and intensely fast pacing has made these tales popular all over the world for 150 years. Editor's introduction. 7 drawings by Hoffmann. xxxiii + 419pp. 5⅜ x 8½.
21793-0 Paperbound $2.25

GHOST AND HORROR STORIES OF AMBROSE BIERCE,
edited by E. F. Bleiler
Morbid, eerie, horrifying tales of possessed poets, shabby aristocrats, revived corpses, and haunted malefactors. Widely acknowledged as the best of their kind between Poe and the moderns, reflecting their author's inner torment and bitter view of life. Includes "Damned Thing," "The Middle Toe of the Right Foot," "The Eyes of the Panther," "Visions of the Night," "Moxon's Master," and over a dozen others. Editor's introduction. xxii + 199pp. 5⅜ x 8½.
20767-6 Paperbound $1.50

THREE GOTHIC NOVELS, *edited by E. F. Bleiler*
Originators of the still popular Gothic novel form, influential in ushering in early 19th-century Romanticism. Horace Walpole's *Castle of Otranto*, William Beckford's *Vathek*, John Polidori's *The Vampyre*, and a *Fragment* by Lord Byron are enjoyable as exciting reading or as documents in the history of English literature. Editor's introduction. xi + 291pp. 5⅜ x 8½.
21232-7 Paperbound $2.00

BEST GHOST STORIES OF LEFANU, *edited by E. F. Bleiler*
Though admired by such critics as V. S. Pritchett, Charles Dickens and Henry James, ghost stories by the Irish novelist Joseph Sheridan LeFanu have never become as widely known as his detective fiction. About half of the 16 stories in this collection have never before been available in America. Collection includes "Carmilla" (perhaps the best vampire story ever written), "The Haunted Baronet," "The Fortunes of Sir Robert Ardagh," and the classic "Green Tea." Editor's introduction. 7 contemporary illustrations. Portrait of LeFanu. xii + 467pp. 5⅜ x 8.
20415-4 Paperbound $2.50

EASY-TO-DO ENTERTAINMENTS AND DIVERSIONS WITH COINS, CARDS, STRING, PAPER AND MATCHES, *R. M. Abraham*
Over 300 tricks, games and puzzles will provide young readers with absorbing fun. Sections on card games; paper-folding; tricks with coins, matches and pieces of string; games for the agile; toy-making from common household objects; mathematical recreations; and 50 miscellaneous pastimes. Anyone in charge of groups of youngsters, including hard-pressed parents, and in need of suggestions on how to keep children sensibly amused and quietly content will find this book indispensable. Clear, simple text, copious number of delightful line drawings and illustrative diagrams. Originally titled "Winter Nights' Entertainments." Introduction by Lord Baden Powell. 329 illustrations. v + 186pp. 5⅜ x 8½. 20921-0 Paperbound $1.25

AN INTRODUCTION TO CHESS MOVES AND TACTICS SIMPLY EXPLAINED, *Leonard Barden*
Beginner's introduction to the royal game. Names, possible moves of the pieces, definitions of essential terms, how games are won, etc. explained in 30-odd pages. With this background you'll be able to sit right down and play. Balance of book teaches strategy — openings, middle game, typical endgame play, and suggestions for improving your game. A sample game is fully analyzed. True middle-level introduction, teaching you all the essentials without oversimplifying or losing you in a maze of detail. 58 figures. 102pp. 5⅜ x 8½. 21210-6 Paperbound $1.25

LASKER'S MANUAL OF CHESS, *Dr. Emanuel Lasker*
Probably the greatest chess player of modern times, Dr. Emanuel Lasker held the world championship 28 years, independent of passing schools or fashions. This unmatched study of the game, chiefly for intermediate to skilled players, analyzes basic methods, combinations, position play, the aesthetics of chess, dozens of different openings, etc., with constant reference to great modern games. Contains a brilliant exposition of Steinitz's important theories. Introduction by Fred Reinfeld. Tables of Lasker's tournament record. 3 indices. 308 diagrams. 1 photograph. xxx + 349pp. 5⅜ x 8. 20640-8 Paperbound $2.50

COMBINATIONS: THE HEART OF CHESS, *Irving Chernev*
Step-by-step from simple combinations to complex, this book, by a well-known chess writer, shows you the intricacies of pins, counter-pins, knight forks, and smothered mates. Other chapters show alternate lines of play to those taken in actual championship games; boomerang combinations; classic examples of brilliant combination play by Nimzovich, Rubinstein, Tarrasch, Botvinnik, Alekhine and Capablanca. Index. 356 diagrams. ix + 245pp. 5⅜ x 8½. 21744-2 Paperbound $2.00

HOW TO SOLVE CHESS PROBLEMS, *K. S. Howard*
Full of practical suggestions for the fan or the beginner — who knows only the moves of the chessmen. Contains preliminary section and 58 two-move, 46 three-move, and 8 four-move problems composed by 27 outstanding American problem creators in the last 30 years. Explanation of all terms and exhaustive index. "Just what is wanted for the student," Brian Harley. 112 problems, solutions. vi + 171pp. 5⅜ x 8. 20748-X Paperbound $1.50

SOCIAL THOUGHT FROM LORE TO SCIENCE,
H. E. Barnes and H. Becker
An immense survey of sociological thought and ways of viewing, studying, planning, and reforming society from earliest times to the present. Includes thought on society of preliterate peoples, ancient non-Western cultures, and every great movement in Europe, America, and modern Japan. Analyzes hundreds of great thinkers: Plato, Augustine, Bodin, Vico, Montesquieu, Herder, Comte, Marx, etc. Weighs the contributions of utopians, sophists, fascists and communists; economists, jurists, philosophers, ecclesiastics, and every 19th and 20th century school of scientific sociology, anthropology, and social psychology throughout the world. Combines topical, chronological, and regional approaches, treating the evolution of social thought as a process rather than as a series of mere topics. "Impressive accuracy, competence, and discrimination . . . easily the best single survey," *Nation.* Thoroughly revised, with new material up to 1960. 2 indexes. Over 2200 bibliographical notes. Three volume set. Total of 1586pp. 5⅜ x 8.
20901-6, 20902-4, 20903-2 Three volume set, paperbound $10.50

A HISTORY OF HISTORICAL WRITING, *Harry Elmer Barnes*
Virtually the only adequate survey of the whole course of historical writing in a single volume. Surveys developments from the beginnings of historiography in the ancient Near East and the Classical World, up through the Cold War. Covers major historians in detail, shows interrelationship with cultural background, makes clear individual contributions, evaluates and estimates importance; also enormously rich upon minor authors and thinkers who are usually passed over. Packed with scholarship and learning, clear, easily written. Indispensable to every student of history. Revised and enlarged up to 1961. Index and bibliography. xv + 442pp. 5⅜ x 8½.
20104-X Paperbound $3.00

JOHANN SEBASTIAN BACH, *Philipp Spitta*
The complete and unabridged text of the definitive study of Bach. Written some 70 years ago, it is still unsurpassed for its coverage of nearly all aspects of Bach's life and work. There could hardly be a finer non-technical introduction to Bach's music than the detailed, lucid analyses which Spitta provides for hundreds of individual pieces. 26 solid pages are devoted to the B minor mass, for example, and 30 pages to the glorious St. Matthew Passion. This monumental set also includes a major analysis of the music of the 18th century: Buxtehude, Pachelbel, etc. "Unchallenged as the last word on one of the supreme geniuses of music," John Barkham, *Saturday Review Syndicate.* Total of 1819pp. Heavy cloth binding. 5⅜ x 8.
22278-0, 22279-9 Two volume set, clothbound $15.00

BEETHOVEN AND HIS NINE SYMPHONIES, *George Grove*
In this modern middle-level classic of musicology Grove not only analyzes all nine of Beethoven's symphonies very thoroughly in terms of their musical structure, but also discusses the circumstances under which they were written, Beethoven's stylistic development, and much other background material. This is an extremely rich book, yet very easily followed; it is highly recommended to anyone seriously interested in music. Over 250 musical passages. Index. viii + 407pp. 5⅜ x 8.
20334-4 Paperbound $2.50

THE TIME STREAM
John Taine
Acknowledged by many as the best SF writer of the 1920's, Taine (under the name Eric Temple Bell) was also a Professor of Mathematics of considerable renown. Reprinted here are *The Time Stream*, generally considered Taine's best, *The Greatest Game*, a biological-fiction novel, and *The Purple Sapphire*, involving a supercivilization of the past. Taine's stories tie fantastic narratives to frameworks of original and logical scientific concepts. Speculation is often profound on such questions as the nature of time, concept of entropy, cyclical universes, etc. 4 contemporary illustrations. v + 532pp. 5⅜ x 8⅜.

21180-0 Paperbound $3.00

SEVEN SCIENCE FICTION NOVELS,
H. G. Wells
Full unabridged texts of 7 science-fiction novels of the master. Ranging from biology, physics, chemistry, astronomy, to sociology and other studies, Mr. Wells extrapolates whole worlds of strange and intriguing character. "One will have to go far to match this for entertainment, excitement, and sheer pleasure . . ."*New York Times*. Contents: The Time Machine, The Island of Dr. Moreau, The First Men in the Moon, The Invisible Man, The War of the Worlds, The Food of the Gods, In The Days of the Comet. 1015pp. 5⅜ x 8.

20264-X Clothbound $5.00

28 SCIENCE FICTION STORIES OF H. G. WELLS.
Two full, unabridged novels, *Men Like Gods* and *Star Begotten*, plus 26 short stories by the master science-fiction writer of all time! Stories of space, time, invention, exploration, futuristic adventure. Partial contents: *The Country of the Blind, In the Abyss, The Crystal Egg, The Man Who Could Work Miracles, A Story of Days to Come, The Empire of the Ants, The Magic Shop, The Valley of the Spiders, A Story of the Stone Age, Under the Knife, Sea Raiders,* etc. An indispensable collection for the library of anyone interested in science fiction adventure. 928pp. 5⅜ x 8.

20265-8 Clothbound $5.00

THREE MARTIAN NOVELS,
Edgar Rice Burroughs
Complete, unabridged reprinting, in one volume, of Thuvia, Maid of Mars; Chessmen of Mars; The Master Mind of Mars. Hours of science-fiction adventure by a modern master storyteller. Reset in large clear type for easy reading. 16 illustrations by J. Allen St. John. vi + 490pp. 5⅜ x 8½.

20039-6.Paperbound $2.50

AN INTELLECTUAL AND CULTURAL HISTORY OF THE WESTERN WORLD,
Harry Elmer Barnes
Monumental 3-volume survey of intellectual development of Europe from primitive cultures to the present day. Every significant product of human intellect traced through history: art, literature, mathematics, physical sciences, medicine, music, technology, social sciences, religions, jurisprudence, education, etc. Presentation is lucid and specific, analyzing in detail specific discoveries, theories, literary works, and so on. Revised (1965) by recognized scholars in specialized fields under the direction of Prof. Barnes. Revised bibliography. Indexes. 24 illustrations. Total of xxix + 1318pp.

21275-0, 21276-9, 21277-7 Three volume set, paperbound $7.75

HEAR ME TALKIN' TO YA, *edited by Nat Shapiro and Nat Hentoff*
In their own words, Louis Armstrong, King Oliver, Fletcher Henderson, Bunk Johnson, Bix Beiderbecke, Billy Holiday, Fats Waller, Jelly Roll Morton, Duke Ellington, and many others comment on the origins of jazz in New Orleans and its growth in Chicago's South Side, Kansas City's jam sessions, Depression Harlem, and the modernism of the West Coast schools. Taken from taped conversations, letters, magazine articles, other first-hand sources. Editors' introduction. xvi + 429pp. 5⅜ x 8½.   21726-4 Paperbound $2.50

THE JOURNAL OF HENRY D. THOREAU
A 25-year record by the great American observer and critic, as complete a record of a great man's inner life as is anywhere available. Thoreau's Journals served him as raw material for his formal pieces, as a place where he could develop his ideas, as an outlet for his interests in wild life and plants, in writing as an art, in classics of literature, Walt Whitman and other contemporaries, in politics, slavery, individual's relation to the State, etc. The Journals present a portrait of a remarkable man, and are an observant social history. Unabridged republication of 1906 edition, Bradford Torrey and Francis H. Allen, editors. Illustrations. Total of 1888pp. 8⅜ x 12¼.
20312-3, 20313-1 Two volume set, clothbound $30.00

A SHAKESPEARIAN GRAMMAR, *E. A. Abbott*
Basic reference to Shakespeare and his contemporaries, explaining through thousands of quotations from Shakespeare, Jonson, Beaumont and Fletcher, North's *Plutarch* and other sources the grammatical usage differing from the modern. First published in 1870 and written by a scholar who spent much of his life isolating principles of Elizabethan language, the book is unlikely ever to be superseded. Indexes. xxiv + 511pp. 5⅜ x 8½. 21582-2 Paperbound $3.00

FOLK-LORE OF SHAKESPEARE, *T. F. Thistelton Dyer*
Classic study, drawing from Shakespeare a large body of references to supernatural beliefs, terminology of falconry and hunting, games and sports, good luck charms, marriage customs, folk medicines, superstitions about plants, animals, birds, argot of the underworld, sexual slang of London, proverbs, drinking customs, weather lore, and much else. From full compilation comes a mirror of the 17th-century popular mind. Index. ix + 526pp. 5⅜ x 8½.
21614-4 Paperbound $3.25

THE NEW VARIORUM SHAKESPEARE, *edited by H. H. Furness*
By far the richest editions of the plays ever produced in any country or language. Each volume contains complete text (usually First Folio) of the play, all variants in Quarto and other Folio texts, editorial changes by every major editor to Furness's own time (1900), footnotes to obscure references or language, extensive quotes from literature of Shakespearian criticism, essays on plot sources (often reprinting sources in full), and much more.

HAMLET, *edited by H. H. Furness*
Total of xxvi + 905pp. 5⅜ x 8½.
21004-9, 21005-7 Two volume set, paperbound $5.50

TWELFTH NIGHT, *edited by H. H. Furness*
Index. xxii + 434pp. 5⅜ x 8½.   21189-4 Paperbound $2.75

La Boheme by Giacomo Puccini,
translated and introduced by Ellen H. Bleiler
Complete handbook for the operagoer, with everything needed for full enjoyment except the musical score itself. Complete Italian libretto, with new, modern English line-by-line translation—the only libretto printing all repeats; biography of Puccini; the librettists; background to the opera, Murger's La Boheme, etc.; circumstances of composition and performances; plot summary; and pictorial section of 73 illustrations showing Puccini, famous singers and performances, etc. Large clear type for easy reading. 124pp. 5⅜ x 8½.
20404-9 Paperbound $1.50

Antonio Stradivari: His Life and Work (1644-1737),
W. Henry Hill, Arthur F. Hill, and Alfred E. Hill
Still the only book that really delves into life and art of the incomparable Italian craftsman, maker of the finest musical instruments in the world today. The authors, expert violin-makers themselves, discuss Stradivari's ancestry, his construction and finishing techniques, distinguished characteristics of many of his instruments and their locations. Included, too, is story of introduction of his instruments into France, England, first revelation of their supreme merit, and information on his labels, number of instruments made, prices, mystery of ingredients of his varnish, tone of pre-1684 Stradivari violin and changes between 1684 and 1690. An extremely interesting, informative account for all music lovers, from craftsman to concert-goer. Republication of original (1902) edition. New introduction by Sydney Beck, Head of Rare Book and Manuscript Collections, Music Division, New York Public Library. Analytical index by Rembert Wurlitzer. Appendixes. 68 illustrations. 30 full-page plates. 4 in color. xxvi + 315pp. 5⅜ x 8½.
20425-1 Paperbound $3.00

Musical Autographs from Monteverdi to Hindemith,
Emanuel Winternitz
For beauty, for intrinsic interest, for perspective on the composer's personality, for subtleties of phrasing, shading, emphasis indicated in the autograph but suppressed in the printed score, the mss. of musical composition are fascinating documents which repay close study in many different ways. This 2-volume work reprints facsimiles of mss. by virtually every major composer, and many minor figures—196 examples in all. A full text points out what can be learned from mss., analyzes each sample. Index. Bibliography. 18 figures. 196 plates. Total of 170pp. of text. 7⅞ x 10¾.
21312-9, 21313-7 Two volume set, paperbound $5.00

J. S. Bach,
Albert Schweitzer
One of the few great full-length studies of Bach's life and work, and the study upon which Schweitzer's renown as a musicologist rests. On first appearance (1911), revolutionized Bach performance. The only writer on Bach to be musicologist, performing musician, and student of history, theology and philosophy, Schweitzer contributes particularly full sections on history of German Protestant church music, theories on motivic pictorial representations in vocal music, and practical suggestions for performance. Translated by Ernest Newman. Indexes. 5 illustrations. 650 musical examples. Total of xix + 928pp. 5⅜ x 8½.
21631-4, 21632-2 Two volume set, paperbound $5.00

THE METHODS OF ETHICS, *Henry Sidgwick*
Propounding no organized system of its own, study subjects every major methodological approach to ethics to rigorous, objective analysis. Study discusses and relates ethical thought of Plato, Aristotle, Bentham, Clarke, Butler, Hobbes, Hume, Mill, Spencer, Kant, and dozens of others. Sidgwick retains conclusions from each system which follow from ethical premises, rejecting the faulty. Considered by many in the field to be among the most important treatises on ethical philosophy. Appendix. Index. xlvii + 528pp. 5⅜ x 8½.
21608-X Paperbound $3.00

TEUTONIC MYTHOLOGY, *Jakob Grimm*
A milestone in Western culture; the work which established on a modern basis the study of history of religions and comparative religions. 4-volume work assembles and interprets everything available on religious and folkloristic beliefs of Germanic people (including Scandinavians, Anglo-Saxons, etc.). Assembling material from such sources as Tacitus, surviving Old Norse and Icelandic texts, archeological remains, folktales, surviving superstitions, comparative traditions, linguistic analysis, etc. Grimm explores pagan deities, heroes, folklore of nature, religious practices, and every other area of pagan German belief. To this day, the unrivaled, definitive, exhaustive study. Translated by J. S. Stallybrass from 4th (1883) German edition. Indexes. Total of lxxvii + 1887pp. 5⅜ x 8½.
21602-0, 21603-9, 21604-7, 21605-5 Four volume set, paperbound $12.00

THE I CHING, *translated by James Legge*
Called "The Book of Changes" in English, this is one of the Five Classics edited by Confucius, basic and central to Chinese thought. Explains perhaps the most complex system of divination known, founded on the theory that all things happening at any one time have characteristic features which can be isolated and related. Significant in Oriental studies, in history of religions and philosophy, and also to Jungian psychoanalysis and other areas of modern European thought. Index. Appendixes. 6 plates. xxi + 448pp. 5⅜ x 8½.
21062-6 Paperbound $2.75

HISTORY OF ANCIENT PHILOSOPHY, *W. Windelband*
One of the clearest, most accurate comprehensive surveys of Greek and Roman philosophy. Discusses ancient philosophy in general, intellectual life in Greece in the 7th and 6th centuries B.C., Thales, Anaximander, Anaximenes, Heraclitus, the Eleatics, Empedocles, Anaxagoras, Leucippus, the Pythagoreans, the Sophists, Socrates, Democritus (20 pages), Plato (50 pages), Aristotle (70 pages), the Peripatetics, Stoics, Epicureans, Sceptics, Neo-platonists, Christian Apologists, etc. 2nd German edition translated by H. E. Cushman. xv + 393pp. 5⅜ x 8.
20357-3 Paperbound $3.00

THE PALACE OF PLEASURE, *William Painter*
Elizabethan versions of Italian and French novels from *The Decameron*, Cinthio, Straparola, Queen Margaret of Navarre, and other continental sources — the very work that provided Shakespeare and dozens of his contemporaries with many of their plots and sub-plots and, therefore, justly considered one of the most influential books in all English literature. It is also a book that any reader will still enjoy. Total of cviii + 1,224pp.
21691-8, 21692-6, 21693-4 Three volume set, paperbound $8.25

THE WONDERFUL WIZARD OF OZ, *L. F. Baum*
All the original W. W. Denslow illustrations in full color—as much a part of
"The Wizard" as Tenniel's drawings are of "Alice in Wonderland." "The
Wizard" is still America's best-loved fairy tale, in which, as the author expresses
it, "The wonderment and joy are retained and the heartaches and nightmares
left out." Now today's young readers can enjoy every word and wonderful picture of the original book. New introduction by Martin Gardner. A Baum
bibliography. 23 full-page color plates. viii + 268pp. 5⅜ x 8.
20691-2 Paperbound $1.95

THE MARVELOUS LAND OF OZ, *L. F. Baum*
This is the equally enchanting sequel to the "Wizard," continuing the adventures of the Scarecrow and the Tin Woodman. The hero this time is a little
boy named Tip, and all the delightful Oz magic is still present. This is the
Oz book with the Animated Saw-Horse, the Woggle-Bug, and Jack Pumpkin-
head. All the original John R. Neill illustrations, 10 in full color. 287pp.
5⅜ x 8. 20692-0 Paperbound $1.75

ALICE'S ADVENTURES UNDER GROUND, *Lewis Carroll*
The original *Alice in Wonderland*, hand-lettered and illustrated by Carroll
himself, and originally presented as a Christmas gift to a child-friend. Adults
as well as children will enjoy this charming volume, reproduced faithfully
in this Dover edition. While the story is essentially the same, there are slight
changes, and Carroll's spritely drawings present an intriguing alternative to
the famous Tenniel illustrations. One of the most popular books in Dover's
catalogue. Introduction by Martin Gardner. 38 illustrations. 128pp. 5⅜ x 8½.
21482-6 Paperbound $1.00

THE NURSERY "ALICE," *Lewis Carroll*
While most of us consider *Alice in Wonderland* a story for children of all
ages, Carroll himself felt it was beyond younger children. He therefore provided this simplified version, illustrated with the famous Tenniel drawings
enlarged and colored in delicate tints, for children aged "from Nought to
Five." Dover's edition of this now rare classic is a faithful copy of the 1889
printing, including 20 illustrations by Tenniel, and front and back covers
reproduced in full color. Introduction by Martin Gardner. xxiii + 67pp.
6⅛ x 9¼. 21610-1 Paperbound $1.75

THE STORY OF KING ARTHUR AND HIS KNIGHTS, *Howard Pyle*
A fast-paced, exciting retelling of the best known Arthurian legends for young
readers by one of America's best story tellers and illustrators. The sword
Excalibur, wooing of Guinevere, Merlin and his downfall, adventures of Sir
Pellias and Gawaine, and others. The pen and ink illustrations are vividly
imagined and wonderfully drawn. 41 illustrations. xviii + 313pp. 6⅛ x 9¼.
21445-1 Paperbound $2.00

Prices subject to change without notice.

Available at your book dealer or write for free catalogue to Dept. Adsci,
Dover Publications, Inc., 180 Varick St., N.Y., N.Y. 10014. Dover publishes more
than 150 books each year on science, elementary and advanced mathematics,
biology, music, art, literary history, social sciences and other areas.